History and Culture of Tamil Nadu

Reconstructing Indian History & Culture
(ISSN 0971-3824)

1. Society in Ancient India; by Sures Chandra Banerji (ISBN 81-246-0000-7)
2. Political Thought in Ancient India; by G.P. Singh (ISBN 81-246-0001-5)
3. Early Indian Historical Tradition and Archaeology; by G.P. Singh (ISBN 81-246-0005-8)
4. Vasantotsava: The Spring Festivals of India; by Leona M. Anderson (ISBN 81-246-0011-2)
5. Ecological Readings in the Veda; by M. Vannucci (ISBN 81-246-0009-0)
6. Vṛndāvana in Vaiṣṇava Literature; by Maura Corcoran (ISBN 81-246-0024-4)
7. Social History of the Tamils (1707-1947); by P. Subramanian (ISBN 81-246-0045-7)
8. Ancient Indian Coinage; by Rekha Jain (ISBN 81-246-0051-1)
9. Buddhism and Socio-Economic Life of Eastern India; by Bimal Chandra Mohapatra (ISBN 81-246-0055-4)
10. Chandragupta Maurya; by P.L. Bhargava (ISBN 81-246-0056-2)
11. Mṛtyu: Concept of Death in Indian Traditions; by Gian Giuseppe Filippi (ISBN 81-246-0072-4)
12. Yama: The Glorious Lord of the Other World; by Kusum P. Merh (ISBN 81-246-0066-X)
13. Sacred Complex of Ujjain; by D.K. Samanta (ISBN 81-246-0078-3)
14. Vedic View of the Earth; by S.R.N. Murthy (ISBN 81-246-0091-0)
15. Society in the Atharvaveda; by B.S. Kharade (ISBN 81-246-0093-7)
16. Orissan History, Culture and Archaeology; by S. Pradhan (ISBN 81-246-0117-8)
17. Education in Ancient India; by Mitali Chatterjee (ISBN 81-246-0113-5)
18. Surā: The Liquor and the Vedic Sacrifice; by M.B. Kolhatkar (ISBN 81-246-0114-3)
19. Human Ecology in the Vedas; by Marta Vannucci (ISBN 81-246-0115-1)
20. Governance in Ancient India; by Anupa Chandra Pandey (ISBN 81-246-0135-6)
21. The Cultural Glory of Ancient India: A Literary Overview; by Sures Chandra Banerji (ISBN 81-246-0137-2)
22. Kauṭilya's Arthaśāstra in the light of Modern Science & Technology; by Sunil Sen Sarma (ISBN 81-246-0187-9)
23. History of Jainism — With Special Reference to Mathurā; by V.K. Sharma (ISBN 81-246-0195-X)
24. Cultural Tourism in India: Museums, Monuments & Arts — Theory and Practice; by S.P. Gupta; Krishna Lal; Mahua Bhattacharya (ISBN 81-246-0215-8)
25. Ancient Indian Historiography — Sources and Interpretations; by G.P. Singh (ISBN 81-246-0228-X)
26. Republics, Kingdoms, Towns and Cities in Ancient India; by G.P. Singh (ISBN 81-246-0237-9)
27. Facets of Ancient Indian History and Culture — New Perception; by G.P. Singh (ISBN 81-246-0238-7)
28. Kamakhya — A Socio-cultural Study; by Nihar Ranjan Mishra (ISBN 81-246-0251-4)
29. History and Culture of Tamil Nadu as Gleaned from the Sanskrit Inscriptions Vol. 1 (up to c. AD 1310); by Chithra Madhavan (ISBN 81-246-0308-1).
30. Life Style of the Vedic People; by Pranati Ghosal (ISBN 81-246-0344-8)
31. History and Culture of Tamil Nadu as Gleaned from the Sanskrit Inscriptions Vol. 2 (up to c. AD 1310 - c. 1885 AD); by Chithra Madhavan (ISBN 81-246-0380-4).

Reconstructing Indian History and Culture, no. 31

History and Culture of Tamil Nadu

— As Gleaned from the Sanskrit Inscriptions —

Volume - 2
(*c*. 1310 – *c*. 1885 AD)

by
Chithra Madhavan

with a foreword by
K.V. Ramesh

D.K. Printworld (P) Ltd.
New Delhi

Cataloging in Publication Data — DK
[Courtesy: D.K. Agencies (P) Ltd. <docinfo@dkagencies.com>]
Madhavan, Chithra, 1996 -

History and culture of Tamil Nadu : as gleaned from the Sanskrit inscription / by Chithra Madhavan : with a foreword by K.V. Ramesh.

2 v., 23 cm — (Reconstructing Indian history & culture, no. 29, 31)

Includes bibligraphical references (p.)
Includes Index.
ISBN 8124603693

1. Inscriptions, Sanskrit — India. 2. Tamil Nadu (India) — Civilization. I. Tittle. II. Series: Reconstruction Indian history & culture; no. 31

DDC 954.82 21

ISBN 81-246-0308-1 (vol. 1) (Hardbound)
ISBN 81-246-0369-3 (vol. 2) (Hardbound)
ISBN 81-246-0370-7 (set) (Hardbound)
ISBN 81-246-0380-4 (vol. 1) (Paperback)
ISBN 81-246-0395-2 (vol. 2) (Paperback)
ISBN 81-246-0396-0 (set) (Paperback)
First published in India in 2007

Published and Printed by:
D.K. Printworld (P) Ltd.
Regd. Office: 'Sri Kunj', F-52, Bali Nagar
Ramesh Nagar Merto Station
New Delhi-110 015
Phones: (011) 2545-3975; 2546-6019; *Fax*: (011) 2546-5926
E-mail: dkprintworld@vsnl.net
Website: www.dkprintworld.com

for

all my teachers

Foreword

Dr. Chithra Madhavan is already known to the world of Indological researchers through the earlier publication of her excellent Doctoral dissertation entitled "Sanskrit Inscriptions of Tamil Nadu–A Historical and Cultural study (upto *c.* 1310 AD). The present monograph is a sequel to that earlier work and incorporates all the research values and methodological virtues of that earlier work.

While the earlier work dealt with the Sanskrit inscriptions of the Pallava, Pāṇḍya and Coḷa periods, the present work deals with the Sanskrit inscriptions of Tamil Nadu of the subsequent period from about 1310 to 1885 AD covering the Vijayanagara, Nāyaka, Later Pāṇḍya and Marāṭha periods. The importance of Dr. Chithra's present work lies in the fact that the advent of the Vijayanagara empire and, later that of the other smaller dynasties, heralds an entirely different scenario as far as the use of Sanskrit in Tamil Nadu inscriptions is concerned. She has rightly pointed out that the Sanskrit inscriptions of this later period have not received adequate attention of researchers.

Dr. Chithra has brought out in great detail as well as accuracy, historical information contained in the Sanskrit portions of these later inscriptions on administration, social and economic life, education and literature as well as religion. Scholars will be greatly benefited and historians will be able to get a clearer comparative picture of the usage of Sanskrit in

Tamil Nadu inscriptions of pre-1310 and post-1310 AD periods through a study of her two volumes in tandem.

A scholar of Dr. Chithra's expertise in Sanskrit will be well-advised to bring out a third volume covering Sanskrit inscriptions of Tamil Nadu from the times of the Pallavas to that of the Marāṭhas, exclusively dealing with the qualitative changes in the diction of Sanskrit inscriptions of Tamil Nadu through the centuries. Such a study will be even more useful and informative if studied in the background of the different changes and degeneration in scripts while composing Sanskrit inscriptions in Tamil Nadu for the entire period covered by Dr. Chithra.

Dr. Chithra deserves to be congratulated for her sustained interest in epigraphical studies at a time when that discipline is fast losing its votaries, whose number anyway has always been meagre.

June 22, 2006

K.V. Ramesh
Formerly Director (Epigraphy) &
(Retd.) Jt. Director general,
Archaeological Survey of India.

Preface

THE present work embodies the result of the research carried out by me from 2001-03 as a recipient of the Junior Research Fellowship in Epigraphy from the Department of Culture, Government of India.

I am greatly indebted to Prof. K.V. Raman, Former Professor and Head, Department of Ancient History and Archaeology, University of Madras, for all his help, encouragement and guidance at every stage of my research. I deem it my good fortune to have had the benefit of his scholarly advice. I also thank Dr. S. Swaminathan, Assistant Superintending Epigraphist, Archaeological Survey of India, for his help.

I wish to thank my parents for their constant support and encouragement throughout the period of my research work. My special thanks to my mother who helped me in the reading and translation of the Sanskrit epigraphs. My heartfelt thanks to Shri L.J. Krishnamurthi and Smt. Shobha Jayaraman for all the help they have rendered to me.

To Dr. K.V. Ramesh, Formerly Director (Epigraphy) and Joint Director General (Retd.), Archaeological Survey of India, I convey my gratitude for going through my book and contributing his scholarly Foreword. My hearty thanks to Shri Susheel K. Mittal of D.K. Printworld (P) Ltd., New Delhi, for the interest and enthusiasm he has shown in publishing this book.

Chithra Madhavan

Contents

Abbreviations

ARE	*Annual Reports on Epigraphy*
CPIK	Copper-Plate Inscriptions belonging to the Śrī Śaṅkarācārya of the Kāmakoṭi Pīṭha.
IA	*Indian Antiquary*
KO	*Koiḷ-Oḻugu*
SII	*South Indian Inscriptions*
SITI	South Indian Temple Inscriptions
TAR	Travancore Annual Report of Epigraphy
TAS	Travancore Archaeological Series
USVAE	Uttankita Sanskrit Vidya-Aranya Epigraphs (Vol. I)

Key to Transliteration

अ *a* (but)	ङ *ṅa* (sing)[1]	न *na* (numb)[4]
आ *ā* (palm)	च *ca* (chunk)[2]	प *pa* (spin)[5]
इ *i* (it)	छ* *cha* (catch him)[2]	फ* *pha* (loophole)[5]
ई *ī* (beet)	ज *ja* (john)[2]	ब *ba* (bin)[5]
उ *u* (put)	झ *jha* (hedgehog)[2]	भ *bha* (abhor)[5]
ऊ *ū* (pool)	ञ *ña* (bunch)[2]	म *ma* (much)[5]
ऋ *ṛ* (rhythm)	ट *ṭa* (start)[3]	य *ya* (young)
ए *e* (play)	ठ* *ṭha* (anthill)[3]	र *ra* (drama)
ऐ *ai* (high)	ड *ḍa* (dart)[3]	ल *la* (luck)
ओ *o* (toe)	ढ* *ḍha* (godhead)[3]	व *va* (vile)
औ *au* (loud)	ण *ṇa* (under)[3]	श *śa* (shove)
क *ka* (skate)[1]	त *ta* (path)[4]	ष *ṣa* (bushel)
ख* *kha* (blockhead)[1]	थ *tha* (thunder)[4]	स *sa* (so)
ग *ga* (gate)[1]	द *da* (that)[4]	ह *ha* (hum)
घ *gha* (loghut)[1]	ध* *dha* (breathe)[4]	

° *ṁ anusvāra* (nasalisation of preceding vowel)

: *ḥ visarga* (aspiration of preceding vowel)

Tamil characters:

ற* r̤ ழ* l̤ ண* n̤

* No exact English equivalents for these letters.

[1] guttural [2] palatal [3] lingual [4] dental [5] labial

Introduction

EPIGRAPHS are the most important source for studying about the history of India. Inscriptions supply the primary source material for the reconstruction of the ancient and medieval history of our country in general and the south in particular.[1]

Among the thousands of inscriptions available in Tamil Nadu, including both lithic and copper-plate records, the majority are composed in the Tamil language. At the same time, starting from the Pallava period (c. fourth century AD), a number of inscriptions were composed in Sanskrit. During the Pāṇḍya and Coḷa periods also this language was frequently used in composing their records. However, while some of the lithic inscriptions of the Pallava, Pāṇḍya and Coḷa periods were written fully in Sanskrit, their copper-plate charters were mostly bi-lingual in nature, i.e. the first part or *praśasti* portion being in Sanskrit prose or verse (or a combination of the two) and the second or operative part of the grant being in Tamil.

During the subsequent periods of the history of Tamil Nadu, when this region was ruled by the kings of the Vijayanagara dynasty, their feudatories, the Nāyakas, the Later Pāṇḍya rulers and also the Marāṭha kings, most of the inscriptions continued to be composed in Tamil. But, at the same time, there are also some lithic inscriptions and numerous

1. T.V. Mahalingam, "Epigraphical Wealth of Tamil Nadu," from Fourth Annual Congress of the Epigraphical Society of India, Madras, 1978, p. 16.

copper-plate charters of these kings which have been composed fully in Sanskrit. As in the case of the Pallava, Pāṇḍya and Coḷa copper-plate epigraphs, some of these charters of the later periods are also bi-lingual in character. They are composed in Sanskrit and the *deśabhāṣā* Tamil, and sometimes Telugu and Kannada were also used.

The Sanskrit lithic inscriptions of the Vijayanagara, Nāyaka and later Pāṇḍya kings found etched on the walls of temples in Tamil Nadu are written in the Grantha script. With regard to the copper-plate epigraphs, the script used in writing the Sanskrit portion is almost always Nandināgari, unlike the copper-plate charters of the Pallava, Pāṇḍya and Coḷa periods in which the Sanskrit part was always written in Grantha. However, even during the Vijayanagara period, in some of the copper-plate records like the Ālampūṇḍi[2] and Soraikkāvūr[3] plates of Virūpākṣa, we find Sanskrit verses written in the Grantha script. The same is the case in many of the copper-plate charters of the later Pāṇḍyas like the Śrīvilliputtūr plates of Abhirāma Pāṇḍya[4], the Pudukkoṭṭai plates of Śrīvallabha and Varatuṅgarāma Pāṇḍya[5] and Daḷavāy-agrahāraṃ plates of Ativīrarāma Pāṇḍya.[6]

In addition to this, there are a few interesting inscriptions of the Vijayanagara period in Tamil Nadu which are in the Maṇipravāḷa style (a unique combination of Sanskrit and Tamil)[7] in which the scripts used are Grantha and Tamil. This

2. *EI*, vol. III, no. 32, pp. 226-28.
3. *EI*, vol. VIII, no. 31, pp. 301-05.
4. *TAS*, vol. I, no. IX, pp. 107-13.
5. *TAS*, vol. I, pp. 64-82.
6. *TAS*, vol. I, no. XIII, pp. 135-43.
7. *EI*, vol. XXIX, no. 9, pp. 76-77; *ARE*, no. 135 of 1936-37.

work, "History and Culture of Tamil Nadu (c. 1310 – c. 1885 AD)" deals with the period beginning from the fall of the second Pāṇḍyan Empire and covering the periods of the Vijayanagara, Nāyaka, later Pāṇḍya and Marāṭha kings. While the Tamil inscriptions of these ages have been analysed in-depth by scholars, the Sanskrit records have not received adequate attention and the aim of this work is to focus on the data gleaned from these Sanskrit inscriptions.

The Sanskrit epigraphs of these ages, although not as numerous or as informative as the Sanskrit inscriptions of the Pallavas, Pāṇḍyas and Coḷas, are, nevertheless, a mine of information about various aspects of life of those times. These records provide data about topics such as the civil administrative system, duties of the numerous ministers and other officials, military administration, social and economic life, education and the literary output of the age and also about the activities in the religious sphere.

In particular, the various benefactions made by the kings to the famous Raṅganāthasvāmi temple at Śrīraṅgam (Tiruchirapalli district), in order to restore it after the Muslim attack on this temple-town, are known from the numerous Sanskrit lithic as well as copper-plate records from this temple.

The accounts of foreign travellers like the narrative of Domingos Paes (written in AD 1520-22) and the chronicle of Ferñao Nuniz (written probably in AD 1535-37)[8] throw much light on the life in the Vijayanagara Empire. Reference has been made to the writings of these travellers wherever necessary in this book. The literary works in Sanskrit and Telugu of these ages have also been referred to in this work to substantiate the data provided by the inscriptions.

---

8. Robert Sewell, *A Forgotten Empire* (*Vijayanagara*), New Delhi, 1988.

The first chapter in this work is entitled "Administration." A number of Sanskrit epigraphs of the period of this study provide data about the duties of the kings as enunciated in the *Dharmaśāstras*, the principles which they adhered to, their crests and emblems and also the names and titles of numerous ministers who helped them in their administrative work.

The second part of this chapter deals with "Military administration." The armies of the Vijayanagara kings were very large and were made up of many divisions. Apart from the information supplied by the epigraphs, the accounts of the foreign travellers who visited the Vijayanagara Empire have also been mentioned in this chapter.

The Vijayanagara rulers were staunch upholders of the principles of *varṇāśrama dharma* (division of society into different groups) as revealed by their epigraphs found in various parts of their empire. The Sanskrit inscriptions of these rulers found in the Tamil country, contain certain titles (*biruda*s) which show their commitment to this principle, and these are outlined in the chapter, "Social and Economic Life."

A lot of information about the brāhmaṇas who were given a high status in the society is forthcoming from these Sanskrit records. Apart from the names of numerous brāhmaṇa scholars well-versed in the Vedic lore, many brāhmaṇas were employed as ministers, officials and generals by the Vijayanagara, Nāyaka, later Pāṇḍya and Marāṭha rulers. Although these inscriptions do not throw any light on their official duties and only highlight their contribution in the religious sphere, yet we come to know about some of the outstanding ministers and generals of the time like Gopaṇa or Gopaṇārya, Muddayya Daṇḍanāyaka and Govinda Dīkṣita.

The names of many of the queens of the Vijayanagara and Nāyaka periods, some of whom were talented composers like Gaṅgā Devī, the queen of Kumāra Kampaṇa and Voḍuva Tirumalāmbā, queen of Acyuta Rāya are also mentioned in this chapter.

Agriculture was the chief occupation of the people and the kings of this period strove to provide a good system of irrigation for the agriculturists. The Sanskrit records provide some information about the crops grown and also the different means of irrigation like tanks and channels used by the agriculturists.

In the third chapter, "Education and Literature," the focus is on the efforts taken by the rulers of the Vijayanagara, Nāyaka, later Pāṇḍya and Marāṭha dynasties to propagate the Brāhmanical system of education. Many of the rulers of these dynasties were very well-educated and some were outstanding scholars who authored books which are read even today. The Sanskrit inscriptions of the period of this study provide plenty of information about the encouragement given to the scholars of the land. Numerous villages (*agrahāras*) were given as tax-free gifts to the brāhmaṇa scholars who were proficient in the Vedas, Purāṇas, epics and other works of ancient India. Some of these donees were also doctors, well-versed in *Āyurveda*. The educational accomplishments of the recipients of these gifts as well as their family background are given in detail in these epigraphs.

The gifts of land made to the *maṭha*s which were among the greatest centres of learning in ancient and medieval India are mentioned in some of the copper-plate charters of these rulers. The pontiffs presiding over these *maṭha*s are spoken of in glowing terms.

Moreover, the rulers of these dynasties also encouraged the poets of their kingdoms. Many of them were commissioned to compose the copper-plate charters of the kings. Although these inscriptions were actually only official documents which recorded the grant of land or money to scholars and to temples, they were composed in verse form by talented poets and are therefore very good pieces of poetry. They are written in numerous metres and are embellished with a variety of *alaṅkāras*. Some of these Sanskrit inscriptions are partially in prose and partially in verse and are thus examples of beautiful *campu-kāvyas*. The names of many of these poets who composed the Sanskrit inscriptions of the period of this study are known to us only through these inscriptions. It is possible that they may have composed other works, but unfortunately none of them have survived till the present day.

The contributions of the rulers, their ministers and other officials of the kingdom to the temples in the Tamil country are given in detail in the chapter on "Religion." The lithic as well as the copper-plate grants in Sanskrit provide a lot of information about the temples, especially the Śrī Raṅganāthasvāmi temple at Śrīraṅgam (Tiruchirapalli district). The efforts of the Vijayanagara rulers to restore this hoary shrine back to its period of glory after the attack of the Muslim forces are evident from a perusal of these inscriptions. The Nāyaka and Marāṭha kings also, following in the tradition of the Vijayanagara rulers, lavished their patronage on the Śrīraṅgam temple. The information about the benefactions given to this shrine are corroborated by the facts mentioned in the Tamil work, *Koil Oḻugu* which is a chronicle of this temple and a very valuable source for the history of this shrine.

The rulers also made munificent gifts to other temples like the Varadarājasvāmi temple in Kāñcīpuram, the Naṭarāja temple in Cidambaram and the Mīnākṣī temple in Madurai and also to smaller shrines, and these have been recorded in this chapter.

The kings of ancient and medieval India were always advised by spiritual preceptors whom they revered and honoured. Many of these *guru*s of the early and later Vijayanagara kings and the role they played in the affairs of this empire are given in this chapter.

In this work, for unavoidable reasons I have retained the district names as given in the volumes of the *Annual Reports on Epigraphy* and *South Indian Inscriptions*, despite many changes having taken place with regard to the names of districts in recent years.

1

Administration

THE Sanskrit inscriptions of the period of the Vijayanagra and the Nāyaka rulers provide some information about the duties of the kings, the viceroys of the different provinces, the names of numerous ministers and other officials of that time, royal crests and emblems as well as some details about the armies of these kings.

Duties of a King

The *Manu-Smṛti* clearly states that the highest duty of a kṣatriya is the protection of his subjects.[1] Kauṭilya in his *Arthaśāstra* also points out that the main duty of a ruler consists in protecting his subjects.[2]

The kings of ancient and medieval India had a large number of onerous duties to perform as per the rules laid down in the *Dharmaśāstras*. Among these, their primary duties were the protection of their subjects and ensuring their welfare and prosperity.

The Sanskrit inscriptions reveal that the kings of the medieval period in south India took these duties very seriously. The Nallūr copper-plate inscription of Harihara II dated AD 1399 describes king Saṅgama as one "by whom all subjects

1. G. Bühler (tr.), *The Laws of Manu*, Delhi, 1993, VII.2.
2. R.P. Kangle, *The Kauṭilīya Arthaśāstra*, Delhi, 1992, 3.1.41.

were protected according to the ancient rules" (*yena pūrvidhanena pālitaḥ sakalāḥ prajāḥ*).[3]

The Śrīraṅgam plates of Deva Rāya I of AD 1428 describe this king as being "by his qualities, the embodiment of the happiness of his subjects" (*pramoda iva mūrto yaḥ prajānām svairguṇaiḥ abhūt*).[4] Similarly, the Kuḍiyāntaṇḍal grant of Vīra-Nṛsiṁha dated AD 1507 as well as another copper-plate insciption of this ruler mention that he ruled his kingdom, "drawing to him the hearts of all his people"(*akhila hṛdayam āvarjya*).[5] The Śrīraṅgam[6] and Kāñcīpuram[7] records of Kṛṣṇadeva Rāya dated AD 1514 and AD 1522 also mention the same facts about Vīra-Nṛsiṁha.

The Kṛṣṇāpuram copper-plate insciption of Sādaśiva Rāya dated AD 1567, speaks of the Nāyaka king of Madurai, Kṛṣṇappa Nāyaka I as "one whose policy was like Manu" (*manunīti*).[8]

Kings as Upholders of Social Order

Society in ancient India rested on the basic code of *varṇāśrama* (division of society into different groups). It was the duty of the rulers to see that *varṇāśrama dharma* was maintained and that the people of the land performed the duties assigned to their respective *varṇa*s (*svadharma*) based on the authority of the Vedas.

The Sanskrit records of ancient Tamil Nadu, of the period of the Pallavas, Pāṇḍyas and the Coḷas repeatedly stress that

3. *EI*, vol. III, no. 19, v. 8, p. 121.
4. *EI*, vol. XVI, no. 8, v. 10, p. 113.
5. *CPIK*, no. III, v. 4, pp. 41-42 & *EI*, vol. XIV, no. 17, v. 14, pp. 237-38.
6. *EI*, vol. XIII, no. 8, v. 14, p. 127.
7. *EI*, vol. XVIII, no. 21A, v. 14.
8. *EI*, vol. IX, no. 52, v. 50, p. 336.

the rulers of these dynasties upheld the laws of the different castes. This was the case in the medieval period also as can be seen from the data supplied by the Sanskrit epigraphs of this age.

An inscription of Harihara II states that this king "upheld the observances of all the castes and orders" (*sarva-varṇāśramācāra pratipālana tatparaḥ*).[9] He also bore the titles *caturvarṇāśrama pālakaḥ* (the supporter of the four castes and orders)[10] and also *vaidikaḥ mārga sthāpana ācāryaḥ* (the master in establishing the ordinanaces prescribed by the Vedas).[11]

Divine Origin

The law books and works on polity in ancient India lay stress on the theory of the divine origin of the king. The *Manu-Smṛti* and the *Arthaśāstra* have dealt with this principle in detail.

The rulers of south India have traditionally assigned a divine origin to their race. In the ancient Tamil country, the Pallavas claimed descent from Lord Viṣṇu (or sometimes Lord Brahmā) as stated in a large number of their copper-plate grants. Similarly, the Pāṇḍyan records mention that these kings belonged to the lunar race (Candra-kula) with the moon as their divine ancestor. The Coḷas belonged to the Solar dynasty (Ravi-kula) and claimed descent from the sun.

The Vijayanagara inscriptions found in the Tamil counrty reveal that these kings took great pride in claiming that they belonged to the race of Yadu, born from the race of the moon (Soma-vaṁśā). These epigraphs also provide some of the titles which the kings of this dynasty bore such as *mahārāja*, *mahārājādhirāja*, *rājaparameśvara*, *pararāja-bhayaṅkara* and *hindu-rāya-suratrāṇa*.

9. *EI*, vol. III, no. 19, v. 5, p. 121.
10. *Ibid.*, line 42, p. 121.
11. *Ibid.*, lines 47-48, p. 122.

Coronation Ceremony

The coronation ceremony was a very important function in ancient and medieval India. The brahmana priests officiated at this ceremony which was witnessed by the officers of the state and feudatory chieftains. In ancient Tamil Nadu, as with other parts of India, this ceremony was a very grand occasion. The panels of historical sculptures found in the Vaikuṇṭhaperumāḷ temple at Kāñcīpuram depict the coronation of numerous kings of the Pallava dynasty.[12] The Sanskrit portion of the Tiruvālaṅgāḍu copper-plate grant of Rājendra Coḷa I gives a graphic description of the coronation ceremony of his father Rājarāja Coḷa I.[13]

Similarly, in the Vijayanagara period also, this function was given utmost importance. A poem called *Kṛṣṇarāyavijayam*, written by Kumāra Dhūrjaṭi gives some details about the coronation of Kṛṣṇadeva Rāya.[14]

Numerous Sanskrit epigraphs found in the Tamil country of the reign of Veṅkaṭa II (AD 1586-1614) mention his coronation and also those of his predecessors, Tirumala and Śrīraṅga Rāya. The Daḷavāy-agrahāram copper-plate grant dated AD 1586 mentions the coronation ceremony (*paṭṭābhiṣekam*) of Tirumala and the numerous gifts granted by him on that occasion.[15] Similarly, the coronation of his son Śrīraṅga Rāya is also mentioned in this record.[16] A verse in this epigraph states

12. C. Minakshi, *The Historical Sculptures of the Vaikuṇṭhaperumāḷ Temple, Kanchi* (Memoirs of the Archaeological Survey of India, no. 63), New Delhi, 1940, p.
13. *SII*, vol. III, no. 205, v. 72, p. 397.
14. S. Krishnaswami Ayyangar, *Sources of Vijayangara History*, Madras, 1919, p. 129.
15. *EI*, vol. XII, no. 21, v. 21, p. 173.
16. *Ibid.*, v. 25, p. 173.

poetically that Veṅkaṭa II, the younger brother of Śrīraṅga Rāya was "anointed according to the prescribed rules by the spiritual preceptor of his *gotra*, the famous Tātārya, who was the ornament of the wise, just as Rāma was anointed by Vaśiṣṭa."[17]

These details are also stated in the Padmaneri[18] and Vellānguḍi[19] copper-plates of Veṅkaṭa II. Describing the coronation ceremony of Śrīraṅga Rāya, these inscriptions state poetically that "by the gifts made by this king at the time of his coronation, poverty was completely wiped out for good men."[20]

Viceroys

During the Vijayanagara period, in continuation of the practice which existed in most parts of India since the ancient days, the eldest son succeeded his father to the throne. The *yuvarāja* (heir-apparent) was sometimes placed in charge of the administration of a part of the kingdom. Similarly, the younger sons and some other members of the royal family were appointed as governors or viceroys of certain provinces.

During the reign of Bukka I (AD 1356-77), his son Kumāra Kaṁpaṇa was governing the Tamil districts of the kingdom as his viceroy.[21] Following the defeat of the Sultān of Madurai by this prince, the whole of south India up to Rāmeśvaram came under the Vijayanagara rule and the conquered territory, together with the remaining parts of the Tamil country, was

---

17. *Ibid.*, v. 28, p. 174.
18. *EI*, vol. XVI, no. 22, pp. 292-96.
19. *EI*, vol. XVI, no. 23, pp. 313-18.
20. *Ibid.*, vv. 28-30.
21. R.C. Majumdar (ed.), *The History and Culture of the Indian People* (vol. VI — The Delhi Sultanate), Bombay, 1990, p. 279.

placed under Kumāra Kaṁpaṇa who was as great an administrator as he was a soldier.[22] Kumāra Kaṁpaṇa has been referred to as Mahāmaṇḍaleśvara in his inscriptions found in the Tamil country.[23]

Similarly, during the reign of Harihara II (AD 1377-1404), his son Virūpākṣa or Virūpaṇa Uḍaiyār was appointed as the viceroy of the Tamil country and he succeeded in putting down a widespread rebellion in this area. The Ālampūṇḍi and the Śoraikkāvūr copper-plate grants dated AD 1383 and 1386 respectively mention his rule. Both these dates fall in the reign of Harihara II. The Ālampūṇḍi inscription records that "having conquered the kings of the Tuṇḍira, Coḷa, Pāṇḍya and Siṁhaḷa countries, he (Virūpākṣa), presented crystals and other jewels to his father."[24]

The Śoraikkāvūr plates record the grant of the village of Śiraikāvūr to a number of brāhmaṇas and he seems to have made the grant as a provinical governor, perhaps with the consent of his father.[25] In this inscription, Virūpākṣa is called Mahāmaṇḍaleśvara Vīra-Virūpākṣa-Uḍaiyār, the son of Mahāmaṇḍaleśvara Rājādhirāja Rājaparameśvara Vīra-Harihara.[26]

In the Tiruvīḻīmilaḻai temple, there are two inscriptions dated AD 1383 and 1385 which belong to the reign of Harihara II and in which his son Virūpākṣa is mentioned as ruling the country.[27]

---

22. *Ibid.*
23. A. Krishnaswami, *The Tamil Country Under Vijayanagara*, Annamalainagar, 1964, p. 67.
24. *EI*, vol. III, no. 32, v. 6, p. 227.
25. *EI*, vol. VIII, no. 31, p. 299.
26. *Ibid.*, lines 42-43, p. 302.
27. *Ibid.*, p. 299, n. 6.

The Madras Museum plates of Śrīgiribhūpāla dated AD 1424, records that Vijayabhūpati or Vijaya I had two sons, Deva Rāya (II) and Śrīgiribhūpāla (also called Śrīgirīndra and Śrīgirīśvara). The former being the elder succeeded to the throne while the second went to Maratakapurī and ruled the country of which it was the capital. It has been suggested that Maratakapurī may be identical with Virinchipuram in North Arcot district.[28]

A copper-plate grant from Śrīraṅgam dated AD 1414 records a gift of a village by Vīra Harihara Rāya Uḍaiyār (III), son of Vīrapratāpa Deva Rāya I, to a trustee of the Śrīraṅgam temple.[29] Harihara Rāya seems to have ruled as a viceroy over the country lying on the banks of the Bhavānī river, or the present-day Coimbatore area. He appears to have ended his life only as a governor and never occupied the position of the king of Vijayanagara.[30]

Emblems

It was a common custom for many of the imperial dynasties in ancient and medieval India to have a crest or emblem which adorned their banners and which were also found in their official documents and royal records. In the Tamil country, the Pallavas had the bull as their royal crest, the Pāṇḍyas, the two carps and the Coḷas, the tiger. The emblems of the kings from outside the Tamil country who ruled over some parts of ancient Tamil Nadu are also known from their inscriptions found here.

The official crest of the mighty Vijayanagara kings who ruled over all of south India was the boar, facing either left or right and surmounted by the figure of a sword or dagger and

28. *EI*, vol. VIII, no. 32, pp. 308-09.

29. *EI*, vol. XVI, no. 15, pp. 224-28.

30. *Ibid*.

those of the sun and moon. These are found on some of the lithic records and copper-plate inscriptions of the emperors of this dynasty. The Śrīraṅgam copper-plates of Deva Rāya II,[31] the Kāñcīpuram[32] and the Udayaṁbākkam[33] plates of Kṛṣṇadeva Rāya, the British Museum plates of Sadāśiva Rāya,[34] the Nīlamaṅgala grant[35] and the Kūniyūr[36] plates of Veṅkaṭa III have on their seals, the figures of a boar and the sun and moon.

The seals of the Ūṇamāñjeri grant of Acyuta Rāya[37] and the Kṛṣṇāpuram plates of Sadāśiva Rāya[38] bear the boar emblem surmounted by the figures of a dagger or sword and the sun and moon. The two copper-plates of Veṅkaṭa II in the British Museum[39] have a seal which bears only the figure of a boar. Some of the coins of king Tirumala Rāya I of the Aravīḍu dynasty bear the boar symbol.[40]

The later Pāṇḍyan rulers adopted the Varāha or Bhūvarāhamūrti as an additional emblem of their family along with their carps and hook as the result of their subordination to the Vijayanagara rulers whose emblem was the boar.[41]

---

31. *EI*, vol. XVIII, no. 21-A, p. 160.
32. *EI*, vol. VIII, no. 8, p. 122.
33. *EI*, vol. XIV, no. 12, p. 168.
34. *EI*, vol. IV, no. 1, p.1.
35. *EI*, vol. XXXVIII, no. 39, p. 212.
36. *EI*, vol. III, no. 334, p. 236.
37. *EI*, vol. III, no. 24, p. 147.
38. *EI*, vol. IX, no. 52, p. 328.
39. *EI*, vol. XIII, no. 22A, p. 225 & *Ibid.*, no. 22B, p. 231.
40. R. Nagaswamy, *Tamil Coins — A Study*, Madras, 1981, pp. 150-51.
41. *TAS*, vol. I, p. 59.

Ministers

The ministers who hepled the rulers in the administration of the land have been assigned a very important place in ancient and medieval India. Kauṭilya in his *Arthaśāstra*, mentions the *amātya* (minister) as one of the seven limbs (*saptāṅga*) of the state, and next only to the king (*svāmi*), the others being country (*janapada*), fortified city (*durga*), treasury (*koṣa*), army (*daṇḍa*) and ally (*mitra*).[42] The necessary qualifications needed for a person to be selected as a minister are also laid out in this text.

The inscriptions of the period of this study show the repsect in which the ministers were held by the kings. The fact that these kings heeded the advice of the ministers and wise men of their courts can be gleaned from the Kāñcīpuram inscription of Kṛṣṇadeva Rāya which mentions that he gave a land-grant to a saint, along with all the rights to the land on the "advice of the learned men of his court."(*purohita purogamaiḥ vidhair vibudhaiḥ śrota pratīkairadhikair gira*)[43] The Kṛṣṇāpuram plates of Sadāśiva Rāya mention that this king was installed on the throne by his sister's husband Rāma Rāya and by the chief ministers (*amātyatilakaiḥ*).[44]

The Kūniyūr copper-plates of Veṅkaṭa III record that Tirumala Nāyaka of Madurai was "anointed to the sovereignty of the whole kingdom by many chiefs of ministers (*mantri-mukhyaiḥ*)."[45]

The Sanskrit inscriptions of the Tamil country of the period of the Pallavas, Pāṇḍyas and Coḷas mention the names and qualifications of a large number of ministers who ably served

42. K.P. Kangle, *The Kauṭilīya Arthaśāstra*, Delhi, 1992, VI.I.I.

43. *EI*, vol. XIII, no. 8, v. 36, pp. 129-30.

44. *EI*, vol. IX, no. 52, v. 29, p. 334.

45. *EI*, vol. III, no. 34, v. 54, p. 246.

their kings. Likewise, the Sanskrit records of the period of this work provide some of the names of the ministers who were employed by the Vijayanagara and the Nāyaka rulers. However, these epigraphs do not mention their duties or qualifications but only the works of charity done by them.

These ministers were known by many titles like *mantri*, *mahāmantri*, *pradhānī*, *mahāpradhānī*, *upapradhānī* and *daṇḍanāyaka*. According to T.V. Mahalingam, the *pradhānī* who generally bore the title *daṇḍanāyaka* was an administrative officer in charge of the general administration of the empire.[46] An inscription found in the Raṅganāthasvāmi temple at Śrīraṅgam of the time of Kumāra Kaṁpaṇa, records a benefaction to this temple by his minister *(mahāmantri)* named Viṭṭhapa, son of Apparasa.[47]

Another minister (*mahāpradhāna*) of Kaṁpaṇa called Duggaṇṇa is mentioned in a record dated AD 1369, from Olagampaṭṭu in North Arcot district.[48] This minister made a gift of a village to a Vaiṣṇava scholar. He may be identified with Duggaṇṇa, noticed as an offficer under the king in a record from Tiruvaḍi near Cuddalore.[49]

Gopaṇa or Gopaṇārya was a brāhmaṇa officer of Kumāra Kaṁpaṇa and initially was a subordinate officer incharge of temples under Somappa Daṇḍanāyaka who was the *mahāpradhānī* and *daṇḍanāyaka* of Kumāra Kaṁpaṇa.[50] Later on, Gopaṇa was appointed Governor of Senji (Ginji) by Kaṁpaṇa.[51] A short Sanskrit epigraph from the Śrī Raṅganāthasvāmi

46. T.V. Mahalingam, *Administration and Social Life Under Vijayanagara*, Madras, 1940, p. 34.
47. *SII*, vol. XXIV, no. 288.
48. *ARE*, 166 of 1941-42.
49. *ARE*, 1941-42, Pt. II, p. 260.
50. A. Krishnaswami, *op. cit.*, p. 55.
51. *Ibid.*, p. 56.

temple, Śrīraṅgam speaks of his valiant efforts in restoring the image of this deity back to the Śrīraṅgam temple after the turbulent conditions during the Muslim invasion of that town.[52]

Muddappa Daṇḍanātha was a great minister of Bukka and in the reign of Harihara II also and was entrusted with the sole responsibility of the government.[53] An inscription dated AD 1379, which repeats an eulogy given to the prime minister in the time of Bukka states, "The king Harihara, committing all the burdens of the kingdom to him (i.e.) Muddappa Daṇḍanātha, was at ease like Hari who places the burden of the earth on the head of the king of serpents."[54]

A very long Sanskrit epigraph of Muddappa Daṇḍanātha also called Muddaya Daṇḍanāyaka is found engraved on the west wall of the second *prākāra* in the Raṅganāthasvāmi temple, Śrīraṅgam.[55]

Apart from Muddappa, Harihara II was assisted by a number of excellent ministers like Sāyaṇa, Iruga or Irugappa-Daṇḍanātha, Guṇḍapa-Daṇḍanātha, Vīra-Bāchaṇṇa-Voḍeya and Mallaṇa-Oḍeyār.[56]

A large number of inscriptions of the period of Virūpākṣa are found in the Raṅganāthasvāmi temple and some mention the benefactions made by his ministers. One of these records mentions that Muddarasa a minister (*mantri*) of this king, who belonged to the Kāśyapa *gotra* made a gift of land for a flower-garden and also gifted twenty cows for maintaining a lamp in

---

52. *EI*, vol. VI, no. 33, p. 330.
53. B.A. Saletore, *Social and Political Life in Vijayanagara Empire* (AD 1346-1646), Madras, 1934, vol. I, p. 259.
54. *Ibid.*, E.C. IX, Dg. 34.
55. *SII*, vol. XXIV, no. 293, pp. 307-08.
56. *EI*, vol. III, no. 19, p. 117.

this temple.[57] Similarly, a *pradhānī* of his named Devarāya also made gifts to this shrine.[58]

One of the chief ministers of Deva Rāya II was Śrīpati, who is stated to have made some structural changes in the Śrīraṅgam temple in a record dated AD 1428 found there.[59] Similarly, a minister named Vaḍamallaṇṇan who is described as the "best among ministers" is mentioned in a long lithic inscription belonging to the reign of Kṛṣṇadeva Rāya found in the Vedanārāyaṇasvāmi temple at Nāgalāpuram in Chengleput district.[60]

There is a reference to a minister of Acyuta Rāya called Virūpākṣa in the Ūṇamāñjerī copper-plate grant of this ruler dated AD 1540.[61] He is described as "a trusted minister" and "the chief of Nāyakas" who was the "moon of the sea of the Adiyappendra Nāyakas." It was at his request that this king granted the village of Uhinai to a number of learned brāhmaṇas.

An inscription from the Ekāmranātha temple, Kāñcīpuram mentions that this king's commander-in-chief named Saḷaka Tirumala, lord of Oṇḍana-maṇḍala, defeated many kings and installed Bhogarāja as governor of Kāñcī.[62]

During the Nāyaka period, the most famous minister was Govinda Dīkṣita who served Sevappa Nāyaka and his successors, Acyutappa and Raghunātha Nāyaka. Unfortunately, none of the Sanskrit inscriptions of this period speak of this illustious minister, but a lithic record written in

57. *SII*, vol. XXIV, no. 297, p. 311; *Ibid.*, no. 296, pp. 310-11.

58. *SII*, vol. XXIV, no. 298, p. 311-12.

59. *SII*, vol. XXIV, no. 321, p. 328.

60. *SII*, vol. XVII, no. 683, pp. 316-17.

61. *EI*, vol. III, no. 24, vv. 49-53, p. 155.

62. *EI*, vol. XXXIII, no. 39, p. 202.

Sanskrit found in the Aruṇacaleśvara temple at Tiruvaṇṇāmalai[63] is believed to have been composed by Govinda Dīkṣita.[64] His son, Veṅkaṭeśvara (Veṅkaṭamakhi) was for some time the minister of Raghunātha's son, Vijayarāghava Nāyaka.[65]

Military Administration

The kings of ancient and medieval India maintained strong and large armies as seen from their epigraphs as well as from the descriptions of numerous battles given in the contemporary literary works. As far as the Tamil country was concerned, the Sanskrit inscriptions of the Pallavas, Pāṇḍyas and Coḷas furnish copious data with regard to the armies maintained in this part of the country. Descriptions of the army divisions, the different weapons used in warfare, the character of the soldiers, military ethics, and even the various musical instruments used in the battles are forthcoming from their Sanskrit records.

Likewise, with regard to the subsequent period in Tamil Nadu history, of the age of the Vijayanagara rulers, the Nāyakas and the later Pāṇḍyas, their Sanskrit epigraphs throw light on the military administration as it existed in those periods.

The Sanskrit epigraphs of the Vijayanagara, Nāyaka and later Pāṇḍya periods, speak of the kings of these dynasties as very great warriors. Bukka I is described as "the very essence of valour" (*vikrama eka rasa*) in the Madras Museum plates of Śrīgiribhūpāla.[66] The Nallūr grant of Harihara II records that one of the titles of this ruler was *raṇa raṅga bhīṣaṇaḥ* (one who

---

63. *ARE*, 422 of 1928-29.

64. *ARE*, 1928-29, Pt. II, p. 87.

65. V. Vriddhagirisan, *The Nayaks of Tanjore*, New Delhi, 1995, p. 123.

66. *EI*, vol. VIII, no. 32, v. 6, pp. 309-10.

is formidable on the battlefield).[67] The Śrīraṅgam plates[68] and the Satyamaṅgalam plates[69] of Deva Rāya II reveal that one of the titles of this ruler was *para-rāja-bhayaṅkaraḥ* (one who terrifies hostile kings).

Weapons wielded by the kings

The different weapons which were wielded by the rulers are also mentioned in the Sanskrit records. The Śrīraṅgam copper-plates of Mallikārjuna mention that Bukka I destroyed his enemies with his sword (*khaḍga*).[70] The same inscription mentions that Deva Rāya II was as skilled in the use of the bow (*dhanurvidyā*) as Dhanañjaya (Arjuna).[71]

Army Divisions

In ancient India, the tradition of the four-fold division of the army, namely, chariots (*ratha*), elephant corps (*gaja*), horses (*turaga*) and infantry (*pada*) was always maintained. Chariots, however, fell into disuse probably after the Saṅgam period, and none of the Sanskrit inscriptions of the ancient Tamil country speak of the use of chariots in the wars waged by the kings. This appears to have been the case in south India in the medieval period also.

Acccording to B.A. Saletore, the armies of the Vijayanagara rulers consisted not of four, but six divisions, thus following the mediaeval precept of Sukra, since an inscription of Deva Rāya I records that he carried out a military expedition, accompanied by the six components of the army, and the Bakhair of Rāma Rāja also mentions it.[72]

67. *EI*, vol. III, no. 19, line 44, p. 122.
68. *EI*, vol. XVI, no. 8, v. 18, p. 114.
69. *EI*, vol. III, no. 5, v. 20, p. 38.
70. *EI*, vol. XVI, no. 28, v. 5, p. 348.
71. *Ibid.*, v. 10, p. 348.
72. B.A. Saletore, *op. cit.*, p. 421.

However, according to T.V. Mahalingam, this epigraph only states that there were six kinds of armies (*vidham*) and not six divisions (*aṅga*).[73] Moreover, the Bakhair of Rāma Rāya, which gives an account of the Vijayanagara army on the battlefield of Rakṣas Tangāḍi, mentions the large numbers of horses, camels, elephants, artillery, bulls and foot-soldiers, but it is not certain if all these actually participated in the war, the camels and bulls probably having been only auxiliaries in the battle.[74]

Elephants

The armies in ancient and medieval India always had a strong elephant force as can be seen from the evidence provided by epigraphical and literary evidence. In the ancient Tamil country, great importance was given to the maintenance and training of the elephant forces as can be gleaned from the works of the Saṅgam period and subsequently from the Tamil and Sanskrit inscriptions of the Pallava, Pāṇḍya and the Coḷa times.

Likewise, the Sanskrit epigraphs of the medieval period discovered in Tamil Nadu point to the active use of the elephant corps in the battles of the rulers of this age. The important role played by the elephants in the armies of the Vijayanagara emperors can be gleaned from the data available in their inscriptions also. The literary works in Sanskrit and Telugu of this period as also the accounts of the foreign travellers who visited the city of Vijayanagara speak of the elephants corps of these kings.

Many of the kings of the medieval period had a fascination for elephants and took personal interest in the training of these

73. T.V. Mahalingam, *op. cit.*, p. 146.

74. *Ibid*.

animals. The work *Sāhitya Sudhā* by Govinda Dīkṣita mentions that Raghunātha Nāyaka was an expert in the training of elephants.[75]

The Satyamaṅgalam copper-plates mention that the army of Pratāpa Deva Rāya I had a large elephant battalion in a very poetic manner: "Through the wind (which was produced) by the flapping of the ears of his elephants on the battlefield, the Tulushka (i.e. Musalmān) horsemen experienced the fate of cotton (i.e. were blown away)."[76]

Apart from the evidence which the epigraphs provide, the literary sources also give a graphic picture of the part played by the elephant troops in the wars of the Vijayanagara kings.

In the Sanskrit poem *Madhurāvijayam* by Gaṅgā Devī, the queen of Kumāra Kaṁpaṇa, which deals with the latter's successful campaign against the Muslim ruler of Madurai, there is a detailed description of the activities of the well-trained war-elephants in battle as well as the heroic efforts of the warriors to fell these mighty animals. The pathetic scene of numerous elephants lying on the battlefield is also poignantly described by this poetess.[77]

The literary work *Rāyavācakamu* written in Telugu prose by a provincial governor of Kṛṣṇadeva Rāya, which gives the details of the battle between this king and the rulers of Bijāpūr, Golkoṇḍa and Bidār, descibes the strength of the war-elephants on either side.[78]

---

75. S. Krishnaswami Ayyangar, *op. cit.*, p. 267.
76. *EI*, vol. III, no. 5, v. 10, p. 37.
77. S. Tiruvenkatachari (ed.), *Madhurāvijayam of Gaṅgā Devī*, Annamalainagar, 1957, pp. 122-26.
78. S. Krishnaswami Ayyangar, *op. cit.*, p. 113.

Similarly, the work *Kṛṣṇarāyavijayam* by Kumāra Dhūrjaṭi, who wrote about the victories of Kṛṣṇadeva Rāya, mentions the strength of the elephant corps in the Vijayanagara army.[79]

The accounts of the travellers from other countries who visited the Vijayanagara kingdom also mention the troops of elephants of these kings. According to Domingos Paes, three or four men were mounted on the back of each elephant which were covered with caparisons of velvet and gold, rich cloths and bells with their heads painted with faces of giants and other kinds of beasts.[80]

Nuniz also describes the elephants as having *howdās* on their backs from which four men fight on each side and that the elephants were completely clothed and had very sharp knives fastened to their tusks with which they did great harm.[81] Others like Abdur Razzak, Nikitin and Varthema have also written about these elephant forces.[82]

The practice of capturing the elephants and horses of the defeated enemy kings has been frequently referred to in the inscriptions of the ancient Tamil country of the period of the Pallavas, Pāṇḍyas and Coḷas. This practice is also mentioned in some Vijayanagara inscriptions. Some of the copper-plate grants of Veṅkaṭa II record that the "troops of elephants, horses, weapons, parasols, etc., of the king Muhammad Shāh, son of Malik Ibrāhim (kings of Golkoṇḍa) were captured by the Vijayanagara army in battle."[83]

---

79. *Ibid.*, pp. 130-31.
80. Robert Sewell, *A Forgotten Empire* (Vijayanagara), New Delhi, 1988, p. 277.
81. *Ibid.*
82 T.V. Mahalingam, *op. cit.*, p. 149.
83. *EI*, vol. IV, no. 39, v. 25, p. 274; *EI*, vol. XVI, no. 23, v. 35; *EI*, vol. XVI, no. 22, v. 31.

The *Rāyavācakamu* mentioned earlier, describes Kṛṣṇadeva Rāya's campaign against the Muslim forces of Bijāpūr, Golkoṇḍa and Bidār and states that this ruler, after seeing his enemies retreat to their respective capitals, ordered the capture of all the ownerless elephants, horses and other paraphernalia of the enemies.

Similarly, the *Acyutarāyābhyudayam* of Rājanātha Diṇḍima mentions that Acyuta Rāya, after defeating the Bijāpūr Sultān, took possession of the latter's horses and elephants. This work also states that this ruler's general defeated the Cera ruler, and obtained from him presents of many elephants and horses which he accepted for his sovereign.[84]

Artillery

Although guns were not used in the wars in ancient India, they seem to have played a major role in the wars of the Vijayanagara period as indicated by epigraphic and literary evidence. The chronicle of Domingos Paes refers to the use of guns in the Vijayanagara army.[85]

The Pudukkoṭṭai plates of the later Pāṇḍyan rulers Śrīvallabha and Varatuṅgarāma Pāṇḍya dated AD 1583, mention a certain Tirumalarāja who was possibly one of the *zamīndārs* who ruled under the Nāyaks of Madurai. He was a chieftain of a place named Cintalapaḷḷi. This inscription states that Tirumalarāja used iron guns which he charged with leaden shots in his wars against his enemies (*lohayantre prakṣipta sīsa-guḷikā*).[86]

84. S. Krishnaswami Ayyangar, *op. cit.*

85. Robert Sewell, *op. cit.*, p. 277.

86. *TAS*, vol. I, no. I, vv. 61-67, pp. 71-72; v. 67, p. 72.

2

Social and Economic Life

THE Sanskrit inscriptions of Tamil Nadu of the period of this study shed some light on society as it existed in the Vijayanagara and Nāyaka ages and also on the economic conditions of those times.

The Vijayanagara rulers were followers of the Brāhmanical religion and thus felt it their duty to protect the institution of caste (*varṇāśrama dharma*). Some of the titles assumed by these kings, as mentioned in their copper-plate grants, reflect their commitment to this cause.

The Nallūr copper-plate grant of Harihara II mentions that this ruler "upheld the observances of all the castes and orders" (*sarva varṇāśramācāra pratipālana tatparaḥ*),[1] and also bore the title *caturvarṇāśrama pālakaḥ* (the supporter of the four castes and orders).[2]

During this period, apart from the four main divisions in the society, there were also a number of other sub-castes. Some of the Vijayangara rulers took upon themselves the duty of protecting not only the four well-known castes, but also the others as well and took the title "protector of all castes in the empire."[3] According to B.A. Saletore, "this meant that especially

1. *EI*, vol. III, no. 19, v. 15, p. 121.
2. *Ibid.*, line 42.
3. *EC*, VIII, TI.14.

in regard to the various sects and subsects, on condition that these latter confined themselves to their own *svadharma* or duties proper to their castes, they could reasonably expect of their rulers the same patronage which was extended by the state to the four great *varṇas*."[4]

The Sanskrit inscriptions found in the Tamil country contain a lot of information about the brāhmaṇas and the important place given to them in society, but unfortunately not much data on the duties and social position of the other castes.

Brāhmaṇas

The brāhmaṇas who were considered the custodians of the sacred brāhmanical literature of the land were greatly honoured by the rulers and by society at large. The majority of the copper-plate inscriptions of the period of this work register gifts of land to the learned and holy brāhmaṇas. Some of these records mention the grant of land to a single learned brāhmaṇa whereas others register many brāhmaṇas as the donees.

The copper-plate grants which record gifts made to the brāhmaṇas give a detailed list of the names of the donees and other information such as the name of their ancestral village, the names of their fathers and *gotra*s, *sūtra*s and *śākhā*s to which they belonged.

The *gotra*s mentioned in the inscriptions are: Ātreya, Āśvalāyana, Āṅgīrasa, Bhārgava, Bhāradvāja, Bādarāyaṇa, Dhanañjaya, Drāhyāyaṇa, Gautama, Gārgya, Gaviṣtra, Gāmagāyana, Hārīta, Jamadagni, Jaimini, Jāmadagneya-Vatsa, Kāśyapa, Kauśika, Kauṇḍinya, Kaṇva, Kāmakkāyana-

4. B.A. Saletore, *Social and Polititcal Life in the Vijayanagara Empire* (AD 1346 - AD 1646), Madras, 1934, vol. II, p. 27.

Viśvāmitra, Kapi, Kāpyāṅgīrasa, Kauśika-Viśvāmitra, Kutsa, Kṛtsa, Lohita, Mauna-Bhārgava, Maudgalya, Maitreya, Niddhruva-Kāśyapa, Parāśara, Potimāṣa, Śathamarṣana, Saṁkṛti, Sāvarṇī, Śrīvatsa, Sālavata, Svatantra-Kapi, Śāṇḍilya, Śāṅkhyāyana, Śaṭhakopa, Saunaka, Rebha-Kāśyapa, Vādhula, Vatsa, Viśvāmitra, Vasiṣṭha, Viṣṇuvardhana, Vādhryaśva and Vācya.

The *sūtra*s to which the donees belonged were Āpastaṁba, Āśvalāyana, Bodhāyana, Drahyāyana, Gadāpastamba, Jaimini, Kātyāyana and Satyaṣādha.

Like in other parts of India, many of the brāhmaṇas followed their traditional professions of teaching and officiating at sacrifices. Some of them were appointed as priests in the temples. This office was usually hereditary. An inscription dated AD 1478, found in the Śaurirāja-Perumāḷ temple in Tirukkaṇṇapuram mentions the sale of temple-land to a certain Śrīraṅgarāja Ācci-Ayyangār, son of Vaṅgipurattu Ācci Ayyangār, whose ancestors were the hereditary *purohita*s of the same temple from the time of Uḍaiyavar (Rāmānuja). The land was presented back to the temple for certain offerings in the mornings.[5]

However, not all the brāhmaṇas devoted themselves to the traditional professions and to scholarly pursuits. Starting from the Pallava, Pāṇḍya and Coḷa periods of the ancient Tamil country, there are numerous epigraphic and literary references to show that many brāhmaṇas served as ministers and officials to the kings and also became high-ranking generals in the army with the title "Brahmādhirāja."

---

5. *ARE*, 524 of 1922.

Similarly, in medieval Tamil Nadu also, of the period of the Vijayanagara, Nāyaka and the later Pāṇḍyan rulers, many brāhmaṇas served the kings in various capacities.

Brāhmaṇas taking up occupations other than those traditionally assigned to them was accepted in ancient India. According to the law-giver Manu, "Twice-born men may take up arms when (they are) hindered (in the fulfilment of) their duties, when destruction (threatens) the twice-born castes in evil times, in their own defence, in a strife for the fees of officiating priests and in order to protect women and brāhmaṇas, he who (under such circumstances) kills in the cause of right, commits no sin."[6]

Inscriptions and literary sources provide the names of many brāhmaṇas of outstanding capacity who served as generals, ministers and officials under the Vijayanagara, Nāyaka and later Pāṇḍyan kings.

Gopaṇa or Gopaṇa-Uḍaiyār (also called Gopaṇārya) who is praised in a Sanskrit inscription dated AD 1371 in the Raṅganāthasvāmi temple, Śrīraṅgam, was an official under Kumāra Kaṁpaṇa and was later made the Governor of Ginji. He was a brāhmaṇa who belonged to the Bhāradvāja *gotra* and Āpasthamba *sūtra.*[7] The chronide of the Śrīraṅgam temple, the *Koiḷ Oḷugu*, mentions that Gopaṇa was an officer under Harihararāya (Harihara II), the brother of Kumāra Kaṁpaṇa who succeded his father Bukka I to the throne at Vijayanagara.[8] A number of Tamil inscriptions speak of Gopaṇa's activities as a general supervisor of temples before his elevation as Governor of Ginji. His role in defeating the Muslim ruler near

6. G. Bühler (tr.), *The Laws of Manu*, Delhi, 1933, VIII.348-49.
7. *EI*, vol. III, p. 225.
8. V.N. Hari Rao, *History of the Śrīraṅgam Temple*, Tirupati, 1976, pp. 124-25.

Śrīraṅgam with a large troop and restoring the image of Raṅganātha to the Śrīraṅgam temple are mentioned in the succeeding chapters.

Similarly, another official of Kumāra Kaṁpaṇa named Anegoṇḍi Vittappar who was the treasury officer of this prince was also a brāhmaṇa who belonged to the Bhāradvāja *gotra*.[9]

A number of brāhmaṇa ministers served the Vijayanagara kings. Mādhava and Sāyaṇa were able brāhmaṇa ministers under Bukka I and Harihara II.[10]

During the reign of Kṛṣṇadeva Rāya, a large number of able brāhmaṇas like Sāḷuva Timma, Nadendla Gopa Mantri, Sāḷuva Govinda Rāja, Rāyas Koṇḍamarasu, Timmarasu, Ayyaparasu, Karaṇika Maṅgarāsayya, Bāchrasayya, Karaṇika Lakṣmināṛāyaṇa and Sāḷuva Narasiṅgarāya Daṇṇāyaka occupied positions of importance in the state.[11]

The fact that this ruler believed in appointing brāhmaṇas to high posts in the kingdom is seen from the statement in his own work *Āmuktamālyada* wherein he says "a king who confers nobility on a brāhmaṇa prospers; for the brāhmaṇa stands at the post of duty even at considerable risk, either to avoid the ridicule of the kṣatriya and śūdra officers or in emulation of the other brāhmaṇa officers in the king's service."[12]

A brāhmaṇa officer named Bhaṇḍāram Veṅkaṭapati, son of Sarvamantri and grandson of Nāgayamātya who belonged

---

9. A. Krishnaswami, *The Tamil Country Under Vijayanagara*, Annamalainagar, 1964, p. 53.
10. T.V. Mahalingam, *Administration and Social Life Under Vijayanagar*, Madras, 1940, p. 241.
11. *Ibid.*
12. K.A. Nilakanta Sastri and N. Venkataramanayya, *Further Sources of Vijayanagara History*, Madras, 1946, p. 154.

to Hārīta *gotra*, Āpastamba *sūtra* and Yajus *śākhā* figures in a copper-plate record of Veṅkaṭa III dated AD 1634. It was at the request of this officer that this king granted a village as an *agrahāra* to a number of Vaiṣṇava brāhmaṇa scholars.[13] It appears that this officer's father and grandfather too were ministers as revealed by their names.

The foreign travellers to the court of the Vijayanagara rulers also mention the respect commanded by the brāhmaṇas of that age. Abdur Razzak states that "the brāhmaṇas are held by him (Deva Rāya II) in higher estimation than all other men."[14] Domingos Paes also gives a detailed account of the brāhmaṇas.[15] He mentions that some of them were officers in the government, while others owned land and "live by their own property and cultivation and the fruits which grow in their inherited grounds." Some were merchants and some were in charge of the temples.[16]

One of the best-known brāhmaṇa ministers of the Nāyaka period was the illustrious Govinda Dīkṣita who served as minsiter to Sevappa Nāyaka, Acyutappa Nāyaka and Raghunātha Nāyaka of Tañjāvūr. He was an orthodox and scholarly brāhmaṇa and an authority on the *Dharmaśāstras* and proved to be an excellent administrator. He was also the author of several books (see Education and Literature).

Acyutappa Nāyaka's great regard for this minister is best seen in his records referring to gifts made by him for the merit of Govinda Dīkṣita.[17] This minister has been credited

13. *ARE*, 1935-36, no. A14.
14. *SII*, vol. I, no. 153, p. 164.
15. R. Sewell, *A Forgotten Empire* (Vijayanagara), New Delhi, 1988, p. 245.
16. *Ibid*.
17. V. Vriddhagirisan, *The Nayaks of Tanjore*, New Delhi, 1995, p. 119.

with the authorship of the Sanskrit verses inscribed in the Aruṇacaleśvara temple, Tiruvaṇṇāmalai in praise of Sevappa Nāyaka.[18]

Veṅkaṭamakhi, a son of Govinda Dīkṣita and the author of the *Caturḍaṇḍī Prakāśīka* mentions that he wrote this work at the instance of Vijayarāghava Nāyaka, son of Raghunātha Nāyaka, when he was minister to him for some time.[19]

The Pudukkoṭṭai plates of the later Pāṇḍyan rulers Śrīvallabha and Varatuṅgarāma Pāṇḍya record that a person named Tirumalairāja who was the chieftain of a place named Chintalapaḷḷi and who was probably a *zamīndār* under the Nāyakas of Madurai had as a minister (*pradhāna*), a brāhmaṇa named Tammarāsa. The latter was also his spiritual teacher. It was due to his influence that Tirumalairāja requested the Pāṇḍyan kings to grant the village of Pudukkoṭṭai (renamed Timmāpuram) to a number of brāhmaṇas. This Tammarāsa who was instumental in bringing into existence the *agrahāra* named Timmāpuram, built in it a temple for Brahmā and a tank.[20]

Many brāhmaṇa families seem to have migrated to the Tamil country from other places. The Tenkāśī inscriptions of Parākrama Pāṇḍya (AD 1422-63) states that God Viśvanātha of Kāśī bade him in his dream to build a temple in the name of Dakṣiṇa Kāśī on the bank of the Citrā river in the Tamil country as the temple (*Śivālaya*) in Uttara Kāśī (Benaras) was in ruins.[21] In accordance with the dream, this ruler built the Viśvanāthasvāmi temple at Tenkāśī.

---

18. *ARE*, 1928-29, Pt. II, p. 87.
19. V. Vriddhagirisan, *op. cit.*, p. 119.
20. *TAS*, vol. I, no. I, vv. 61-83, pp. 71-72.
21. N. Sethuraman, *The Later Pāṇḍyas* (1371-1759 AD), Paper presented at the Nineteenth Annual Congress of the Epigraphical Society of India, Tiruchirapalli, 1993, p. 4.

The Tenkāśī inscriptions of Parākrama Pāṇḍya reveal that many brāhmaṇas from the northern regions came to this place.[22] Probably, they sought asylum in the south when the Benaras temple was destroyed by the Muslims.[23]

The Kaḍalāḍi plates of Acyuta Rāya mentions the grant of the village of Kaḍalāḍi, situated in Paḍaivīḍu-mahārājya (possibly in North Arcot district) to a brāhmaṇa scholar named Rāmacandra Dīkṣita who again allotted it to numerous brāhmaṇas.[24] These donees belonged to an important sect of brāhmaṇas, the Poysala Kannaḍa sect, the only sub-sect of Kannaḍa brāhmaṇas where Sāmavedins are found.[25]

The Veḷḷāṇguḍi copper-plate inscription of Veṅkaṭa II mentions a grant of land to a large number of learned brāhmaṇas by this king at the request of Kṛṣṇappa Nāyaka II of Madurai.[26] This record adds that this Nāyaka ruler gave money to brāhmaṇas from other kingdoms to redeem their lands which they had to return to their kings as they were unable to pay the taxes properly.

It thus appears that the govenment of other kings was so oppressive, even in the case of brāhmaṇas and consequently much more so in the case of other castes that the former had, on account of their inability to make good the heavy taxes imposed upon their lands, to abandon them; whereas the government of Kṛṣṇa-Mahīpati was so good as to attract brāhmaṇas from other countries to seek the benefit of his munificence.[27] This statement appears to be a fact as most of

22. *ARE*, 569 of 1917; *ARE*, 1918, p. 158, para, 56.
23. N. Sethuraman, *op. cit.*
24. *EI*, vol. XIV, no. 22, vv. 40-104, pp. 317-22.
25. *Ibid.*, p. 313.
26. *EI*, vol. XVI, no. 23, vv. 53-98, pp. 313-17.
27. *Ibid.*, p. 301.

the donees of this grant were residents of the Telugu country and had possibly come to the Tamil country at the invitation of the Nāyaka kings who were themselves of Telugu origin. Similarly, the brāhmaṇa donees mentioned in the Padmaneri copper-plate inscriptions seem to have come from distant lands.[28]

A copper-plate epigraph dated AD 1686 records that Mahādeva Sarasvatī, disciple of Candraśekhara Sarasvatī of the maṭha of Kāñcī gave to a brāhmaṇa named Rāma Śāstrī who belonged to the Hoysaḷa Karnāṭa sect (i.e. the Karnāṭakas of the Hoysaḷa country) of the Āśvalāyana *sūtra* and Kāmakkāyana Viśvāmitra *gotra,* land in the village of Melupākkam, some money and two house-sites.[29]

Other Castes

In some of the Sanskrit epigraphs of Tamil Nadu, we find a mention of the, *rathakāras*, whose profession, as indicated by the name itself, was the manufacture of chariots. An interesting inscription of Kulottuṅga Coḷa I (AD 1071-1122) from Uyyakkoṇḍāṉ-Tirumalai deals in detail with the status and profession of an *anuloma* class called *rathakāras*.[30] Architecture, building coaches and chariots, erecting *gopuras* of temples with images on them, preparation of instruments required by brāhmaṇas in their sacrificial ceremonies, building *maṇḍapas* and making jewels for kings were the means of livelihood for the *rathakāras*.[31]

In the period of this study, the Ḍaḷavāy-agrahāram plates of Ativīrarāma Pāṇḍya dated AD 1595 refers to this community.

---

28. *EI*, vol. XVI, no. 22, p. 291.
29. *CPIK*, pp. 133-36.
30. *ARE*, 479 of 1908.
31. *ARE*, 1909, Pt. II, p. 94.

This record states that this inscription was engraved on copper-plates by Purandara, the maker of chariots (*rathakāra*).[32] It is therefore obvious that the people of this community continued in their hereditary profession through the ages.

Queens

The Sanskrit inscriptions of Tamil Nadu of the periods of the Pallavas, Pāṇḍyas and Coḷas and also those of their vassal-chieftains mention many of the queens of these dynasties. These royal ladies, although they did not play any major role in the administration, are seen actively participating in the spheres of religion and culture. The numerous temples of the Tamil country, as well as the deserving scholarly folk received gifts in the form of land and money from these ladies. From their descriptions found in these epigraphs, it can be seen that many of them were extremely well-versed in the fine-arts and also enjoyed an exalted position in their respective kingdoms as elsewhere in south India at that time.

The Sanskrit inscriptions of the Vijayanagara, Nāyaka and Marāṭha rulers found in the Tamil country also contain plenty of information about the names and the activities of the queens of these dynasites.

The Ālampūṇḍi[33] and Śoraikkāvūr[34] copper-plate grants of Virūpākṣa mention that the queen of Saṅgama, the reputed founder of the Vijayanagara dynasty was Kāmākṣī and that their son was Bukka I. The Nallūr grant of Harihara II mentions that he was the son of Bukka I and his queen Gaurī.[35] While the Satyamaṅgalam plates of Deva Rāya II[36] record the same

32. *TAS*, vol. I, no. XIII, p. 143.
33. *EI*, vol. III, no. 32, v. 3, p. 227.
34. *EI*, vol. VIII, no. 31, v. 3, p. 301.
35. *EI*, vol. III, no. 19, v. 14, p. 121.
36. *EI*, vol. III, no. 5, v. 7, p. 37.

facts, the Śrīraṅgam plates of the same king refer to her as Gaurāmbikā.[37]

The Ālampūṇḍi epigraph states that Bukka's son Harihara II married Mallādevī, who belonged to the family of Rāmadeva and their son was Virūpākṣa.[38] The Śoraikkāvūr plates state that this queen was the granddaughter of Rāmadeva at the beginning,[39] but in a verse at the end of this record[40] which also occurs in the Sanskrit play *Nārāyaṇīvilāsam* by Virūpākṣa, she is called as the daughter of king Rāma. According to V. Venkayya, Mallādevī may have been the daughter of the Yādava ruler of Devagiri named Rāmacandra.[41] According to Robert Sewell, if Rāma is to be identified with Rāmacandra of Devagiri, it is unlikely that Mallādevī was his daughter, given the reign periods of Rāmacandra and Harihara I, and that she was possibly his granddaughter.[42] According to T.A. Gopinatha Rao, a possible solution to this puzzle is that Rāmacandra of Devagiri may have had an (otherwise unknown) son named Rāmabhūpati (mentioned in verse 17 of the Śoraikkāvūr plates) who was the father of Mallādevī, the mother of Virūpākṣa.[43]

Some lithic epigraphs of Virūpākṣa from the Raṅganāthasvāmi temple, Śrīraṅgam also provide some data about his parents. One of these states that Virūpākṣa was the son of Harihara, grandson of Bukka and the daughter's son (*dauhitra*) of Rāmabhūpati.[44] Another record states that he was

37. *EI*, vol. XVII, no. 8, v. 8, p. 113.
38. *EI*, vol. III, no. 32, v. 5, p. 227.
39. *EI*, vol. VIII, no. 31, v. 5, p. 301.
40. *Ibid.*, v. 17, pp. 304-05.
41. *Ibid.*, p. 225.
42. *IA*, vol. XXXIV, p. 19.
43. *EI*, vol. VIII, no. 31, p. 299, n.6.
44. *SII*, vol. XXIV, no. 292, p. 306.

the son of Harihara by Mallāmbikā and the daughter's son of Rāmadeva of Yadukula.[45]

The Satyamaṅgalam inscription of Deva Rāya II records that the queen of Harihara II was Mallāmbikā.[46] As the names Mallādevī and Mallāmbikā are very similar, it is possible to consider them as identical.[47] The very same inscription states that Harihara's son by Mallāmbikā was Pratāpa Deva Rāya I (who was a brother of Virūpākṣa I).[48]

Another lady of the royal household is mentioned in the Ālampūṇḍi copper-plate grant of Virūpākṣa which states that this ruler gifted to some brāhmaṇas the village of Ālampūṇḍi and that this village had been the object of a previous grant by his father Harihara II and had at that time received the name Jannāmbikābdhi.[49] The pronouns *mama* and *maya* in lines 17 and 21 of this record show that both the previous grant and the present donation of Virūpākṣa were made at the instance of a princess who was a sister of Harihara and consequently the paternal aunt of Virūpākṣa and whose name must have been Jannāmbikā because the village Ālampūṇḍi received the surname Jannāmbikābdhi (Jannāmbikā-samudram) after her own name.[50]

The Satyamaṅgalam plates of Deva Rāya II mention that the consort of Pratāpa Deva Rāya I was Hemāmbikā and their son was Vijaya-Bhūpati (Vijaya Rāya I).[51] The Śrīraṅgam plates

45. *SII*, vol. IV, no. 294, p. 309.
46. *EI*, vol. III, no. 5, v. 9, p. 37.
47. *EI*, vol. III, no. 32, p. 225.
48. *EI*, vol. III, no. 5, v. 9, p. 37.
49. *EI*, vol. III, no. 32, vv. 9-10, p. 227.
50. *Ibid.*, p. 225.
51. *EI*, vol. III, no. 5, v. 11, p. 37.

of Deva Rāya II repeat the same facts but the name of this queen is given as Demāmbikā.[52]

Both the Satyamaṅgalam[53] and the Śrīraṅgam[54] grants of Deva Rāya II state that Nārāyaṇāmbikā was the consort of Vīra-Bhūpati (also called Vīra Vijaya) and their son was Deva Rāya II. The Śrīraṅgam epigraph also states that Deva Rāya II made a grant of land to God Raṅganātha at Śrīraṅgam in the name and for the benefit of his mother Nārāyaṇāmbikā (Nārāyaṇādevī auva).[55]

Although none of the Sanskrit records of Deva Rāya II found in the Tamil country mention the names of his queens, epigraphs from other places reveal that he had three wives named Ponnalā Devī, Bhīmā Devī and Kamalā Devī.[56] Deva Rāya II had a son by his queen Ponnalā Devī called Mallikārjuna.[57] Deva Rāya II had an elder sister called Harimā who married Saluva Tippa.[58]

Many of the inscriptions of the kings of the Tuluva dynasty provide the names of the consorts of the rulers. The Kuḍiyāntaṇḍal copper-plates[59] as well as another epigraph of Vīra-Nṛsiṁha,[60] the son of Narasa Nāyaka, mention his ancestor, Timma whose wife was Devakī, to whom was born Īśvara whose wife was Bukkamā and that their son was Narasa (Nāyaka). Narasa had two sons Vīra-Nṛsiṁha and Kṛṣṇadeva

52. *EI*, vol. XVII, no. 8, v. 12, p. 113.
53. *EI*, vol. III, no. 5, vv. 13-14, p. 38.
54. *EI*, vol. XVII, no. 8, vv. 13-14, p. 113.
55. *Ibid.*, lines 44-45, p. 114.
56. H.M. Nagaraju, *Devarāya II and His Times*, Mysore, 1991, p.12.
57. *Ibid.*, p. 13.
58. *Ibid.*, p. 18.
59. *EI*, vol. XIV, no. 17, vv. 6-8, pp. 236-37.
60. *CPIK*, VV. 6-7, pp. 39-40.

Rāya by his queens Tippagi and Nagalā respectively.[61] These very same facts are repeated in many of the records of Kṛṣṇadeva Rāya like the two grants from Śrīraṅgam, the Kāñcīpuram and the Udayaṁbākkam plates.

The copper-plate grants of Acyuta Rāya like the Kaḍalāḍi[62] and the Ūṇamāñjerī[63] plates mention the same details. However, the last mentioned grant adds that the king Nṛsiṁha (Nāyaka) from a third wife, Obalāmbikā-Devī had one more son named Acyutendra, a younger brother of Kṛṣṇadeva Rāya.[64]

The British Museum plates of Sadāśiva Rāya,[65] while giving all the details found in the Ūṇamāñjerī plates, also go on to state that Narasa had two sons by Odāmbikā, namely Raṅga and Acyuta Rāya. Raṅga, whose queen was Timmāmbā had a son Sadāśiva Rāya, while Acyuta Rāya's son was called Veṅkaṭa Rāya. The Kṛṣṇāpuram plates of Sadāśiva also echo the same details.[66]

This record also mentions a sister of Sadāśiva Rāya who was married to a king named Rāma. It was this Rāma who made the ministers install Sadāśiva Rāya on the throne of Vijayanagara after the brief rule of Veṅkaṭa Rāya or Veṅkaṭadeva Rāya who ascended the throne after Acyuta Rāya.[67]

According to F. Kielhorn, in another Vijayanagara inscription, this Rāma is distinctly called as Kṛṣṇadeva Rāya's

61. *Ibid.*, VV. 12-13, p. 237.
62. *EI*, vol. XIV, no. 22, vv. 6-7.
63. *EI*, vol. III, no. 24, vv. 7-8, p. 15.
64. *Ibid.*, V. 14, p. 152.
65. *EI*, vol. IV, no. 1, vv. 5-14, p. 12.
66. *EI*, vol. IX, no. 52, vv. 12-14, p. 332.
67. *Ibid.*, vv. 27-30, p. 334.

daughter's husband and this statement, as well as the one given in the above-mentioned British Museum plates, could be best reconciled by taking the word *bhaginī* (sister) of this inscription as denoting a cousin of Sadāśiva's, the daughter of his paternal uncle, Kṛṣṇadeva Rāya.[68]

In addition to the data supplied by the epigraphs, are the accounts of the foreign travellers who visited Vijayanagara. According to Domingos Paes, Kṛṣṇadeva Rāya had twelve lawful wives of whom there were three principal ones. He adds that each one of these wives had a house to herself with women guards and many women servants.[69] All the queens had very large sums of money, treasure and personal ornaments. With regard to the three principal queens, he states that they had each the same, one as much as the other, so that there may never be any discord or ill-feeling among them; all of them are great friends, and each one lives by herself.[70]

From the epigraphs found at Tirumala, it is known that Kṛṣṇadeva Rāya visited the Veṅkaṭācalapati temple in AD 1513 along with his two consorts, the senior queen Tirumala Devī and the junior queen Chinnājiammā (Cinna Devī). The former gifted a gold cup for offerring milk to the Lord and a gold plate for perfumes and Chinnājiammā also presented a similar gold cup to the deity.[71] Another epigraph of Kṛṣṇadeva Rāya speaks of other gifts of land and ornaments to this deity for the merit of his father Narasa and his mother Nāgajammā.[72] Superb bronze images of Kṛṣṇadeva Rāya with Tirumala Devī and Cinna Devī are found in the Tirumala temple.

---

68. *EI*, vol. IV, no. 1, p. 4.
69. Robert Sewell, *op. cit.*, pp. 247-48.
70. *Ibid.*, p. 249.
71. Sadhu Subrahmanya Sastri, *Tirupati Sri Venkateswara*, Tirupati, 1998, p. 211.
72. *Ibid.*

Acyuta Rāya's two queens Varadā Devī Amman (Varadāmbikā) and Tirumala Devī (Tirumalāmbā) are known from many epigraphs of the period of this ruler. Varadā Devī was the chief-queen (*paṭṭamahiṣī*) as seen from records at different places.[73] Her son was the crown-prince Cikka Veṅkaṭādri.

Tirumala Devī was a gifted Sanskrit poetess who composed the Sanskrit *campu-kāvya* called *Varadāmbikāpariṇayam* dealing with the marriage of Acyuta Rāya and Varadāmbikā.[74] She composed another Sanskrit work *Bhaktisañjīvi* and many Sanskrit verses about the benefactions of her husband which have been engraved in many places including the Raṅganāthasvāmi temple, Śrīraṅgam and the Varadarājasvāmi temple, Kāñcīpuram (see Chapter on Education and Literature). She was known as Oduva (Voduva) Tirumalāmbā and was a reader (*Oduva*) at the Vijayanagara court before she became the co-queen (*rājamahiṣī*).[75]

In the *Varadāmbikāpariṇayam* she describes herself in the colophon as "the favourite of king Acyuta."[76] This queen is also known from two Telugu works *Vijayavilāsam* and *Raghunāthābhyudayam* which also mention that her sister Mūrtimāmbā was given in marriage to Cinna Cevappa Nāyaka along with the governorship of Tañjāvūr as dowry.[77]

A Tamil epigraph found at the Śrīraṅgam temple registers a gift of money and land by Acyuta Rāya on the occasion of his visit to this temple with his two queens Oduva Tirumalai

73. *ARE*, no. 330 of 1929-30; *ARE*, 181 of 1922.
74. T.V. Mahalingam, *op. cit.*, p. 355.
75. *EI*, vol. XXIV, no. 41, p. 287.
76. *Ibid.*
77. S. Krishnaswami Ayyangar, *Sources of Vijyayanagara History*, Madras, 1919, p. 170.

Amman and Varadā Devī and prince Cikka Veṅkaṭādri.[78] Another epigraph mentions a land grant by Triumalai Amman to this temple.[79]

The chief queen Varadā Devī is known to have made a gift of six villages to the Śrī Veṅkateśvara temple, Tirumala and later arranged for offerrings to Lord Govindarāja during his *brahmotsava* and other occasions and also to Goddess Alarmelmaṅgā and to Tirumaṅgai Āḷvār and to Āṇḍāl.[80] Two portrait-images of Acyuta Rāya and his queen Varadājiamman (Varadā Devī) standing in *añjali* pose are seen in the Śrī Veṅkaṭeśvara temple, Tirumala.[81]

This queen and her son also accompanied Acyuta Rāya on his visit to the Varadarājasvāmi temple, Kāñcīpuram as seen from a Sanskrit epigraph in this shrine which states that this king performed the *mukta-tulābhāra* ceremony (weighing oneself against an equal weight of pearls) of himself and his queen Varadāmbikā Devī at Kāñcī.[82]

Some details about the queens of the Araviḍu dynasty are also found in the epigraphs. The Veḷḷāṅguḍi plates[83] of Veṅkaṭa II trace the history of the family from Tata Pinnama, Somideva, Vīra-Rāghava, Pinnama II, Araviti Bukka who married Bāllāmbikā, Rāmarāja I whose wife was Lakkāmbikā, Śrī-raṅgarāja who married Tirumalāmbikā and their three sons Rāmarāja II, Tirumala and Veṅkaṭādri. Tirumala married Veṅgalāmbā and had two sons, Śrīraṅgarāya and

78. *SII*, vol. XXIV, no. 409, pp. 395-96.
79. *SII*, vol. XXIV, no. 407, pp. 393-94.
80. Sadhu Subrahmanya Sastry, *op. cit.*, pp. 236-37.
81. K.V. Raman, *Sculpture Art of Tirumala Tirupati Temple*, Tirupati, 1993, p. 56.
82. *ARE*, 511 of 1919.
83. *EI*, vol. XVI, no. 23, vv. 7-16.

Veṅkaṭapatideva Rāya. The latter's four queens were Veṅkaṭāmbā, Rāghavāmbā, Pedobāmāmbā and Kṛṣṇamāmbā.

Most of these details are also found in the Daḷavāy-agrahāram plates[84] and two other inscriptions of this ruler found in the British Museum. The first of the British Museum plates[85] gives the names of his queens as Veṅkaṭāmbā, Rāghavāmbā, Pedobāmāmbā and Pinavobāmāmbā. However, the second of these plates records their names as Veṅkaṭāmbā, Pedobāmāmbā, Kṛṣṇamāmbā and Koṇḍamāmbā.[86]

Queens of the Madurai Nāyakas

The names of some of the queens of the Nāyaka kings of Madurai are also mentioned in a few copper-plate grants of this period. The Kṛṣṇāpuram plates of Sadāśiva Rāya, dated AD 1567 which records a land grant by this king to the temple of Veṅkaṭanātha, constructed by Kṛṣṇappā Nāyaka I mentions that this Nāyaka king was the son of Viśvanātha Nāyaka and his queen Nāgamā.[87]

The Daḷavāy-agrahāram copper-plate grant dated AD 1586 which records the gift of a village by Veṅkaṭa II to some brāhmaṇas at the request of Vīrabhūpa (Vīrappa Nāyaka) records that the latter was the son by queen Lakṣmamā of Kṛṣṇanṛpati (Kṛṣṇappā Nāyaka I) and the grandson of Viśvanātha Nāyaka.[88]

The Veḷḷāṅguḍi plates, dated AD 1598 also of the reign of Veṅkaṭa II records that the queen of Kṛṣṇappā Nāyaka I was Lakṣmyāmbikā (also known as Lakṣmamā as seen in the

84. *EI*, vol. XII, no. 21, vv. 9-35, pp. 171-74.

85. *EI*, vol. XIII, no. 22A, v. 26, p. 228.

86. *Ibid.*, no. 22B.

87. *EI*, vol. IX, no. 52, v. 54, p. 336.

88. *EI*, vol. XII, no. 21, v. 75, p. 117.

previous record). Their son was Vīrabhūpati (Vīrappa Nāyaka) who married Tirumalāmbikā and their son was Kṛṣṇa-Mahīpati (Kṛṣṇappā Nāyaka II).[89] The Padmaneri copper-plate grant of Veṅkaṭa II also states the above-mentioned details.[90]

Queens of the Tañjāvūr Nāyakas

Some information about the queens of the Tañjāvūr Nāyakas is also available from a few Sanskrit epigraphs and also from literary sources. Sevappa Nāyaka was the first ruler of this dynasty and his queen Mūrtimāmbā was the sister-in-law of the Vijayanagara emperor Acyuta Rāya during whose reign Sevappa ruled over Tañjāvūr. The literary works such as the *Tañjāvūri Āndhra Rājula Caritamu* and also the *Tañjāvūri Vāri Caritam* say that Sevappa got Tañjāvūr from the emperor as *strīdhana* for his wife.[91] The *Raghunāthābhyudayam* of Rāmabhadrāmbā, the *Vijayavilāsam* and the *Raghunāthābhyudayam* of Vijayarāghava Nāyaka, all refer to the marriage of Sevappa with the sister of Acyuta Rāya's queen.[92]

A lithic inscription discovered in the Pagalapattu-maṇḍapa in the Raṅganāthasvāmi temple in Śrīraṅgam dated AD 1567, records that Acyutappa was the son of Cinna-cevva (Sevappa Nāyaka) and his queen Mūrtiāmbā.[93] A copper image of Mūrtiāmbā, about 60 cm in height, is seen in Madhyārjuna temple at Tiruviḍaimarudūr (Tanjavur district).[94] In this portrait, this Nāyaka queen is shown standing in a posture of

---

89. *EI*, vol. XVI, no. 23, vv. 71-76, p. 315.
90. *EI*, vol. XVI, no. 22, vv. 58-77.
91. V. Vriddhagirisan, *op. cit.*, p. 24.
92. *Ibid.*
93. *EI*, vol. XXIV, no. 488, p. 466.
94. R. Nagaswamy "Tanjore Nayak Bronzes" from "*South Indian Studies - II*," Madras, 1979, p. 165.

adoration, wearing a long *sarī* in typical Vijayanagar fashion. On the pedestel of this image is an inscription in sixteenth century Tamil characters reading Mūrtiammāḷ, the Tamil form of Mūrtiāmbā.[95]

Some of the queens of these dynasties were very well educated and even composed excellent works in Sanskrit (see Chapter on Education and Literature).

In some of the copper-plate records, the land grants given to the brāhmaṇa donees by the kings consisted of villages which were named after the queens of the ruling dynasties.

The Padmaneri copper-plate grant of Veṅkaṭa II records that this king gave the village of Padmaneri to many brāhmaṇas at the request of Kṛṣṇappā Nāyaka II in AD 1598. This village was surnamed Tirumalāmbikāpuram, presumably after Kṛṣṇappa Nāyaka's mother, the queen of Vīrappa Nāyaka whose name was Tirumalāmbikā.[96]

A copper-plate epigraph dated AD 1581 of the later Pāṇḍyan ruler, Abhirāma Sundareśa Varatuṅgarāma registers a gift of the village Śolaiseri as an *agrahāra* to brāhmaṇas and also mentions that it was given under the new name Śivakāmasundarī-caturvedimaṅgalam in honour of his queen.[97]

The naming of villages after the queens of the royal dynasties was obviously a continuation of the tradition found in the ancient Tamil country and attested to by many inscriptions of that period. The famous Karandai copper-plate grant of Rājendra Coḷa I (AD 1012-44), records that he gave to

---

95. R. Nagaswamy "Tanjore Nāyak Bronzes" from "*South Indian Studies - II,*" Madras, 1979, p. 165.
96. *EI*, vol. XVI, no. 22, pp. 292-96.
97. *ARE*, 1932-33, no. A9.

numerous brāhmaṇas an *agrahāra* called Tribhuvanamahādevī (caturvedimaṅgalam) after his mother's name.[98]

Brāhmaṇa Women

The numerous copper-plate grants of the Tamil country of the ancient and medieval periods always record the names of the donees who were usually brāhmaṇa scholars to whom land and money were gifted. Women as a rule never figured in the list of donees. However, the Veḷḷāṇguḍi plates of Veṅkaṭa II which record the gift of an *agrahāra* to a large number of brāhmaṇas and gives a list of the donees, mentions some brāhmaṇa ladies also as donees.[99] It is very rare to see the allotment of shares to women in the *agrahāra*s which are conferred on brāhmaṇas.[100] Their names, given in this record are Veṅkaṭāmbā, wife of Sarva Bhaṭṭa, Ammannārī, wife of Tippavojhla Vallam Bhaṭṭa and Mallamā, wife of Vāsudeva-Gaṇapatyārya.

The brāhmaṇa women of this age also presented gifts to temples in their own right as seen from the evidence supplied by the Sanskrit epigraphs.

An inscription found in the Raṅganāthasvāmi temple, Śrīraṅgam dated AD 1428, of the period of Deva Rāya II records the gift of a gold *kalaśa* to God Raṅganātha by a sister of Cakrarāya named Periyaperumāḷ.[101] Cakrarāya was responsible for carrying out a number of repairs in this temple.

The Śrīraṅgam copper-plate grant of Mummaḍi Nāyaka dated AD 1358 records that this Telugu chieftain granted the

---

98. K.G. Krishnan, *Karandai Tamil Saṅgam Plates of Rājéndra Choḷa I*, New Delhi, 1984, vv. 65-67, p. 200.
99. *EI*, vol. XVI, no. 23, pp. 321-29.
100. *Ibid.*, p. 302.
101. *SII*, vol. XXIV, no. 322, pp. 328-29.

village of Koṭṭāllapaṟṟu to his teacher, Parāśara Bhaṭṭa VII, who evidently enjoyed the income from this village before his death. This interesting inscription records that his mother Jaganmātā wanted to give away the property to her relatives, but thinking that Lord Śrī Raṅganātha was her truest and nearest relative, made a gift of this village to that God along with all her other belongings such as gardens and houses.[102]

Economic Life

Agriculture was the main occupation of the people of the Tamil country. The Sanskrit epigraphs repeatedly mention that villages were granted by the kings to learned brāhmaṇas as *agrahāra*s in recognition of their scholarship and for their livelihood. Similarly, the rulers also gifted many villages to temples as a source of income. These villages were often situated near rivers and were very fertile, yielding an abundance of crops.

Crops

Some of the inscriptions which record the grant of villages to scholars by the kings often contain descriptions of these fertile areas and the crops grown there. The Nallūr copper-plate grant of Harihara II records the gift of the village of Nallūri or Śrīnallūr, which is described as being "resplendent with an abudance of corn."[103] This record also mentions that this village had many ponds, wells and tanks.[104]

The Madras Museum plates of Śrīgiribhūpāla which mentions a grant of a village named Nīpataṭāka to a doctor named Sampatkumāra-Paṇḍita records that this village was

102. *EI*, vol. XIV, no. 3, vv. 46-50, p. 94.

103. *EI*, vol. III, no. 19, v. 23, p. 122.

104. *Ibid.*, p. 123.

rich in crops, watered by the Nāgakulya channel and also "adorned with various gardens."[105]

The village of Kuḍiyāntaṇḍal, in Chengleput district which was granted by Vīra-Nṛsiṁha to the pontiff of the Kāñcī Maṭha named Mahādeva Sarasvatī is described in this grant as "looking beautiful with plenty of coconut, mango, jackfruit, palmyra and other types of vegetation (*nālikera-āmra-panasa-tāḷa-hintāḷa-śobhitam*)."[106]

The village of Śrī Kṛṣṇāpuram which included a number of other villages and which was presented as a *sarvamānya* gift by Sadāśiva Rāya to the temple of Lord Veṅkaṭanātha is described in the Kṛṣṇāpuram record of Sadāśiva Rāya as an excellent one in which a number of cereals grew.[107]

Likewise, the Kūniyūr copper-plate grant of Veṅkaṭa III states that the village of Kūniyūr produced an abundance of all types of grains.[108]

Irrigation

South India has always been dependent on monsoonal rains. The kings of ancient and medieval India, realizing the difficulty suffered by the agriculturists during times of drought, tried their best to alleviate their distress by building tanks and reservoirs and digging wells and irrigation canals.

The fact that the Vijayagnagara rulers paid great attention to the construction of tanks can be seen from the famous record of Bhāskara Bhavadūra, son of Bukka I who constructed the Porumāmiḷḷa tank (Cuddapah district, Andhra Pradesh), in AD 1369 and inscribed all the details about this construction,

105. *EI*, vol. VIII, no. 32, vv. 13-20, pp. 310-11.
106. *EI*, vol. XIV, no. 17, v. 31, p. 239.
107. *EI*, vol. IX, no. 52, vv. 70-82, p. 337.
108. *EI*, vol. III, no. 34, v. 45, p. 245.

probably to ensure that future kings should know about the technology of tank construction.[109]

The Portuguese traveller, Ferrao Nuniz mentions in his writings that Kṛṣṇadeva Rāya constructed a large tank in Nāgalāpura (Karnataka), a new city built by him with the help of Joao della Ponte, a Portuguese mason.[110] In his famous work *Āmuktamālyada*, Kṛṣṇadeva Rāya states that the prosperity of a state would increase only when tanks and irrigation canals are constructed and favour is shown to poor cultivators in the matter of taxation and services.[111]

The inscriptions of the ancient Tamil country of the period of the Pallavas, Pāṇḍyas and Coḷas record the construction of numerous tanks and the digging of wells and canals to help irrigate the fields. The Vijayanagara and the other dynasties which subsequently ruled over the Tamil country also paid great attention to irrigation as seen from their epigraphs.

Tanks and Channels

A number of tanks and channels were dug to irrigate the villages as mentioned in the Sanskrit inscriptions. The Madras Museum plates of Śrīgiribhūpāla mention that the village of Nīpataṭāka which was altered into Vijayarāyapura was given to a brāhmaṇa named Sampatkumāra-Paṇḍita. This fertile village was watered by the Nāgakulya channel, a branch of the Kāverīpāka channel.[112]

The village granted, Nīpataṭāka is evidently a Sanskrit translation of a Tamil name, Kaḍapperi, a village in North

109. *EI*, vol. XIII, no. 4, p. 97 ff.
110. R. Sewell, *op. cit.*, pp. 364-65.
111. *Āmuktamalyada*, Canto. IV, v. 236.
112. *EI*, vol. VIII, no. 32, vv. 13-20, pp. 310-11.

Arcot district situated five miles east of the anicut or masonry dam across the Pālār river. It is situated on the Kāverīpākkam channel which flows from the Pālār river and is irrigated by a branch of it.[113]

The Kṛṣṇāpuram copper-plate grant of Sadāśiva Rāya gives a beautiful description of the village of Śrī Kṛṣṇāpuram which was granted to the temple of Veṅkaṭeśa. It is stated in this inscription that this village was situated on the banks of the river Tāmaraparaṇī. Among the landmarks mentioned is a channel called after Sundara Pāṇḍya.[114]

The village of Gaṅgāvarappaṭṭi which was one of the villages granted by king Veṅkaṭa II to a number of brāhmaṇas is described in the Daḷavāy-agrahāram plates of this king as being watered by the river (and channel) coming from the village of Mūngīlaṇai.[115]

The Padmaneri grant of Veṅkaṭa II records the gift of the village of Padmaneri (identified with a village near Nānguneri in Tirunelveli district) and mentions that the village received a regular supply of water from the Śyāmā-nadi anicut and possessed the ownership of the two dams across the mountain streams of Coḷagiri and Vaḷḷigiri as also numerous canals.[116]

The copper-plate grants of the time of the later Pāṇḍyas also provide the names of many channels and tanks. The Śrīvilliputtūr plates of Abhirāma Pāṇḍya which mention the grant of the village named Kṣīrārjunapura renamed Parākrama-Pāṇḍyapura to some brāhmaṇas mentions that the tank of Kāḷi was fixed as the southern boundary of this village. The channel

113. *Ibid.*, p. 309.

114. *EI*, vol. IX, no. 52, vv. 46-57, pp. 335-36.

115. *EI*, vol. XII, no. 21, vv. 41-66, pp. 175-77.

116. *EI*, vol. XVI, no. 22, lines 107 ff.

of this tank was fixed as the boundary on the west and the tank of Śrī Devī was fixed as the boundary on the north.[117]

Similarly, the Pudukkoṭṭai plates of Śrīvallabha and Varatuṅgarāma Pāṇḍya,[118] the Daḷavāy-agrahāram plates of Varatuṅgarāma Pāṇḍya (AD 1588),[119] and the Daḷavāy-agrahāram plates of Ativīrarāma Pāṇḍya[120] mention many tanks and channels which were used for purposes of irrigation.

A number of inscriptions record that many of the villages gifted to the scholarly brāhmaṇas as well as to temples were situated on the banks of the river Kāverī, this marking them out to be very fertile villages irrigated by the waters of this river.[121]

The Śrīraṅgam lithic inscription of Sadāśiva Rāya gives some interesting information regarding flood-control measures adopted in the island of Śrīraṅgam during the period of the Coḷas.[122] The frequent floods of the river Kāverī south of Śrīraṅgam, had been encroaching into the soil of this place towards the direction of the temple. A devotee named Nalantigaḷ Nārāyaṇa Jīyar at this place arranged for a stream to be cut out, branching off the right bank of the southern branch of the Kāverī (Tentirukkāverī), so that a large volume of the water might flow out and the effect of erosion into the soil of Śrīraṅgam (i.e. on the north bank of the Kāverī) would be minimized. A type of coarse grass, which served as a

117. *TAS*, vol. I, no. IX, pp. 109-10.

118. *TAS*, vol. I, no. I, pp. 64-82.

119. *TAS*, vol. I, no. XII, pp. 126-33.

120. *TAS*, vol. I, no. XIII, pp. 135-43.

121. *EI*, vol. XVIII, no. 17, vv. 25-31, pp. 141-42; *EI*, vol. XVI, no. 8, lines 41-74, pp. 114-15; *EI*, vol. XVIII, no. 21, vv. 26-40, pp. 162-64; *EI*, vol. XII, no. 38, vv. 27-44, pp. 352-54.

122. *EI*, vol. XXIX, no. 9, pp. 76-77.

protection to the boundary on that side was planted on the left bank. The waters of the Kāverī were partially dried up along the south bank.

However, due to the cutting of this stream to the right of the Kāverī, water entered the fields of the cultivators of Cintāmaṇi village. The Jīyar gave them lands in Koḷakuṭṭai village in exchange, but still dissatisfied, the former approached the Coḷa king. The latter asked for the Jīyar's explanation and was pleased with his representation.

Special Privileges

Certain families of artisans were specially chosen by the rulers for carrying out their orders and were thus more privileged than the others of their kind. The Sanskrit epigraphs of the Pallavas and the Coḷas reveal that some families of goldsmiths, weavers and engravers of the royal edicts were hereditary employees of these kings.

Similarly, in the Vijayanagara and later Pāṇḍya periods, we find the same person or persons being appointed for certain purposes like the writing of the royal orders on the copper-plates and on the walls of temples.

The Nallūr grant of Harihara II mentions that a sculptor (*śilpī*) named Muddaṇa, who was the "best among the masters (of the writers) of edicts" (*śāsanācārya-varyeṇa*) caused this edict to be engraved by the order of Harihara.[123]

The Śrīraṅgam copper-plate grant of Mallikārjuna mentions in a verse at the very end that this document was engraved by Vīraṇa, son of Muddaṇācārya and praised as being virtuous (*suguṇaḥ*) and intelligent (*dhīmān*).[124]

---

123. *EI*, vol. III, no. 19, v. 35, p. 123.

124. *EI*, vol. XVI, no. 28, v. 38, p. 351.

The Kuḍiyāntaṇḍal[125] as well as another copper-plate grant of Vīra-Nṛsiṁha[126] mention at the end of the document that Vīraṇāsāri (Vīraṇācārya), son of Mallaṇāsāri (Mallaṇācārya) was the engraver of this document.

A lithic inscription of Kṛṣṇadeva Rāya found in the Vedanārāyaṇasvāmi temple (Chengleput district) states that this long epigraph in Sanskrit verse was engraved by Mallaṇācārya.[127] Similarly, the two copper-plate records of this king from Śrīraṅgam record that they were engraved by Mallaṇācārya.[128] The Kāñcīpuram[129] and the Udayaṁbākkam grants of Kṛṣṇadeva Rāya,[130] the Ūṇamāñjerī[131] and Kaḍalāḍi[132] plates of Acyuta Rāya state that Vīraṇācārya, son of Mallaṇācārya engraved these records.

The Kṛṣṇāpuram plates of Sadāśiva Rāya record that Vīraṇācārya engraved this document.[133] A grant of Veṅkaṭa II[134] records that the engraver was Kāmyācārya, son of Gaṇapāya and younger brother of Vīraṇa, while the Daḷavāy-agrahāram plates,[135] the Padmaneri plates[136] and the Veḷḷānguḍi plates[137] of this king mention that the engraver of these charters

125. *EI*, vol. XIV, no. 17, v. 33, p. 240.

126. *CPIK*, v. 33, pp. 45-46.

127. *SII*, vol. XVII, no. 677, p. 311.

128. *SII*, vol. XVIII, no. 21A, v. 48, p. 164; *Ibid.*, 21B, v. 45, p. 169.

129. *EI*, vol. XIII, no. 8, v. 46, p. 130.

130. *EI*, vol. XIV, no. 12, v. 45, p. 174.

131. *EI*, vol. III, no. 24, v. 111, p. 158.

132. *EI*, vol. XIV, no. 22, v. 106, p. 322.

133. *EI*, vol. IX, no. 52, v. 107, p. 339.

134. *EI*, vol. XIII, no. 22-B, v. 83, p. 235.

135. *EI*, vol. XII, no. 21, v. 201, p. 185.

136. *EI*, vol. XVI, no. 22, v. 154, p. 296.

137. *EI*, vol. XVI, no. 23, line 559, p. 318.

was Vīraṇācārya (also called Vīraṇamahācārya), the son of Gaṇapāya.

The Nīlamaṅgala[138] and the Kūniyūr[139] copper-plate charters of Veṅkaṭa III mention that Acyuta Rāya, son of Gaṇapārya and the grandson of Vīraṇācārya inscribed these edicts. Thus, Vīraṇamahācārya, Kāmaya and Acyuta were brothers following the same profession.

Of the Sanskrit inscriptions of the later Pāṇḍya dynasty, only one epigraph, the Pudukkoṭṭai plates of Śrīvallabha and Varatuṅgarāma Pāṇḍya[140] mention that the document was engraved on copper-plates by Nārāyaṇa.

It can thus be seen that the engravers of the copper-plate epigraphs of the Vijayanagara kings found in the Tamil country belonged to one illustrious family who were patronized by this royal house. Many of these copper-plate grants reveal that the engravers were given one share of the land grant made as a gift to temples or to scholarly brāhmaṇas.

Medicine

Many of the Sanskrit records of the ancient period from Tamil Nadu reveal that the system of medicine (*Āyurveda*) was of a very high standard in those days. Medical practitioners were given a respected place in society and this practice continued in the succeeding periods also as many of the Vijayanagara and later Pāṇḍyan epigraphs speak of the gifts bestowed on doctors.

The Madras Museum plates of Śrīgiribhūpāla record that this ruler made a grant of land to a few brāhmaṇas, among

---

138. *EI*, vol. XXXVIII, no. 39, v. 56, pp. 220-21.
139. *EI*, vol. III, no. 34, v. 126, p. 250.
140. *TAS*, vol. I, no. 1, v. 186, p. 81.

whom the chief donee was Sampatkumāra-Paṇḍita (or Sampatsuta), who was a very learned medical man.[141] He is described in this inscription as "the foremost among all physicians" (*bhiṣajam-agrayāyin*) and the renowned son of the great Govinda-Paṇḍita who was also well-versed in the *Āyurveda* and the Vedāṅgas.

The Daḷavāy-agrahāram plates of Varatuṅgarāma Pāṇḍya (AD 1582) record that this ruler gave a village named Muruganeri to a doctor named Candraśekhara, son of Chokkapa Paṇḍita.[142]

Temples

The temples of the Tamil country, besides being religious institutions, were also the hub of the social and economic life of a town or village. The temples of the period of this study were very wealthy institutions. The kings endowed many villages to these temples, the income from which was used for the performance of worship, festivals and maintenance.

The temple provided employment to a very large number of persons beginning from the brāhmaṇa priests who performed worship, accountants, managers, watchmen, treasurers and superintendents of stores among others. Moreover, a number of articles for *pūja*, repairs, etc., indirectly provided employment to a very large number of people.

The Sanskrit inscriptions do not directly mention the employment of or salaries given to the temple-staff. But the inscriptions in the temples, especially from the Raṅganāthasvāmi temple, Śrīraṅgam clearly mention the numerous repairs undertaken by Uttamanambi, a trustee of this temple and the members of his family for the restoration

141. *EI*, vol. VIII, no. 32, vv., 13-14, p. 310.
142. *TAS*, vol. I, no. XI, vv. 19-28, pp. 121-22.

of this shrine following the attacks of the Muslim armies. These repairs must have necessitated the employment of a large workforce in addition to the staff employed to carry on the routine work of temple administration.

Tātācārya, who was the spiritual preceptor of Veṅkaṭa II was the manager of the Varadarājasvāmi temple in Kāñcīpuram, another large Vaiṣṇava shrine of that period. A Sanskrit epigraph found in this temple mentions that he was the manager of the temple affairs (*śrī kārya dhurandhara*) with a staff of subordinates under him.[143]

143. *SITI*, vol. III, pt. II, p. 1354.

3

Education and Literature

In the Tamil country as with the whole of India, the value of education was realized from very early times. Learning was traditionally imparted through institutions like the temple, *maṭha* and the *agrahāras* where the brāhmaṇas resided.

The main source of knowing about these educational institutions is through a study of inscriptions. The Pallava, Pāṇḍya and Coḷa rulers did their utmost for the dissemination of learning. The inscriptions of the Vijayanagara, Nāyaka, later Pāṇḍya and Marāṭha rulers found in the Tamil country show that these rulers also did likewise. The focus of this chapter is on the data supplied by the Sanskrit inscriptions about the state of education and the literary output of the period of this study.

The kings of ancient and medieval India had always traditionally encouraged and honoured the Sanskrit scholars of their land and some of these kings themselves were great scholars, poets and dramatists.

It was mandatory for the princes of the royal families of ancient and medieval India to be well-educated as it was vital for the head of the state to possess the knowledge required for conducting the affairs of the kingdom in an able and efficient manner. The law-givers of ancient India like Manu[1]

1. Bühler, G., tr., *The Laws of Manu*, Delhi, 1993, Ch. VII. 43.

and Kauṭilya[2] have repeatedly stressed the need for princes to be taught various disciplines at a tender age. Not only had they to study the scriptures but also had to undergo training in the military sphere. These princes also traditionally underwent rigorous training in the fine arts.

The kings of the Vijayanagara, Nāyaka, later Pāṇḍyan and Marāṭha dynasties were great patrons of learning as seen from the extraordinary support that they extended to the scholars of their land and also their zeal in the dissemination of Brāhmanical learning. The numerous Sanskrit and Tamil inscriptions as well as the literary works of Tamil Nadu reveal the condition of education during these ages.

During the reign of Bukka I, his son Kumāra Kaṁpaṇa led an army into the Tamil country and inflicted a crushing defeat on the Muslim ruler of Madurai, thus putting an end to the Sultanate of Madurai after forty years. This military excursion of Kumāra Kaṁpaṇa was the subject of a beautiful Sanskrit poem called *Madhurāvijayam* or *Kamparāyacaritam* by his queen Gaṅgā Devī. This quasi-historical work records in detail the campaign of this Vijayanagara prince into the Tamil country and an account of his victory over the Madurai Sultān.[3]

This poem is composed in elegant Sanskrit and resembles the *Raghuvaṁśa* in style. Gaṅgā Devī was a great student of Sanskrit classics and well-versed in the Vedic lore.[4] She mentions the names of Kālidāsa, Bhaṭṭa Bāṇa, Bhāravi, Daṇḍin, Bhavabhūti, Vyāsa and Vālmīki and in a single verse devoted to each, she brings out the special merit of the poet.[5] Gaṅgā

---

2. Kangle, K.P., *The Kauṭilīyam Arthaśāstram*, Delhi, 1992. 1.5.8.
3. S. Tiruvenkatachari, *Madhurāvijayam of Gaṅgā Devī*, Annamalainagar, 1957.
4. *Ibid.*, Canto I.
5. *Ibid.*

Devī's work reveals this royal lady to be a very gifted poetess among the galaxy of great poets of Sanskrit literature.

It was during the period of the early Vijayanagara rulers that the illustrious Śrī Vaiṣṇava scholar, Vedānta Deśika (AD 1268-1369) lived in the Tamil country. He wrote about one hundred and thirty-nine works in Sanskrit, Tamil, Prākṛt and Maṇipravāḷa.

Vedānta Deśika lived for a number of years at Śrīraṅgam. According to tradition, when the Muslims attacked Śrīraṅgam in AD 1323, Vedānta Deśika fled to Satyamaṅgalam (sometimes identified with a place called Satyagalam near Kollegal).[6]

According to the literary works, the *Guruparamparāprabhāvam* and the *Koiḷ Oḻugu* (a chronicle of the Śrīraṅgam temple), on the eve of a Muslim invasion of Śrīraṅgam, the temple authorities removed the image of Aḷagiyamanavāḷa-perumāḷ of this temple to Tirunārāyaṇapuram (Melkote near Mysore) and to many other places and finally to Tirupati.[7] One of the Vijayanagara officers, Gopaṇa Uḍaiyār who resided at Senji (Ginji) took this image from Tirupati (Tirumala) to Siṅgapuram (near Senji) where it was worshipped. He defeated the Muslims with the help of a strong force and brought back the image of the Lord to Śrīraṅgam and reconsecrated the God and His two consorts.

According to the *Guruparamparā*, on this occasion he was praised by the Vaiṣṇava preceptor, Vedānta Deśika in a Sanskrit verse in which Gopaṇa's heroic activities are extolled.[8] An inscription dated AD 1371, containing this verse along with another similar one make up a subjoined inscription, engraved

---

6. V.N. Hari Rao, *History of the Śrīraṅgam Temple*, Tirupati, 1976, p. 119.
7. *EI, vol. VI, no. 33*, p. 322 ff.
8. *Ibid.*, p. 322.

on the east wall of the second *prākāra* of the Śrīraṅgam temple.[9]

According to the literary work, *Prapannāmṛtam,* the verses in this inscription were composed by Vedānta Deśika, who returned to Śrīraṅgam from his exile and witnessed in great delight the re-consecration of the images.[10]

Harihara II

Harihara II (AD 1377-1404), who succeeded Bukka I to the throne at Vijayanagara, strove for the spread of Vedic learning in his empire. The Nallūr copper-plate charter of this ruler records that he gave to Vedic scholars named Aubhala-Yajvan and his younger brother Nṛsiṁha-Yajvan, the village called Śrīnallūr.[11]

This inscription mentions a number of *biruda*s (titles) of Harihara II, one of them being *Vedabhāṣya-prakāśakaḥ* (the publisher of the commentaries on the Vedas).[12] This *biruda* clearly refers to the commentaries on the Vedas which were published under the king's authority by Sāyaṇācārya, the celebrated Vedic scholar who was a minister of Saṅgama II and Harihara II.[13]

The Madras Museum plates of Śrīgiribhūpāla, the younger brother of Devā Rāya II describe Harihara II as "fully accomplished in learning (*siddha sārasvata*)."[14]

9. *Ibid.*, p. 330.
10. V.N. Hari Rao, *op. cit.*, p. 125
11. *EI*, vol. III, no. 19, vv. 29-31, p. 123.
12. *Ibid.*, p. 122.
13. *Ibid.*, p. 118.
14. *EI*, vol. VIII, no. 32, v. 7, p. 310.

Virūpākṣa

Virūpākṣa, the son of Harihara II, who ascended the throne on the death of his father, ruled for only one year. He was a scholar who composed two Sanskrit dramas, namely the *Nārāyaṇīvilāsam* in five acts and the *Unmattarāghava* in one act describing Rāma's lamentations on the loss of Sītā.[15]

An inscription found at the Raṅganāthasvāmi temple, Śrīraṅgam consisting of two verses mentions the benefactions of this ruler to Lord Raṅganātha.[16] The first of these verses is the opening verse in the *Nārāyaṇīvilāsam* in which the *sūtradhāra* introduces king Virūpākṣa as the author of that play. As this verse is apparently copied from that drama, it may be surmised that the king took keen interest in popularizing this composition.[17]

Some of the copper-plate inscriptions of Virūpākṣa record his gifts of land to brāhmaṇas who were scholars well-versed in the Vedas. The Śoraikkāvūr copper-plate grant of Virūpākṣa dated AD 1386, records that he gave an *agrahāra* to fourteen brāhmaṇas of Vijayasudarśanapuram which consisted of the village of Chiraikkāvūr and a field.[18]

The Ālampūṇḍi copper-plates of Virūpākṣa state that he granted to many learned brāhmaṇas, the village of Ālampūṇḍi which had been the object of a previous grant by Harihara II and had then received the surname Jannāmbikābdhi.[19] It

15. R.C. Majumdar, *The History and Culture of the Indian People* (vol. VI, The Delhi Sultanate), Bombay, 1990, p. 469.

16. *ARE*, no. 86 of 1938-39; *SII*, vol. XXIV, no. 291, p. 306.

17. B.Bh. Chhabra, N. Lakshminarayana Rao & M. Ashraf Hussain, Ten Years of Indian Epigraphy (1937-46) from *Ancient India* (Bulletin of the Archaelogical Survey of India), no. 5, Jan. 1949, p. 57.

18. *EI*, vol. VIII, no. 31, vv. 7-12, p. 301.

19. *EI*, vol. III, no. 32, vv. 9-12, pp. 227-28.

appears that both Harihara's as well as Virūpākṣa's grants were made at the instance of a princess who was a sister of Harihara II and aunt of Virūpākṣa, whose name must have been Jannāmbikā because the village of Ālampūṇḍi received the surname Jannāmbikābdhi (Jannāmbikā-samudram) after her own name.[20]

Deva Rāya I

Deva Rāya I (AD 1406-22), too was a patron of scholars. They were invited to his court and the "Pearl Hall" of the palace where he honoured distinguished poets, philosophers and artists by bathing them in showers of gold coins and gems is immortalized in literature.[21] During his reign, Vijayanagara became an important centre of learning in south India.

An inscription of the period of this king, dated AD 1410-11, contains the information that Deva Rāya I made Bhūpati, son of Bukka as Governor of the Tamil country. The latter granted the village of Nelvāyi, situated in Tuṇḍiramaṇḍala as an *agrahāra* to Vāmana, son of Govinda-yajvan of the Bhāradvāja *gotra* and who had studied the three Vedas.[22]

Deva Rāya II

Deva Rāya II (AD 1422-46), was a scholar himself and also patronized the poets and scholars of his land. He appears to have been the author of the *Ratiratna-dīpikā* and the *Brahmasūtravṛtti*, a gloss on the *Brahmasūtras* of Bādarāyaṇa, following the Advaita tradition of Śaṅkara.[23] His court was

---

20. *EI*, vol. III, no. 32, vv. 9-12, p. 225.
21. R.C. Majumdar, *op. cit.*, p. 288.
22. *ARE*, 1972-73, no. A11.
23. *Vijayanagara Sexcentenary Commemmoration Volume*, Dharwar, 1936, p. 397.

the meeting place of Jaina, Śrīvaiṣṇava, and Vīraśaiva scholars.[24] Among the Sanskrit scholars of his reign the greatest was Sarvajña Siṅgama who wrote the *Nāṭakaparibhāṣā*, *Saṅgīta-sudhākara*, *Saṅgīta-cintāmaṇi* and *Rasārṇava-sudhākara*. Some of the other Sanskrit scholars were Vāmanabhaṭṭa who wrote *Bhāva-śṛṅgāra-bhūṣaṇa*, Komaṭi Vema the composer of *Śṛṅgāra-dīpikā*; Sāḷuva Gopa Tippa the grandson of Harimā, a sister of Deva Rāya II and his viceroy of Muḷubāgal, who wrote *Kāmadhenu*, a commentary on Vāmana's *Kāvyālaṅkāra* and *Tāla-dīpikā*; Maggeya Māyideva's compositions were *Anubhāva-sūtra* and *Viśeṣārtha-prakāśīkā*; *Vaiśya-Vaṁśa-sudhārṇava* was written by Kalācala Mallinātha; a commentary on *Amara* was composed by Bommalakaṇṭi Appalācārya under the patronage of Sarvajña Siṅgama; Irugappa Daṇḍanātha, the army general of Deva Rāya who was also a scholar wrote *Nānārtha-ratnamālā*.[25]

Other poets at Deva Rāya's court were Candra-kavi who has described himself as a *aṣṭa-bhāṣā-kavi* (a poet in eight languages) and thus he must have composed in Sanskrit too, and Rājaśekhara who composed the Śrīraṅgam copper-plate grant of this king.[26]

The other copper-plate grants of this ruler like the Satyamaṅgalam and Śrīraṅgam charters were also composed by talented poets, but whose names have, unfortunately, not been inscribed on these plates. Deva Rāya II thus, apart from patronizing the great Sankritists mentioned above, also made some other talented scholars compose his royal records and encouraged them to reveal their talent.

---

24. S. Srikanta Sastri, Development of Sanskrit Literature Under *Vijayanagara from Vijayanagara Sexcentenary Commemoration Volume*, Dharwar, 1936, p. 309.
25. H.M. Nagaraju, *Devaraya II and His Times*, Mysore, 1991, p. 184.
26. *Ibid*.

Deva Rāya II also encouraged the scholars by granting them many villages. The Satyamaṅgalam plates of Deva Rāya II dated AD 1424, record the gift of a village named Ciṭeyāṭyūru which he surnamed Devarāyapura after himself as an *agrahāra* along with presents (*dakṣiṇā*) to eight excellent brāhmaṇas (*dvijottama*) of the Bhāradvāja *gotra* who were masters of the *Ṛk-śākhā*.[27]

An epigraph inscribed at Attipākkam in South Arcot district in characters of the fifteenth century, belonging to either the reign of Deva Rāya I or Deva Rāya II, mentions a grant to a brāhmaṇa who was well-versed in the Vedas and Śāstras and who belonged to the Bhāradvāja *gotra* and the *Āpasthamba-sūtra*.[28]

Another copper-plate grant dated AD 1424, issued by prince Śrīgiribhūpāla, the younger brother of Deva Rāya II, who ruled over the province of Maratakapurī states that he made a grant of a village (*agrahāra*) named Nīpataṭāka to Sampatkumāra-Paṇḍita. The donee is described in this epigraph as a very renowned physician and the son of Govinda-Paṇḍita who was well-versed in the *Āyurveda* and Vedāṅgas.[29]

This village Nīpataṭāka had been given away to the same donee by (the donor's father) Vijayabhubhuj (Vijaya I or Vijayabhūpāla). It appears that due to some reason it had lapsed in the interval.[30] At the time of Śrīgiribhūpāla's grant, the village was renamed as Vijayarāyapura or Vijayarātpura, evidently in honour of its original donor, Vijayarāja.[31]

---

27. *EI*, vol. III, no. 5, vv. 25-32, pp. 38-39.
28. *ARE*, 263 of 1968-69.
29. *EI*, vol. VIII, no. 32, vv. 13-20, pp. 310-11.
30. *Ibid.*, p. 308.
31. *Ibid.*

Vīra-Nṛsiṁha

There are very few Sanskrit records in the Tamil country of the reign of Vīra Nṛsiṁha, the eldest son of Narasa Nāyaka and who ruled only for a brief period from AD 1503-09. One of these inscriptions, a copper-plate epigraph dated AD 1508 records the grant of the village Sadarimaṅgalam situated in Kulottuṅga-Coḷa-vaḷanāḍu to a scholar named Hastigiri Dīkṣita of Saṁkṛti *gotra, Bodhāyana-sūtra* and *Yajus śākhā*. The village was renamed Vīra-Śrī-Narasiṁhendrapuram. The donee in turn, distributed the land in this village to several brāhmaṇas of various *śākhās* and *gotras*.[32]

Kṛṣṇadeva Rāya

Another versatile scholar-king of this dynasty was Kṛṣṇadeva Rāya (AD 1509-29). He authored works like *Madālasācaritra, Satyavadhūpreṇanam, Śakalakathāsāra Saṁgraham, Śuktinaipuṇī Jñānacintāmaṇi, Rasamañjarī,* and the famous Sanskrit play called *Jāmbavatīkalyāṇam*, which was enacted before the people assembled to witness the spring (Caitra) festival of Śrī Virūpākṣa in the city of Vijayanagara.[33] He also composed the *Āmuktamālyada* or Viṣṇucittīya, one of the great *kāvyas* of Telugu literature. In Kṛṣṇadeva Rāya's court flourished many Sanskrit scholars and poets.

The work, *Bāla Bhārata Vyākhyā*, a commentary on *Bāla Bhārata* (which summarizes the whole story of *Mahābhārata* in twenty cantos by Agastya, the court-poet of Pratāparudra of Wārrangal) by Sāḷuva Timma, the prime minister of Kṛṣṇadeva Rāya; *Candrikā*, a commentary on Kṛṣṇamiśra's play *Prabodhacandrodaya* by Sāḷuva Timma's nephew Gopa; *Saṅgīta*

---

32. *ARE*, 1954-55, no. A9.
33. T.V. Mahalingam, *Administration and Social Life Under Vijayanagara*, Madras, 1940, p. 365.

Sūryodaya, a work on music dedicated to Kṛṣṇadeva Rāya by Lakṣmīnārāyaṇa; and *Ratirahasya* by Haribhaṭṭa, who also translated cantos VI, XI and XII of the *Bhāgavata* into Telugu were some of the works of this period. Lolla Lakṣmīdhara, a great and versatile scholar, authored many works on astronomy, astrology, law and other subjects and also wrote a commentary on the *Saundaryalaharī* of Śaṅkarācārya.[34]

Apart from these scholars who are known to the present day by their works, this ruler also encouraged other poets who composed his royal charters and whose names would be unknown but for their legacy left behind on stone and copper-plate inscriptions.

Like his predecessors, Kṛṣṇadeva Rāya also granted *agrahāras* to learned brāhmaṇas. A copper-plate grant of this ruler from the Raṅganāthasvāmi temple, Śrīraṅgam dated AD 1514 records that he gave the village of Eṇṇākudi which was situated on the south bank of the river Kāverī under the new name Kṛṣṇarāyapuram to a brāhmaṇa named Allāla-Bhaṭṭa, son of Varadarājārya, who was a master of the six systems of philosophy (*ṣaḍ-darśanyambudi*) and the Vedas, who officiated as the priest during the *Go-sahasra mahādāna*. This inscription further praises the donee as "Goddess Sarasvatī in male form and being of good conduct and intelligence."[35]

Another copper-plate grant from the Raṅganāthasvāmi temple, Śrīraṅgam, also of the period of Kṛṣṇadeva Rāya, dated AD 1528 records that this ruler made a grant of an *agrahāra* to a number of brāhmaṇas of various *gotras*, *sūtras* and *śākhās* who were well-versed in the Vedas and fit to recieve land grants.

34. T.V. Mahalingam, *Administration and Social Life Under Vijayanagara*, Madras, 1940, p. 366.

35. *EI*, vol. XVIII, no. 21A, vv. 29-35, p. 163.

The village granted was Vaḍambūr-Ekāmbarapuram situated on the south bank of the river Kāverī and its name was changed to Kṛṣṇarāyapuram at the time of the grant.[36]

Apart from the above-mentioned inscriptions, there are many other copper-plate grants of the period of Kṛṣṇadeva Rāya which record his gift of *agrahāras* to the scholars in the Vedas and other religious texts.[37]

Acyuta Rāya

Acyuta Rāya (AD 1530-42), the brother and successor of Kṛṣṇadeva Rāya was also a good scholar and has been credited with the authorship of the work *Tāḷamahodadhi*, which was commentated on by Somanātha, his contemporary.[38] Rājanātha Diṇḍima, the court poet of Acyuta Rāya wrote the Sanskrit poem, *Acyutarāyābhyudaya* during the lifetime of this ruler. He also composed the *Bhāgavatacampū*, a work dedicated to his patron. Acyuta Rāya, continuing in the tradition of his predecessors, was a patron of the learned. In the Kṛṣṇāpuram copper-plates of Sadāśiva Rāya, he is described as one "who made gifts satsifying the desires of the learned" (*vidvadiṣṭa pradātā*).[39]

The patronage extended to poets and scholars during the period of Acyuta Rāya is evident from the data revealed by an inscription of this king engraved on the wall of the Sabhānāyaka shrine in the Ekāmranātha temple in Kāñcīpuram.[40] This bilingual record mentions in the Sanskrit portion an important event which took place when Bhogarāja,

36. *EI*, vol. XVIII, no. 21B, vv. 26-40, pp. 166-68.
37. *ARE*, 1953-54, A no. 18; *ARE*, 1954-55; A no. 10; *ARE*, 1936-37, A no. 10.
38. T.V. Mahalingam, *op. cit.*, p. 366.
39. *EI*, vol. IX, no. 52, v. 24, p. 334.
40. *EI*, vol. XXXIII, no. 39, pp. 200-04.

who was appointed by Saḷaka Tirumala, the commander-in-chief of Acyuta Rāya, was the governor at Kāñcī. This Bhogarāja, who was a devotee of Lord Ekāmranātha summoned an assembly of learned Śaiva brāhmaṇas, Māheśvaras and temple officers before this deity, and on that occasion, this assembly listened to four literary works in Sanskrit composed by Śrīnivāsa Yajvan. One of these was the *Śivabhaktivilāsa*, a poem (*kāvya*) dealing with an account of the lives of the sixty-three devotees (Nāyaṉmars) of Śiva, and another was the *Caraṇādistava* (called *Pādādikeśastava* in the Tamil portion). The other two works were *Bhogāvaḷi* and *Nāmāvaḷi*.

The theme of the *Śivabhaktivilāsa* is the same as that of the Tamil poetical work entitled *Periyapurāṇam*, also known as *Tiruttoṇḍarpurāṇam*, composed by Śekkiḻār in the first half of the twelfth century AD.[41] The *Caraṇādistava*, probably the same as the *Ekāmranāthastava* as also the *Bhogāvaḷi* and the *Nāmāvaḷi* were compositions on Lord Ekāmranātha of Kāñcī.[42]

Some details about the poet, Śrīnivāsa Yajvan are also found in this epigraph. He is mentioned as the son of Sītārāma of the Bhāradvāja *gotra* and his native place was Cheyarūr. He was well-versed in the *Sāmaveda* and had performed the Vājapeya sacrifice.

This record also speaks of the gifts this talented poet received for these compositions. The *sabhā* is said to have made presents of ornaments and clothes to him and also purchased a house for him in Kāñcī for his permanent residence. He was also to receive a *śivamāna* of rice daily and five *bhāras* of grains and five *paṇas* every month and this grant was to be enjoyed hereditarily. The members of the *sabhā* were entrusted with

41. *EI*, vol. XXXIII, no. 39, p. 201.

42. *Ibid*.

the responsibility of seeing that this gift continued uninterruptedly. The munificence of the gifts made to the poet is sufficient indication of the patronage that men of letters enjoyed during this period.[43]

Apart from the scholars and poets of his reign mentioned above, there also lived many talented inscriptional poets who received support and encouragement from the royal court by commissioning them to draft the royal copper-plate charters.

Many great Vedic scholars also received gifts of land from Acyuta Rāya as seen from the evidence supplied by some of his copper-plate grants. The Kaḍalāḍi plates of Acyuta Rāya record the grant of the village of Kaḍalāḍi, *alias* Paṭendal by this ruler to Rāmacandra Dīkṣita who is described as the "best of brāhmaṇas" (*bhūmideva agrayāyin*). The latter in turn, distributed the land among forty-six brāhmaṇas after taking some shares for himself. Among the donees, twenty-four were *Ṛgvedins* (*Bahvṛca*), fifteen were *Yajurvedins* (*Yajuṣa*) and two *Sāmavedins* (*Sāmagas*).[44]

The Ūṇamāñjerī copper-plate grant of Acyuta Rāya dated AD 1540 mentions that this ruler granted the village Uhinai which was also known as Acyutendra Mahārāyapura to forty-eight brāhmaṇas learned in the Vedas and famous for their knowledge of the Śāstras. Twenty-one of these donees were students of the *Ṛgvedins* (*Bahvṛca*), eighteen students of the *Yujurveda* (*Yajuṣa*) and one was a student of the *Sāmaveda* (*Sāmaga*).[45]

One of Acyuta Rāya's queens, Tirumalāmbā or Tirumala Devī was a very talented poetess. She wrote the Sanskrit campūkāvya *Varadāmbikāpariṇayam*, the theme of this work

---

43. *Ibid.*
44. *EI*, vol. XIV, no. 22, vv. 40-104, pp. 316-22.
45. *EI*, vol. III, no. 24, pp. 151-58.

being the marriage of Acyuta Rāya with Varadāmbikā. This quasi-historical work gives a clear picture of this king's life and ends with the installation of his son Veṅkaṭādri as *yuvarāja*.[46]

A bilingual inscription found at the Raṅganāthasvāmi temple at Śrīraṅgam records in the introductory portion in Tamil that when Acyuta Rāya performed a *tulābhāra* ceremony, his queen (*rājamahiṣī*) Oḍuva Tirumalaidevī-Ammaṇavargaḷ composed two Sanskrit *śloka*s and had them engraved at several holy places, Śrīraṅgam being one of them, so that the descendents of prince Cikka Veṅkaṭādri may rule as emperors (*sārvabhaumas*).[47] The two Sanskrit verses are then engraved, which refer to the gift of Ānandanidhi. The second of these verses in Śārdūlavikrīḍita metre, with a pun on the word *nava* is very poetic:

> "Though (themselves) *nava* (nine), how can the *nidhi*s (of Kubera) attain equality with the Ānandanidhi of king Acyuta of renowned valour, which has earned *nava* (new) celebrity (or eulogy) for, while the former are surrounded by hosts of demons and seized by crowds of serpents, the latter is protected by meritorious deeds and is covered (only) by the assemblage of the good?"

Voḍūva Tirumalammā composed a Sanskrit verse (AD 1533) to commemorate the gift of *suvarṇameru* by Acyuta Rāya and the verse is inscribed in the Viṭṭhala temple of Hampi.[48] It is possible that the three verses recording the king's celebration of the *tulābhāra* of pearls at Kāñcīpuram in company with his queen Varadāmbikā and prince Cikka-Veṅkaṭādri were also

46. T.V. Mahalingam, *op. cit.*, p. 266.
47. *EI*, vol. XXIV, no. 41, pp. 289-90.
48. *ARE*, 709 of 1922; see also T.V. Mahalingam, *op. cit.*, p. 367.

her compositions.[49] It may be inferred that poetess Tirumalāmbā (composer of *Varadāmbikāpariṇayam*) was identical with Oduva Tirumalaidevī-ammaṉavargaḷ (Voḍūva Tirumalāmmā), who was originally a "reader" (*oduva*) at the royal court and subsequently rose to the position of co-queen (*rājamahiṣī*) herself.[50] She was one of the galaxy of poetesses, royal and otherwise, who attained to literary fame under the patronage of the Vijayanagara kings.[51]

Rāmarāja is spoken of in the British Museum plates of Sadāśiva as "a king Bhoja in exercising imperial sway over the sentiments of poetry" (*sāhitya rasa sāmrājya bhoga bhojamahībujaḥ*).[52] From this epithet, it is clear that Rāmarāja was a poet or at least a patron of poets.[53]

Śrīraṅga Rāya

The Ariviḷimaṅgalam copper-plate grant dated AD 1577 of the reign of Śrīraṅga Rāya (AD 1572-85), states that at the request of Sevappa Nāyaka of Tañjāvūr, the Vijayanagara emperor, Śrīraṅgadeva Rāya granted the village of Arumoḷimaṅgalam *alias* Acyutappasamudra to the Madhva guru Vijayīndra Tīrtha.[54] The grant of the village which was situated south of the river Kāverī had already been made by Acyuta (Acyutappa Nāyaka), son of Sevappa Nāyaka, but now the formal sanction from the Vijayanagara overlord had been obtained and the village was given to the donee.[55]

---

49. *EI*, vol. XXIV, p. 286.
50. *EI*, vol. XXIV, p. 287.
51. *Ibid.*
52. *EI*, vol. IV, no. 1, v. 142, p. 21.
53. *Ibid.*, p. 4.
54. *EI*, vol. XII, no. 38, vv. 27-44, pp. 352-54.
55. *Ibid.*, p. 342.

Veṅkaṭa II

Veṅkaṭa II (AD 1586-1614), was also a patron of learned men. Many of his copper-plate inscriptions record the grant of villages to the brāhmaṇa scholars. The Vilapāka epigraph of this ruler dated AD 1601 records the gifts of the village Vilapāka, surnamed Jvaraharaliṅgasamudra to Tiruvengaṭanāthārya, son of Ananta Bhaṭṭa who was conversant with the eighteen Purāṇas and belonged to the Śrīvatsa *gotra*, Āpasthamba *sūtra* and *Yajus śākhā*.[56]

An epigraph, dated AD 1602, registers a grant by Veṅkaṭa II of four villages Chittūru, Māṁbāka, Agaram and Pūruvalupāka, situated in Accarapāka of Padaivīdu-mahārāja to a brāhmaṇa named Vāsudeva-Bhaṭṭa of Ātreya *gotra*, *Āśvalāyana sūtra* and *Ṛk-śākhā*. The four villages were constituted into one unit and renamed Dattātreyapuram.[57]

Another copper-plate record dated AD 1586 mentions that he gifted two villages named Yāṁpeḍu *alias* Veṅkaṭa-mahārāya Samudram and Battulapaḷḷi also styled Veṅkaṭendra-mahārāya Samudram to a brāhmaṇa named Kaimili Kṛṣṇam Bhaṭṭa.[58]

According to an inscription dated AD 1611, this ruler granted the village of Chittūru surnamed Raghupati-samudram with its hamlet situated in Paḍaivīḍu-mahārājya to the brāhmaṇa Ammalācārya, who was well-versed in Ubhaya Vedānta, Tarka, Mahābhāṣya and the eighteen Purāṇas.[59]

A copper-plate grant of this ruler dated AD 1613, mentions the grant of a village named Kātrapāḍi-Ciṇatimmāpuram also

56. *EI*, vol. IV, no. 39, vv. 43-52, pp. 276-77.
57. *ARE*, 1957-58, no. A32.
58. *EI*, vol. XIII, no. 22A, pp. 230-31.
59. *ARE*, 1935-36, no. A13.

known as Kṛṣṇāñjamasamudram to a very large number of brāhmaṇas of various *gotras* and *śākhās*.[60]

In AD 1608, Veṅkaṭa II presented a *sarvamānya* gift of the village of Kṛṣṇapura in Paḍaivīḍu-rājya to Tūpil Nārāyaṇācārya, son of Appayācārya of the Kauśika *gotra*, *Āpastamba sūtra* and *Yajus śākhā* who was a great devotee of Raghuvīra (Lord Rāma) and a scholar in the *Śrīmad Rāmāyaṇa*.[61]

The *guru* of Veṅkaṭa II was Eṭṭūr Kumāra Tirumala Tātācārya also known as Lakṣmīkumāra and Koṭikanyādānam Tātācārya who officiated at his coronation ceremony and made numerous benefactions to the Śrī Varadarājasvāmi temple at Kāñcī as attested to by numerous Sanskrit and Tamil inscriptions found there.

Tātācārya was an eminent scholar and was the author of a work of philosophy called *Sātvika Brahma Vidyā Vilāsa*.[62] He also wrote the *Pāṇḍuraṅga-māhātmya* about the Viṣṇu temple at Panḍharpur in Maharashtra.[63]

Tātācārya composed a poem of twenty Sanskrit verses called *Hanumadviṁśati* in praise of God Hanumān, consecrated in the temple on the banks of Tātasamudram (Aiyangārkulam) at Kāñcī, dug by and named after him. These verses are engraved on the walls of the temple of Hanumān at Aiyangārkulam[64] and also at many places in the Varadarājasvāmi temple.[65]

---

60. *EI*, vol. XIII, no. 22B, pp. 233-35.
61. *ARE*, 1931-32, no. A2.
62. T.V. Mahalingam, *op. cit.*, p. 368.
63. *Ibid*.
64. *ARE*, 92 of 1923.
65. *ARE*, 651, of 1919; see also K.V. Raman, *Śrī Varadarājasvāmi Temple, Kāñcī*, Delhi, 1975, p. 83.

The great scholar Appaya Dīkṣita was also patronized by Veṅkaṭa II. This scholar enjoyed the patronage of Cinna Bomma Nāyaka, viceroy at Velūr, during the reign of Veṅkaṭa II.[66] Appaya Dīkṣita has been credited with the authorship of a hundred and four works. Although there are some Tamil inscriptions which give some information about his activities, there are no Sanskrit epigraphs in which he is mentioned.

Veṅkaṭa III

Veṅkaṭa III (AD 1630-42), was also a patron of learned men. The Kūniyūr[67] and the Nīlmaṅgala[68] plates record that when he was anointed king, the learned (of his kingdom) were presented with plenty of gold (*tadā abhiṣiktāḥ sudhīyaḥ api hemna*). These records also state that he gave wealth to wise men. The Kūniyūr record, in the concluding portion, states that Veṅkaṭa III was "a moon to the lilies (which are) learned men" (*sudhījana-kuvalaya-candraḥ*).[69] This inscription also mentions that at the request of Tirumala Nāyaka of Madurai, Veṅkaṭa III gave the village of Kūniyūr which was surnamed Muddukṛṣṇāpuram to a number of learned brāhmaṇas.[70]

The Nīlamaṅgala copper-plates dated AD 1632, also of the reign of Veṅkaṭa III, records the gift of the village Nīlmaṅgala also called Rāghavaśrīpura and its hamlets Kottanūr-Māṇambākkam to a learned brāhmaṇa named Nāgam Bhaṭṭa.[71]

Another copper-plate grant dated AD 1634, records the gift of the village Chittūru, purchased from Ambalācārya (same

66. S. Krishnaswami Ayyangar, *Sources of Vijayanagara History*, Madras, 1919, pp. 250-51.
67. *EI*, vol. III, no. 34, v. 32, p. 244 (Kūniyūr plates).
68. *EI*, vol. XXXVIII, no. 39, v. 32, p. 218 (Nīlamaṅgala plates).
69. Kūniyūr plates, *op. cit.*, v. 124, p. 250.
70. *Ibid.*, VV. 38-40, pp. 224-25.
71. Nīlamaṅgala plates, *op. cit.*, vv. 40-52, pp. 219-21.

as Ammalācārya who received this village from Veṅkaṭa II) together with the hamlet Karanai surnamed Prasanna-veṅkaṭapuram as an *agrahāra* to a number of Vaiṣṇavas by the king at the request of a brāhmaṇa officer named Bhaṇḍāram Veṅkaṭapati by Veṅkaṭa III.[72]

Nāyaka Kings of Madurai

The Nāyaka rulers of Madurai, following in the footsteps of their Vijayanagara overlords, were also patrons of scholars.

The Kūniyūr plates speak of Vīrappa Nāyaka of Madurai as one who was "the support of scholars" (*bhūdānām ālambanam*).[73] According to the Veḷḷāṅguḍi plates, Kṛṣṇa-mahīpati (Kṛṣṇappā Nāyaka II), the son of Vīrappa Nāyaka was very well-read in all the Nīti-śāstras.[74]

Many of the rulers of this dynasty gave grants of villages to the scholarly brāhmaṇas. The Daḷavāy-agrahāram copper-plate grant of Veṅkaṭa II dated AD 1586 records that at the request of the Madurai Nāyaka prince, Vīra-Bhūpa (Vīrappa Nāyaka), the son of Kṛṣṇappa Nāyaka I, king Veṅkaṭapati granted to a number of brāhmaṇas well-versed in the Vedas and Śāstras, the village of Gaṅgāvarappaṭṭi, together with a few other villages, clubbed under the name Vīrabhūpa-samudram.[75]

Another copper-plate inscription of Veṅkaṭa II, the Veḷḷāṅguḍi plates dated AD 1598, mentions that at the request of Kṛṣṇa-Bhūpati (Kṛṣṇappā Nāyaka II), the son of Vīra-Bhūpati and Tirumalāmbikā, king Veṅkaṭa II granted as an

---

72. *ARE*, 1935-36, no. A14.
73. Kūniyūr plates, *op. cit.*, v. 51, p. 245.
74. *EI*, vol. XVI, no. 23, v. 80, pp. 315-16 (Veḷḷāṅguḍi plates).
75. *EI*, vol. XII, no. 21, vv. 41-79, pp. 175-78 (Daḷavāy-agrahāram plates).

agrahāra to a large number of scholarly brāhmaṇas, the village of Veḷḷāṅguḍi together with three villages, all clubbed together under the name Vīrabhūpa-samudram.[76]

The names of the donees given in this inscription reveal that they were residents of the Telugu country who had already migrated into the Tamil country or had come down south at the invitation of the donor.[77] It appears that the Nāyaka kings of Madurai who were themselves Telugus by birth encouraged large numbers of Telugu brāhmaṇas to settle down in the Madurai and Tirunelveli regions.[78]

The Veḷḷāṅguḍi plates also praise Kṛṣṇa-bhūpati as creating many *agrahāra*s for brāhmaṇas and protecting them. This record adds that he granted enough money to brāhmaṇas of other kingdoms to redeem their lands which they had lost to their kings owing to their inability to pay the taxes.

The Padmaneri copper-plate grant of Veṅkaṭa II dated AD 1598, mentions that this king gave the village of Padmaneri to numerous brāhmaṇas at the request of Kṛṣṇappa Nāyaka II. The village, surnamed Tirumalāmbāpuram, presumably after Kṛṣṇappa Nāyaka's mother, was divided by this king into eighty-three shares and bestowed on a number of brāhmaṇas of different *gotra*s and *sūtra*s who were very well-versed in the Vedas.[79] This inscription also praises Kṛṣṇappa Nāyaka as having founded numerous *agrahāra*s for the exclusive use of brāhmaṇas proficient in the Śāstras and bestowed villages on them in perpetuity.

The Kūniyūr copper-plate inscription of Veṅkaṭa III dated AD 1634, records that the village of Kūniyūr was given by this

---

76. Veḷḷāṅguḍi plates, *op. cit.*, vv. 53-98, pp. 313-17.

77. *Ibid.*, p. 302.

78. *Ibid.*

79. *EI*, vol. XVI, no. 22, vv. 46-80, pp. 292-96 (Padmaneri plates).

king at the request of Tirumala Nāyaka to a number of brāhmaṇas "who were celebrated for their learning in the Śāstras and deeply versed in the Vedas."[80] This village was surnamed Muddukṛṣṇapuram evidently after Muddukṛṣṇa (Muttu Kṛṣṇappa Nāyaka), the father of Tirumala Nāyaka.

Nāyaka Kings of Tañjāvūr

The Nāyakas of Tañjāvūr were also great patrons of scholars and did a lot to promote learning in their land. Sevappa Nāyaka, the first Tañjāvūr Nāyaka chief made a grant of a village to the learned Madhva *guru*, Vijayīndra Tīrtha in AD 1577, who in turn distributed it among many scholarly brāhmaṇas.[81]

Sevappa's son and successor Acyutappa too was a patron of learning and granted *agrahāras* to many learned brāhmaṇas. A copper-plate inscription of Sadāśiva Rāya dated AD 1564, records the grant of the village of Muḍigoṇḍān-puttūr in Kulottuṅga-coḷa-vaḷanāḍu to a learned brāhmaṇa named Veṅkaṭārya, son of Aubalārya, belonging to Śrīvatsa *gotra*, *Āpastamba sūtra* and *Yajus śākhā*. This gift was made on the representation of Rāmarāja by Acyuta, son of Sevappa Nāyaka.[82]

Acyutappa's grandson, Vijayarāghava Nāyaka, continuing in the tradition of his family presented many *agrahāras* to scholars as attested by many copper-plate epigraphs of his reign.

One of these dated AD 1656, registers the gift of a village called Alamelumaṅgāpuram as an *agrahāra* to Vaiṣṇava

80. Kūniyūr plates, *op. cit.*, vv. 40-48, p. 245.

81. *EI*, vol. XII, no. 38, vv. 27-44, pp. 352-54 (Ariviḷimaṅgalam plates).

82. *ARE*, 1951-52, no. A9.

brāhmaṇas who were learned in the Vedas.[83] Another copper-plate inscription of Vijayarāghava Nāyaka, dated AD 1659, records gifts of lands to several Śrī Vaiṣṇavas of various *gotras* and *sūtras* of the village of Śrī Campakamannārupuram.[84] Another copper-plate grant of this king, dated in the same year appears to refer to the same gift mentioned above, consisting of forty-two shares in the *agrahāra* newly constituted, by clubbing together two villages on the same occasion.[85]

Govinda Dīkṣita, the illustrious brāhmaṇa minister who served Sevappa Nāyaka, his son Acyutappa and grandson Raghunātha Nāyaka was a very great Sanskrit scholar. He was the author of the poem *Sāhitya Sudhā*.[86] He wrote commentaries on the *Jaimini Sūtras* and *Kaumārila Darśana*.[87] He was proficient in the six systems of philosophy (*ṣaḍ-darśanas*) and was a master of Advaita and was called Advaita Vidyācārya. He was also an authority on the Dharmaśāstras. He was the elder contemporary of the famous Advaita scholar Appaya Dīkṣita and the latter held him in very high esteem.[88]

It was at the instance of Govinda Dīkṣita that the *Tiruvaiyāṟṟu Purāṇam* was translated from Sanskrit into Tamil in AD 1605, during the reign of Acyutappa Nāyaka.[89]

Only one Sanskrit inscription of Govinda Dīkṣita has been discovered.[90] This inscription etched in the Aruṇācaleśvara

83. *ARE*, 1921-22, no. A10.
84. *ARE*, 1949-50, no. A29.
85. *ARE*, 1949-50, no. A50.
86. S. Krishnaswami Ayyangar, *op. cit.*, p. 267.
87. V. Vriddhagirisan, *The Nayaks of Tanjore*, New Delhi, 1995, p. 121.
88. *Ibid*.
89. *EI*, vol. XII, no. 38, pp. 343-44.
90. *ARE*, 422 of 1928-29.

temple, Tiruvaṇṇamalai consists of two verses praising Sevappa Nāyaka by Govinda Sūri who is believed to be Govinda Dīkṣita.[91]

Two of Dīkṣita's sons were also great scholars. Yajñanārāyaṇa Dīkṣita wrote the famous works *Sāhitya Ratnākara, Raghunāthavilāsa Nāṭaka* and the *Alaṅkāra Ratnākara.* He studied under his father as well as from Raghunātha Nāyaka who taught him all the Śāstras including Vyākaraṇa, Tarka, Mīmāṁsā and Vedānta.[92]

His brother Veṅkaṭeśvara, also known as Veṅkaṭamakhi, wrote a number of commentaries as well as a treatise on Vedic trignometry. He was also a well-known authority on music and wrote the *Saṅgīta Sāmrājya* and the very well-known work *Caturdaṇḍiprakāśīkā.*[93]

Later Pāṇḍyan kings

Some of the rulers of the later Pāṇḍyan dynasty were also scholars. The Pudukkoṭṭai plates state that Varatuṅgarāma Pāṇḍya was "famous like Bhoja" (in literary capacity) (*bhoja iva*).[94]

Aḻagan Perumāḷ Abhivīrarāma *alias* Śrīvallabha was a great Tamil scholar who translated the Sanskrit poem *Naiṣadam* into Tamil called *Naidadham.* He wrote the *Kūrma Purāṇa* and *Kāśī Kāṇḍam* in Tamil.[95]

---

91. *ARE,* 1928-29, Pt. II, p.87.
92. V. Vriddhagirisan, *op. cit.,* p. 122.
93. *Ibid.*
94. *TAS,* vol. I, no. I, V. 32, p. 69.
95. N. Sethuraman, *The Later Pāṇḍyas* (1371-1759 AD), Paper presented at the 19th Annual Congress of the Epigraphical Society of India, Tiruchirapalli, 1993, p. 10.

The Daḷavāy-agrahāram plates of Ativīrarāma Pāṇḍya (1595 AD) mention that Abhirāma Pāṇḍya also known as Ativīrarāma and Śrīvallabha, was very learned in the Tamil language (*kalaṣodbhava jiṣṇuvāṇī tadbhūṣaṇaśca*).[96]

Many of the epigraphs of the later Pāṇḍyan kings also refer to the grant of land to scholars. The Śrīvilliputtūr plates of Abhirāma Pāṇḍya dated AD 1552 records that this ruler made the village of Kṣīrārjunapura into an *agrahāra* named Parākrama Pāṇḍyapura and granted it free of tax to eminent scholarly brāhmaṇas. The new name seems to have been conferred on it after the name of the king's father and would appear to have already been granted earlier to the brāhmaṇas by his predecessors.[97]

A copper-plate record dated AD 1581 registers a grant made by Abhirāma Sundareśa Varatuṅgarāma, son of Kulaśekharadeva Parākrama Pāṇḍya of the village Śolaiseri *alias* Nayinaragaram as an *agrahāra* to brāhmaṇa scholars under the new name Śivagāmasundarī-caturvedimaṅgalam, in honour of his queen.[98]

The Daḷavāy-agrahāram plates of Varatuṅgarāma Pāṇḍya dated AD 1582 also records a grant of a village named Muruganeri to a brāhmaṇa donee named Candraśekhara, son of Cokkappa Paṇḍita of Kāśyapa *gotra, Bodhāyana-sūtra* and *Yajus śākhā*. The donee was a doctor.[99]

The Pudukkoṭṭai copper-plate grant of Śrīvallabha and Varatuṅgarāma Pāṇḍya dated AD 1583 states that the villages of Pudukkoṭṭai, Illuppaiyaḍippaṭṭi, Valaṅgaimigāmaṉ and Śivakāḷaiyākkuṟuchchi were granted by these kings to a

96. *TAS*, vol. I, no. XIII, v. 17, p. 137.
97. *TAS*, vol. I, no. IX, pp. 109-13.
98. *ARE*, 1932-33, A. no. 9.
99. *TAS*, vol. I, no. XI, vv. 19-28, pp. 121-22.

number of learned brāhmaṇas of various *gotras* and *śākhās*.[100]

The Daḷavāy-agrahāram plates of Vartuṅgarāma Pāṇḍya, dated AD 1588, states that this king also called as Vīra-Pāṇḍya and Abhirāma Sundareśvara set-up many villages for brāhmaṇas.[101] He also granted the village of Silarippaṭṭi to Govinda-Bhaṭṭa, son of Udayam-Bhaṭṭa, who was a student of *Ṛgveda*.[102]

Another copper-plate grant, the Daḷavāy-agrahāram plates of Ativīrarāma Pāṇḍya dated AD 1595, states that prince Abhirāma *alias* Ativīra granted, at the request of Rāmakṛṣṇappa Nāyaka, the village of Nandikkuḍi under the name Ativīrarāmapura to a number of brāhmaṇas.[103]

A Sanskrit lithic inscription found in the *mahāmaṇḍapa* of the Viśvanāthasvāmi temple at Tenkāśī dated AD 1615 records that king Varaguṇa Śrīvallabha set-up on the bank of the river Citrā, an image of Gaṇeśa named Yajñeśa during a sacrifice and there presented to the sacrificial priests an excellent *agrahāra* named Abhiṣekapura situated in front of the deity at Tenkāśi.[104]

Marāṭhas

Although the Sanskrit inscriptions of the Marāṭha rulers do not speak much about the patronage given by these kings to education, it is well known from other sources that the Marāṭha kings of Tañjāvūr were great patrons of scholars. Many of the kings of this dynasty were eminent scholars themselves and authored many works on diverse subjects which included *Āyurveda* and music. Their court became the centre of literature

100. *TAS*, vol. I, no. I, vv. 41-61, pp. 69-71.
101. *TAS*, vol. I, no. XII, vv. 15-17, p. 129.
102. *Ibid.*, vv. 24-30.
103. *TAS*, vol. I, no. XIII, vv. 22-29, pp. 137-38.
104. *TAS*, vol. I, no. XIV, p. 147.

and art. Here was an enormous literary output in Sanskrit, Telugu and Tamil and it embraced every form of composition: epics, dramas, romantic pieces, burlesques, treatises on medicine, astrology and music.[105]

These kings granted a number of *agrahāra*s to learned brāhmaṇas where they could pursue their scholarly activities in peace. Shāji II's love for learning was so great that in AD 1693, he renamed Tiruvisanallūr as Shāhjirājapuram and gifted it to forty-six learned men of his court. This village was the seat of scholarship in languages, literature, philosophy and medicine throughout the Marāṭha period and some of the most distinguished men were Telugus.[106]

The Marāṭha rulers also invited many of their own countrymen speaking the Marathi language and planted a considerable colony of Marāṭhā and Gurjara brāhmaṇas in the Tañjāvūr kingdom.[107]

Maṭhas

The *maṭha*s attached to many of the temples in ancient and medieval India, both Vaiṣṇava and Śaiva, were great centres of Brāhmanical learning. According to the Sanskrit lexicon, *Amarakośa*, the *maṭha* is a place where "pupils and their teachers reside" (*maṭhāścātrādi nilayaḥ*).[108] These *maṭha*s were usually presided over by a pontiff and education and food was supplied to the inmates, usually made possible by lavish royal grants as also by the benefactions made by the common people.

105. C.K. Srinivasan, *Maratha Rule in the Carnatic*, Annamalainagar, 1944, p. 370.
106. K.R. Subrahmanian, *The Marāṭha Rajas of Tanjore*, Madras, 1928, p. 29.
107. *EI*, vol. XVI, p. 302.
108. Satyadeva Mishra (ed.), *Amarakośa*, Varanasi, 1972, II.2.8.

According to K.A. Nilakanta Sastri, "the temple and the *maṭha* were two great gifts of medieval Hinduism to South India."[109] While the former stood as a symbolic expression of the religious impulse of the people, the latter was an institution that stood for the propagation of certain schools of thought, of the imparting of religious education in the particular way which was agreeable to the founder.[110]

The inscriptions of the ancient Tamil country reveal that the Tamil kings gave numerous grants of land and money to the *maṭhas* of their choice. In the later period of the history of Tamil Nadu, the Sanskrit inscriptions of the Vijayanagara and Nāyaka kings reveal that this practice continued in these ages also.

The Vijayanagara rulers made many benefactions to the *maṭha* at Śṛṅgerī (in Karnataka) which was founded by the great Advaita philosopher and teacher, Śaṅkarācārya. The heads of this *maṭha,* like Vidyātīrtha and Vidyāraṇya, played a very important role in laying the foundation of the mighty Vijayanagara empire. The Sanskrit inscriptions of Tamil Nadu of the Vijayanagara times contain much information about the famous sage Vidyāraṇya (see chapter on Religion), but do not mention anything about the grants given to his *maṭha* or about the other pontiffs who succeeded him.

However, the Vijayanagara epigraphs often mention the Kāmakoṭi *maṭha,* located in Kañcīpuram and to which many of these rulers made many endowments. These records give the names of the pontiffs of this *maṭha* to whom the grants were made. The first of these is a copper-plate epigraph of the reign of Vīra-Nṛsiṁha, the elder brother of Kṛṣṇadeva Rāya, dated

109. K.A. Nilakanta Sastri, *The Coḷas*, Madras, 1984, p. 635.

110. T.V. Mahalingam, *op. cit.*, p.331.

AD 1506. According to this record, this ruler granted two villages named Elichchūr and Veṇpākkam to Mahādeva Sarasvatī, disciple of Sadāśiva Sarasvatī (*sadāśiva śiṣyaḥ*) who is described in this record in glowing terms as a *paramahaṁsa-parivrājakācārya*, seeking liberation (*mumukṣave*), whose body is smeared with ashes (*bhasmadhūḷita gātrāya*), adorned with *rudrākṣa* garlands (*rudrākṣāvaḷi dhāriṇe*), who is a great person (*mahātmane*), who is unaffected by the effects of cold and heat (*śītoṣṇādhi dvandva duḥkha vyatītāya*), who has thoroughly studied all the Śāstras (*samasta-śāstra-pāthodhi pāragāya*), is also a *tapasvī* (*tapasvine*), who has attained the eight *yoga sādhanās*, namely *yama, niyama,* etc. (*aṣṭāṅga yoga yuktāya*), who is full of grace (*dayāśīlāya*), who is of bright intellect (*dhīmate*) and resembles Lord Śiva himself (*śivarūpiṇe*).[111]

Another record of the same ruler mentions that he gave the village of Kuḍiyānṭaṇḍal (Chengleput district) to this same teacher, who is described in exactly the same glowing terms as in the previous record.[112]

A copper-plate grant of Kṛṣṇadeva Rāya (AD 1521), records that this ruler gave to Candracūḍa Sarasvati, the disciple of Mahādeva Sarasvati, the villages of Poḍavūr (this name was converted to Kṛṣṇarāyapuram at the time of this grant) and Kāṭapaṭṭu. This inscription praises this pontiff as a talented and high-souled saint, who was the disciple of Mahādeva Sarasvatī (*mahādeva sarasvatyāḥ śiṣyaḥ*), a devotee of Śiva (*śiva cetase*), the famous commentator on all the Śāstras (*vyākhyātākhila śāstrāya*), an expert in Māyāvāda (*māyāvādāmbudīndave*) and who was a resident of Kāñcīpuram (*kāñcīpuranivāsinaḥ*).[113]

111. *CPIK*, no. II, pp. 24-26.
112. *CPIK*, no. III, pp. 42-46; *EI*, vol. XIV, no. 17, pp. 236-40.
113. *EI*, vol. XIII, no. 8, p. 129 (Kāñcīpuram plates of Kṛṣṇadeva Rāya).

Another copper-plate epigraph of the same ruler dated AD 1527, records a grant of the village Udayaṁbākkam (Chengleput district) to Sadāśiva Sarasvatī, the disciple of Candraśekhara Sarasvatī (or Candracūḍa Sarasvatī).[114]

Thus, Sadāśiva Sarasvatī the donee of this grant, was the pupil of Candracūḍa Sarasvatī, the donee of the earlier grant. Sometime in the interval between the two grants (AD 1521 and AD 1527) Candracūḍa must have passed away and must have been succeeded by his disciple Sadāśiva.[115] The four grants mentioned above give the names of four successive pontiffs of the Kāmakoṭi Maṭha at Kāñcīpuram, namely, Sadāśiva, Mahādeva, Candracūḍa and Sadāśiva, who were contemporaneous with the Vijayanagara kings Vīra-Nṛsiṁha and Kṛṣṇadeva Rāya (from AD 1506-29).[116] One of the pontiffs of this *maṭha*, the third in apostolic descent from Sadāśiva (AD 1527), composed a work, *Guru-rāja-ratna-mālā-stava* in which the names of the above-mentioned teachers are given in the same order.[117]

Later, this *maṭha* seems to have been shifted to Gajāraṇyakṣetram or Jambūkeśvaram (near Tiruchirapalli).[118] An inscription of the period of Vijayaraṅga Cokkanātha of Madurai (AD 1708), in Sanskrit and Telugu records the grant of lands in some villages in Tiruchirapalli district and some lands on both sides of the river Kāverī for the conduct of worship, offerings and charities in the Śaṅkarācārya Maṭha at

---

114. *EI*, vol. XIV, no. 12, vv. 32-43, pp. 173-74 (Udayambakkam grant of Kṛṣṇadeva Rāya).

115. *EI*, vol. XIV, no. 12, vv. 32-43; *EI*, vol. XIV, no. 12, vv. 32-43, p. 169.

116. *Ibid*.

117. *EI*, vol. XIV, no. 17, pp. 233-34.

118. T.V. Mahalingam, *op. cit.*, p. 336.

Jambūkeśvaram.[119] The document records that the grant was made by this ruler at the instance of the then presiding *guru* of the *maṭha*, whose name is unfortunately not given in this record, but who is described as *Lokaguru Śrīmad Śaṅkarācārya Svamulavāru*. He and his line of disciples on the pontifical throne were to enjoy the lands and to protect the charities.

The above inscriptions show the reverence of these rulers towards the pontiffs of these *maṭhas*, who were very learned and holy men as those records themselves indicate. The benefactions of these kings must have gone a long way in helping the maintenance of the *maṭhas*, especially, the boarding and lodging of the disciples who came there to imbibe the teachings of these scholars and to continue the tradition of the *maṭha*.

Poet-Composers of the Sanskrit Inscriptions

The Sanskrit inscriptions found in different parts of India have been composed by great scholars and the poetry contained therein reveals that some of them must have been poets of great calibre. The Sanskrit inscriptions of the ancient Tamil country of the period of the Pallavas, Pāṇḍyas and Coḷas are mostly written in the form of poems, although some are in prose. The names and personal qualifications of these poets are also inscribed at the very end of these epigraphs. A study of these poems shows the high level which Sanskrit poetry had attained in the ancient Tamil country and also the skill of these poet-scholars.

In the subsequent periods also in the Tamil country, we find the Sanskrit copper-plate epigraphs of the period of the Vijayanagara, Nāyaka and later Pāṇḍyan kings to be mostly in verse form and an in-depth study of these reveals that these

119. *EI*, vol. XVI, no. 12, pp. 94-96.

poems were written by eminent Sanskrit poets. Once again, the names of these poet-composers are found engraved at the end of the records along with some details about their family and their educational qualifications.

The Nallūr inscription of Harihara II states that the composer of the verses of this charter (*śāsana śloka karta*) was Mallanārādhyavṛttika, who had frequently performed sacrifices and who was the son of Koṭiśāradhya.[120]

The Śrīraṅgam copper-plate grant of Deva Rāya II, which is mostly in Sanskrit verse, except for a portion in Tamil, records that it was composed by Rājaśekhara.[121] However, no details about this composer of this charter are given.

A detailed study of the inscription clearly shows the literary skill of this poet who had composed these forty-eight verses in different metres, and was chosen by his king to compose this royal grant.

The composer of the official records of Kṛṣṇadeva Rāya and Acyuta Rāya in the Tamil country was the poet named Sabhāpati. Both the Śrīraṅgam copper-plate charters of this ruler mention at the end that Sabhāpati composed the documents at the command of Kṛṣṇadeva Rāya.[122] The Kāñcīpuram epigraph of this ruler mentions that it was composed by Urukavi. According to the editors of this inscription, the name Urukavi, perhaps means "great poet," but a blank in the next line of the epigraph may well be filled in with the word Sabhāpati, as the metre of that word requires it.[123] Sabhāpati was the famous rhymester of Kṛṣṇadeva Rāya's

---

120. *EI*, vol. III, no. 19, v. 35, p. 123 (Nallūr grant of Harihara II).
121. *EI*, vol. XVIII, no. 17, v. 41, p. 143.
122. *EI*, vol. XVIII, no. 21A, v. 47, p. 164; *ibid.*, no. 21B, v. 44, p. 169.
123. *Ibid.*, p. 126.

court. Urukavi was probably another name for Sabhāpati or a title assumed by him.[124] The Udayambākkam grant of this king also mentions this gifted poet as the composer of this record.[125]

The same poet also wrote the verses of the Kaḍalāḍi[126] as well as Ūṇamāñjerī copper-plate grants of Acyuta Rāya.[127] The British Museum[128] and Kṛṣṇāpuram[129] copper-plates of Sadāśiva Rāya mention that these documents were composed by Sabhāpati Svayambhu, who was obviously the son of Sabhāpati. The Arivilimaṅgalam plates of Śrīraṅgarāya also mentions clearly at the end of the record that this deed was drafted by Svayambhu, son of Sabhāpati.[130]

Some of the records of Veṅkaṭa II like the Daḷavāy-agrahāram plates,[131] the Padmaneri plates,[132] the British Museum plates[133] and the Veḷḷāṅguḍi plates[134] were composed by Kṛṣṇakavi, the son of Kāmakoṭi and grandson of Sabhāpati. However, the second of the British Museum plates of the same ruler, which consist of the same thiry-eight verses at the beginning, state that the stanzas subseqent to the *praśasti* were

124. *Ibid.*
125. Udayambākkam grant, *op. cit.*, v. 44, p. 174.
126. *EI*, vol. XIV, no. 22, v. 105, p. 322 (Kaḍalāḍi plates of Acyuta Rāya).
127. *EI*, vol. III, no. 24, v. 110, p. 158 (Ūṇamāñjerī plates of Acyuta Rāya).
128. *EI*, vol. IV, no. 1, v. 151, p. 22 (British Museum Plates of Sadāśiva Rāya).
129. *EI*, vol. IX, no. 52, vv. 105-06, p. 339 (Kṛṣṇāpuram plates of Sadāśiva Rāya).
130. Ariviḷimaṅgalam plates, *op. cit.*, v. 65, p. 355.
131. *EI*, vol. XII, no. 21, v. 200, p. 185.
132. Padmaneri plates, *op. cit.*, vv. 152-53, p. 296.
133. *EI*, vol. XIII, no. 22A, v. 64, p. 231.
134. Veḷḷāṅguḍi plates, *op. cit.*, lines 557-58, p. 318.

composed by Cidambara-kavi, the nephew of Śivasūrya-kavi.[135]

The Nīlamaṅgala[136] and Kūniyūr[137] copper-plate grants of Veṅkaṭa III were composed by Rāmakavi, the son of Kāmakoṭi and grandson of Sabhāpati.

The Daḷavāy-agrahāram grant of Veṅkaṭa II composed by Kṛṣṇa Kavi, as mentioned earlier, contains many verses found in the Maṅgalampāḍ grant of Veṅkaṭa II where it is stated that the composer of the verses was one Cidambara-kavi, sister's son of Śivasūrya, the king of poets, whereas, the Kūniyūr, Vilāpakkam, Koṇḍyāta and Kallakurśi grants, which contain many of the verses of the Daḷavāy-agrahāram plates are said to be the compositions of Rāma, the son of Kāmakoṭi and the grandson of Sabhāpati; a similar grant belongs to the Kūdli Śṛṅgerī Svāmī's Maṭha, and the writing is claimed there by Kṛṣṇakavi Kāmakoṭi, the grandson of Sabhāpati.[138]

It appears that there is a great deal of divergence in the statement as to the actual authorship of the composition, and it seems that some of the earlier members of the family, perhaps Sabhāpati, was the actual author, and every time his verses were repeated and added to by drawing up fresh documents by the later members of the family, the composition was claimed to be his by the copyist.[139]

Among the Sanskrit copper-plate grants of the later Pāṇḍyas, the Daḷavāy-agrahāram plates of Varatuṅgarāma Pāṇḍya dated AD 1582 were composed by a poet named Nārāyaṇa.[140] The Pudukkoṭṭai plates of Śrīvallabha and

135. *EI*, vol. XIII, no. 22B, v. 82, p. 235.

136. Nīlmaṅgala plates, *op. cit.*, v. 5, p. 220.

137. Kūniyūr plates, v. 125, p. 250.

138. *EI*, vol. XII, p. 163.

139. *Ibid.*

140. *TAS*, vol. I, no. XI, v. 44, p. 124.

Varatuṅgarāma Pāṇḍya were written by Abhirāma Sabhāpati Kāmākṣī[141], while the Daḷavāy-agrahāram plates of Ativīrarāma Pāṇḍya were composed by Rājanātha-kavi, son of Svayambhū.[142]

Thus, it seems that even in the period of the later Pāṇḍyan rulers, who were the vassals of the kings of Vijayanagara, the descendents of Sabhāpati continued to be the composers of the royal documents of their kings.

Apart from the copper-plate epigraphs, there are also many lithic inscriptions of the period of the Vijayanagara, Nāyaka and the later Pāṇḍyan kings which mention the names of the composers of the epigraphs.

A Sanskrit record found in the second *prākāra* of the Raṅganāthasvāmi temple, Śrīraṅgam speaks of a grant of land to this temple by Vyāsa Bhāratī Yogi, who was a disciple of Parivrājaka Rāmacandra Sarasvatī for offerings to Lord Raṅganātha.[143] This inscription, dated AD 1429, of the period of Deva Rāya II, mentions that the donor himself composed this epigraph.

An undated epigraph in Sanskrit verse found at the Varadarājasvāmi temple at Kāñcīpuram which mentions the benefactions of Rāmarāya to the Varadarāja and Ekāmranātha temples states that Ahobala-dīkṣita was the composer.[144] It is likely that this poet was the spiritual preceptor of Viṭṭaladeva and Cinna Timma, cousins of Rāmarāya who conducted successful campaigns in the southern areas of the Vijayanagara empire.[145]

---

141. *TAS*, vol. I, no. I, vv. 184-85, p. 80.
142. *TAS*, vol. I, no. XIII, v. 85, p. 142.
143. *ARE*, 55 of 1938-39; *SII*, vol. XXIV, no. 323, p. 329.
144. *ARE*, 656 of 1919.
145. *SII*, vol. XXIV, no. 455, p. 437.

Similarly, a bilingual record found in the Vaikuṇṭha-nārāyaṇa Perumāḷ temple at Ākkūr of the period of Perumāḷ Kulaśekhara Pāṇḍya mentions that the two Sanskrit verses found in this inscription were composed by Bhaṭṭa Narasiṁha and Bhaṭṭa Devaratha respectively.[146]

The lithic inscriptions of the Tañjāvūr Nāyaka period also provide the names of the poets who composed these Sanskrit epigraphs. A bilingual inscription of Sevappa Nāyaka found at the Aruṇācaleśvara temple at Tiruvaṇṇāmalai mentions that the four Sanskrit verses of this record were composed by Śrīnivāsa Dīkṣita of Śaktimaṅgalam.[147] The first verse mentions that Sevappa constructed, or rather completed the tall *gopura* of eleven storeys in this temple, while the second of these verses states that this *gopura* was constructed at the request of two sages (*tapasvins*) named Śivāneśa and Lokanātha. In the third verse, the poet of this epigraph gives some interesting details about himself and his family. His parents were Āṇḍampiḷḷai and Lakṣmī and he had a son named Keśava Dīkṣita and that he had a title (*biruda*) "Divāpradīpa."

From these facts, it is possible to identify this poet with Śrīnivāsa Dīkṣita of Satyamaṅgalam, a village in the Vellore taluk of North Arcot district, who was much honoured in the court of the Tañjāvūr Nāyaka kings, especially that of Raghunātha, from whom he is said to have recieved the surname "Ratnakheṭadvani" in commemoration of a particularly fine Sanskrit verse he had composed describing the beauty of the evening twilight.[148]

The inscription adds that this poet had two more sons named Ardhanārīśvara Dīkṣita and Rājacūḍāmaṇi Dīkṣita, the

146. *ARE*, 230 of 1925.

147. *ARE*, 419 of 1928-29.

148. *ARE*, 1928-29, Pt. II, pp. 86-87.

latter having attained much success as an author. The last verse is an eulogistic stanza in praise of this *gopura*.

Another inscription from the same *gopura* contains two Sanskrit verses by a person named Govinda Sūri, who mentions that he was a dependent of Sevappa Bhūpa (Sevappa Nāyaka) and expresses his gratitude for the favours received by composing verses in praise of his patron.[149] In all probability, the author of these verses is identical with Govinda Dīkṣita, who became the minister of Sevappa's successor, Acyutappa and Raghunātha and rose to fame on account of his administrative capacity and his pious and charitable disposition.[150]

It can thus be seen that the rulers of the medieval Tamil country were very keen to promote Sanskrit and to encourage the poets of their land. Apart from the royal charters inscribed on copper-plates by the talented poets, even the lesser-known poets who composed only a couple of stanzas which were inscribed on the temple walls, were allowed to etch their names alongside to survive for all time. The composers of these lithic epigraphs have openly declared their gratitude to their patrons and the honours and titles bestowed on them by these kings.

Literary Beauty of the Sanskrit Inscriptions

The talent of the composers of the Sanskrit inscriptions of the period of this work is evident. These epigraphs are composed in a variety of metres and embellished with different *alaṅkāras*. Many of the copper-plate grants of the Vijayanagara period are bilingual as has been mentioned earlier, but many of them have been composed wholly in Sanskrit verse.

---

149. *ARE*, 1928-29.

150. *ARE*, 1928-29, Pt. II, p. 87.

The Kuḍiyāntaṇḍal copper-plate inscription of Vīra-Nṛsiṁha consists of thirty verses composed in the *Anuṣṭubh, Śārdūlavikrīḍita, Hariṇī, Śragdhara* and *Mālinī* metres.[151]

The Śrīraṅgam copper-plate grant of Kṛṣṇadeva Rāya is composed in fifty verses in metres like *Śragdhara, Anuṣṭubh, Gītī* and *Śālinī.*[152] Similarly, the Udayambākkam plates of the same ruler consists of fifty verses in *Anuṣṭubh, Śārdūlavikrīḍita, Śragdhara, Hariṇī* and *Doḍhaka* metres.[153]

Some of the copper-plate inscriptions of the later Vijayanagara kings like Veṅkaṭa II are extremely long records consisting of a large number of verses. The Padmaneri grant of Veṅkaṭa II consists of one hundred and fifty nine verses composed in as many as fifteen metres like *Anuṣṭubh, Śārdūlavikrīḍita, Rathoddhata, Śragdhara, Vasantatilakā, Pṛthvī, Śikhariṇī, Mālinī, Śailaśikha, Indravajra, Puṣpitāgra, Upajāti, Āryā, Śālinī* and *Doḍhaka.*[154]

Likewise, the Daḷavāy-agrahāram[155] and the Vellānguḍi plates[156] of this ruler are very lengthy documents and composed in numerous metres in beautiful style.

A few of the copper-plate inscriptions of the later Pāṇḍyan rulers like the Pudukkoṭṭai plates of Śrīvallabha and Varatuṅgarāma Pāṇḍya[157] which consists of one hundred and ninety-seven verses are some of the longest records of the period of this study.

---

151. *EI*, vol. XIV, no. 17, pp. 236-40 (Kuḍiyāntaṇḍal grant of Vīra-Nṛsiṁha).
152. *EI*, vol. XVIII, no. 21A, v. 162-64.
153. Udayambākkam plates, *op. cit.*, pp. 170-174.
154. Padmaneri plates, *op. cit.*, v. 5, pp. 292-96.
155. *EI*, vol. XII, no. 21, pp. 171-85.
156. Veḷḷāṅguḍi plates, *op. cit.*, pp. 313-18.
157. *TAS*, vol. I, no. I, pp. 64-82.

Apart from the inscriptions which are fully in verse, there are some which are a mixture of prose and verse, marking them out to be delightful campū-kāvyas. There are also a few epigraphs which have only a couple of verses at the beginning or end, and the major section of which is in prose. An inscription of Muddaya-Daṇḍanāyaka found in the Raṅganāthasvāmi temple, Śrīraṅgam is prefaced and ends with Sanskrit verses, but is couched in prose in between.[158] The prose passage consists of a long string of epithets (*birudāvaḷī*), beautifully arranged in different patterns such as *anuprāsa*, *sāṁkhyapūrva*, *akṣaramālā* and *antādi*.[159]

The poets of the Sanskrit inscriptions of south India were very well-acquainted with the works of the classical Sanskrit writers like Kālidāsa, Bāṇa and Bhāravi. Ravikīrti, the author of the famous Aihoḷe inscription (7th century AD) openly compares himself with Kālidāsa and Bhāravi.[160] Many of the composers of the Sanskrit epigraphs of the Pallavas, Pāṇḍyas and Coḷas have freely borrowed ideas and expressions from the works of the great poets of ancient India.[161]

Similarly, in the Sanskrit inscriptions of the Vijayanagara period also, we notice that the composers of the inscriptions have been influenced by the illustrious poets and composers of prose of the classical age. An invocatory verse in praise of Śiva found in a very large number of the copper-plate grants of the Vijayanagara and later Pāṇḍyan rulers and which runs as follows:

---

158. *SII*, vol. IV, no. 505, pp. 143-44; *SII*, vol. XXIV, no. 293, p. 307.

159. V.S. Subrahmanian, Characteristic Features of Sanskrit Inscriptions from, *South Indian Studies* (Dr. T.V. Mahalingam Commemoration Volume), Mysore, 1990, p. 198.

160. *EI*, vol. VI, no. 1, v. 37, p. 7.

161. Chithra Madhavan, *History and Culture of Tamil Nadu — Vol. I (upto c. 1310 AD)*, New Delhi, 2005, p. 206.

namas-tuṅga-śiras-cumbi-candra-cāmara-cāvare,
trailokya-nagar-ārambha-mūla-stambhāya-śaṁbhave,

is identical with the opening verse of Bāṇa's *Harṣacarita.*[162]

Maṇipravāḷa Style

A very unique development in the writing of inscriptions in the *maṇipravāḷa* style began in the ancient period in the Tamil country. This style involves the use of clusters of Sanskrit expressions along with fine Tamil expressions sometimes set in the form of versified prose.[163]

The very first inscription written in this style is the Madurai (Vaigai river bed) inscription of Pāṇḍyan Chendaṉ of the second half of the seventh century AD.[164] The *maṇipravāḷa* style was put to great use by the Vaiṣṇava commentators of the *Divya-Prabandham* and woven into a special dialect of their own.[165]

During the Vijayanagara period we find some *maṇipravāḷa* inscriptions. One such epigraph is a record of Sadāśiva Rāya dated AD 1545, found in the Raṅganāthasvāmi temple, Śrīraṅgam,[166] which contains some information about a Vaiṣṇava preceptor, named Nantigaḷ Nārāyaṇa Jīyar who was associated with the administration of the Śrīraṅgam temple and who did yeoman service with regard to flood control in this temple town. The scripts used in this inscription are Grantha and Tamil and the language provides a good example

162. V. Subrahmanian, *op. cit.*, p. 197.
163. K.G. Krishnan, Sanskrit Inscriptions of Tamil Nadu, from *Svasti Śrī* (B. Ch. Chhabra Felicitation Volume), New Delhi, 1984, p. 23.
164. *EI*, vol. XXXVIII, no. 4, pp. 27-33.
165. K.G. Krishnan, *op. cit.*
166. *EI*, vol. XXIX, no. 9, pp. 71-78.

of the typical Vaiṣṇava style with a fair admixture of Sanskrit and Tamil words.[167]

Similarly, another *maṇipravāḷa* inscription discovered at Tiruvānaikāval near Śrīraṅgam belongs to the period of Veṅkaṭa II. This record, which mentions the selection of a married person to the pontificate of the Pāśupata Maṭha at Tiruvānaika which had till then been conferred on a celibate only is couched in a very ornate *maṇipravāḷa* style.[168] The quaint style of the record bristles with bombastic quotations from several works in seeming support of this transition.[169]

Apart from their mastery over the Sanskrit language and skill in expression, a perusal of their inscriptions reveals that these composers were great scholars who were well-acquainted with the epics and Purāṇas. Their knowledge of Vaiṣṇava and Śaiva mythology is revealed in their compositions.

Vaiṣṇava Mythology

Lord Viṣṇu is referred to in many of the copper-plate epigraphs of the Vijayanagara rulers by his various names and epithets like Nārāyaṇa, Raṅganātha, Veṅkaṭeśa, Upendra, Keśava, Ādikeśava, Mādhava, Śauri and Śārṅgadhara. The poets of these Sanskrit inscriptions composed beautiful invocatory verses in praise of Lord Viṣṇu.

The Vijayanagara rulers contributed much to the enrichment and expansion of the Śrī Raṅganāthasvāmi temple at Śrīraṅgam (Tiruchirapalli district). One invocatory verse in the Śrīraṅgam plates of Deva Rāya II is in praise of Lord Raṅganātha of this shrine: "May God Nārāyaṇa who is pleased

167. *EI*, vol. XXIX, no. 9, p. 71.

168. *ARE*, 135 of 1936-37.

169. *ARE*, 1936-37, Pt. II, p. 91.

to recline on (the serpent) Śeṣa in (the island of) Śrīraṅgam, on the bank of the tank Candrapuṣkariṇi on the sands of the Kāverī, adored by Brahmā, and who is attended by the Goddesses Lakṣmī and Bhū (Earth), protect you."[170]

Two inscriptions of the later Pāṇḍya kings, the Pudukkoṭṭai plates of Śrīvallabha and Varatuṅgarāma Pāṇḍya[171] and the Daḷavāy-agrahāram plates of Varatuṅgarāma Pāṇḍya (dated AD 1588)[172] contain a stanza extolling Viṣṇu.

VEṄKAṬEŚA

Many of the copper-plate charters of Veṅkaṭa II such as the Daḷavāy-agrahāram plates,[173] the two British Museum plates,[174] the Veḷḷāṅguḍi plates,[175] and the Padmaneri plates[176] mention "Salutations to Lord Veṅkaṭeśvara" (*śrī veṅkaṭeśāya namaḥ*) as the very first line in these inscriptions. The Nīlamaṅgala[177] and Kūniyūr[178] records of Veṅkaṭa III, likewise open with the same auspicious sentence.

All the above-mentioned records also end with the auspicious term Śrī Veṅkaṭeśa. The seal of the Veḷḷānguḍi, Kūniyūr and Nīlamaṅgala grants also bear the legend "Śrī Veṅkaṭeśa." This is not surprising as the later Vijayanagar kings were ardent devotees of Lord Veṅkaṭeśvara of Tirumala.

---

170. *EI*, vol. XVIII, no. 17, v. 3, p. 140.
171. *EI*, vol. I, no. 1, v. 2, p. 64.
172. *TAS*, vol. I, no. XII, v. 3, p. 127.
173. *EI*, vol. XII, no. 21, v. 1, p. 171.
174. *EI*, vol. XIII, no. 22A, p. 226; *ibid.*, no. 22B, p. 232.
175. Veḷḷāṅguḍi plates, *op. cit.*, p. 313.
176. Padmaneri plates, *op. cit.*, p. 292.
177. Nīlamaṅgala plates, *op. cit.*, v. 1., p. 213.
178. Kūniyūr plates, *op. cit.*, v. 1., p. 240.

VARĀHA

The boar-incarnation or Varāhāvatāra seems to have been a favourite deity of the Vijayanagara rulers.

In the earlier Sanskrit inscriptions of the ancient Tamil country, of the times of the Pallavas, Pāṇḍyas and Coḷas, there are absolutely no invocatory verses to Varāha. Only one inscription of the fourteenth century of the period of the Kākatiya king, Pratāparudra II contains a verse in praise of Varāhāvatāra.[179]

There are a very large number of copper-plate charters of the Vijayanagara kings which contain invocatory verses in praise of the Varāhāvatāra. The very first verse of the Ālampūṇḍi plates of Virūpākṣa states, "Adoration to the primeval boar, whose (pair of) tusks have the shape of the syllable *Oṁ*, who is sporting in the pond (which is) the Śruti (Veda), and who possesses firm power (or who carries the constant Goddess of Fortune)."[180] Likewise, the Śoraikkāvūr plates of the same king contains a similar verse in praise of the boar incarnation.[181]

The Madras Museum plates of Śrīribhūpāla opens with the sentence "Salutations to Bhūvarāha" (*bhūvarāhāya namaḥ*)[182] while the third verse again praises him thus: "Salutations to that effulgence, whose form is that of the boar, whose arm bristled (with pleasure) at the loving embrace of the Earth (when he brought Her up from the bottom of the sea) and which increases our happiness and plenty."[183]

179. *EI*, vol. VII, no. 18, v. 1, p. 130.

180. *EI*, vol. III, no. 32, v. 1, p. 226 (Ālāmpūṇḍi plates of Virūpākṣa).

181. *EI*, vol. VIII, no. 31, v. 1, p. 30 (Śoraikkāvūr plates of Virūpākṣa).

182. *EI*, vol. VIII, no. 32, line. 1, p. 309 (Madras Museum plates of Śrīgiribhūpāla).

183. *Ibid*.

The copper-plate grants of Deva Rāya II from Śrīraṅgam, one dated AD 1434[184] and the other in AD 1428[185] and the Satyamaṅgalam plates[186] of this ruler, also contain very poetic verses in praise of the boar-incarnation of Viṣṇu.

Similarly, the copper-plate inscriptions of the other rulers of this dynasty invariably contain beautiful invocatory verses to Varāha. The Śrīraṅgam plates of Mallikārjuna[187] has a short verse praising this God, while the Nallūr inscription of Harihara II contains three beautiful verses in adoration of Varāha.[188]

The other copper-plate inscriptions which have verses about Varāha are the Śrīraṅgam plates of Harihara-Rāya Uḍaiyār (III),[189] the Kuḍiyāntaṇḍal grant of Vīra-Nṛsiṁha,[190] the Ariviḷimaṅgalam plates of Śrīraṅgarāya II,[191] the Kāñcīpuram plates,[192] Śrīraṅgam plates[193] and the Udayambākkam plates[194] of Kṛṣṇadeva Rāya, the Kaḍalādi[195] and Ūṇamāñjerī plates[196] of Acyuta Rāya, the British Museum

184. *EI*, vol. XVIII, no. 17, v. 2, p. 140.

185. *EI*, vol. XVI, no. 8, v. 3, p. 113.

186. *EI*, vol. III, no. 5, v. 2, p. 37.

187. *EI*, vol. XVI, no. 28, v. 1, p. 347 (Śrīraṅgam plates of Mallikārjuna).

188. Nallūr Inscription, *op. cit.*, vv. 2,4 & 5., p. 120.

189. *EI*, vol. XVI, no. 15, lines 1-5, p. 224 (Śrīraṅgam plates of Harihara Rāya Uḍaiyār III).

190. Kuḍiyantaṇḍal plates, *op. cit.*, v. 2., p. 236.

191. Ariviḷimaṅgalam plates, *op. cit.*, v. 2., p. 350.

192. *CPIK*, v. 2, p. 68.

193. *EI*, vol. XVIII, no. 21A, v. 2; *ibid.*, no. 21B, v. 2.

194. Udayambākkam plates, *op. cit.*, v. 2., p. 170.

195. Kaḍalāḍi plates, *op. cit.*, v. 3.

196. Ūṇamāñjerī plates, *op. cit.*, v. 2., p. 151.

plates[197] and the Kṛṣṇāpuram plates of Sadāśiva Rāya,[198] the Daḷavāy-agrahāram plates[199] and the Veḷḷāṅguḍi plates of Veṅkaṭa II.[200]

It is interesting to note that starting from the Nallūr grant of Harihara II, a large number of the copper-plate inscriptions carry the very same verse praising Varāha thus: "Let it protect you — the staff-like tusk of Hari, who disported himself as a boar, (placed) on which (tusk), the Earth resembled a parasol, with the golden mountain (Meru) as its point."

It is interesting to note that a firman issued by the emperor of Delhi in AD 1710, in favour of his Holiness, the Svāmi Paramahaṁsa Parivrājakācārya of the Maṭha at Kāñcī contains this verse about Varāha at the beginning of the record.[201]

Apart from inscriptions of the Vijayanagara dynasty, other records such as the Śrīraṅgam plates of Mummaḍi Nāyaka contain beautiful invocatory verses in praise of Varāha.[202]

The later Pāṇḍya rulers also adopted the practice of beginning their inscriptions with stanzas extolling Varāha. The Daḷavāy-agrahāram plates of Varatuṅgarāma Pāṇḍya (dated AD 1582) begin with three verses in praise of this deity.[203] The Daḷavāy-agrahāram plates of Ativīrarāma Pāṇḍya also opens with a benediction to this God.[204]

---

197. British Museum plates of Sadāśiva Rāya, *op. cit.*, v. 2., p. 12.
198. Kṛṣṇāpuram plates, *op. cit.*, v. 2., pp. 331-32.
199. *EI*, vol. XII, no. 21, v. 3., p. 171.
200. Veḷḷāṅguḍi plates, *op. cit.*, v. 3, p. 313.
201. *CPIK*, p. 116.
202. *EI*, vol. XIV, no. 3, v. 3, p. 90.
203. *TAS*, vol. I, no. XI, vv. 1-3, pp. 117-18.
204. *TAS*, vol. I, no. XIII, v. 2, p. 135.

Some of the verses praising this deity, found in the epigraphs of the later Pāṇḍyas are the very same as those inscribed in the grants of the Vijayanagara rulers.

RĀMA

The seventh incarnation of Lord Viṣṇu as Rāma, which figures in a large number of Sanskrit epigraphs of the Tamil country, starting from the Pallava age, also finds frequent mention in the inscriptions of the Vijayanagara period. The Kuḍiyāntaṇḍal plates of Vīra-Nṛsiṁha state that this ruler and Kṛṣṇa Rāya (Kṛṣṇadeva Rāya) were born to Narasa Nāyaka of Tippajī and Nāgalā Devī just as Rāma and Lakṣmaṇa were born to Pankiratha (Daśaratha) of Kauśalyā and Sumitrā.[205]

The inscriptions of Veṅkaṭa II such as the Daḷavāy-agrahāram plates,[206] the Veḷḷāṅguḍi plates,[207] the two British Museum plates[208] and the Padmaneri plates[209] which contain the same set of introductory verses, mention that this ruler was anointed king by his spiritual preceptor, Tātayārya just as Rāma was anointed by Vaśiṣtha.

All the above-mentioned inscriptions of Veṅkaṭa II contain an invocatory verse in praise of Lord Rāma. "I take refuge in that pair of objects which is to be worshipped by the Gods (and) at whose meritorious touch, a stone became the best of women."

In the Sanskrit inscriptions of the dynasty of the later Pāṇḍyas too, there are introductory verses in praise of Rāma. The very first verse of the Śrīvilliputtūr plates of Abhirāma

---

205. *EI*, vol. XIV, no. 17, vv. 12-13, p. 237.
206. *EI*, vol. XII, no. 21, v. 28., p. 174.
207. Veḷḷāṅguḍi plates, *op. cit.*, p. 313.
208. *EI*, vol. XIII, no. 22A, & 22B, v. 25.
209. Padmaneri plates, *op. cit.*, v. 29.

Pāṇḍya states: "Supreme is this victorious (Rāma) in the world, whose wife is Jānakī, who is the lord of the bearer of Jahnu's daughter (Śiva) and of the earth, pure blue in complexion like a cloud, whose lotus-feet are illuminated by the gems in the diadems of the Gods and whose glory is praised by Brahmā, Śiva and Indra."[210]

It is interesting to note that many of the kings of this dynasty had names ending in Rāma like Kaliyugarāman, Avanivendarāman, Rājakularāman, Abhirāman, Āhavarāman, Ativīrarāman, Guṇarāman, Varatuṅgarāman, etc.[211]

KṚṢṆA

The incarnation of Lord Viṣṇu as Kṛṣṇa, of whom there is no direct reference in any of the Sanskrit inscriptions of the Tamil country in the pre-Vijayanagara age, however finds mention in many of the records of the period of this study.

The poets of the Sanskrit charters of the period of this work refer to the Kṛṣṇa-*avatāra* often. The Madras Museum plates of Śrīgiribhūpāla, while tracing the mythological ancestry of the kings of the Vijayanagara dynasty, record that in the lunar race was born Yadu in whose lineage Viṣṇu was born as a partial incarnation (i.e. Kṛṣṇa).[212]

The Kuḍiyāntaṇḍal grant of Vīra-Nṛsiṁha mentions that Timma, whose wife was Devakī, was famous among the princes of Tuluva (dynasty) just as Kṛṣṇa shone in the race of Yadu.[213] The record also mentions that from the son of this Devakī was born king Narasa, just as Kāma (Manmatha) was born of Kṛṣṇa, the son of Devakī.[214]

210. *TAS*, vol. I, no. IX, v. 1, p. 107.
211. *TAS*, vol. I, p. 59.
212. *EI*, vol. VIII, no. 32, v. 5, p. 309.
213. Kuḍiyāntaṇḍal plates, *op. cit.*, v. 6, p. 236.
214. *Ibid.*, v. 8, p. 237.

This very same idea is also expressed in many of the charters of other kings of this dynasty. The Pudukkoṭṭai copper-plates of Śrīvallabha and Varatuṅgarāma Pāṇḍya also has a stanza in praise of Lord Kṛṣṇa at the very beginning of this epigraph.[215]

BHŪDEVĪ

The poets of the Sanskrit charters of the Pallavas, Pāṇḍyas and the Coḷas composed a number of beautiful invocatory verses on Lakṣmī or Śrī the consort of Viṣṇu, but it is surprising to note that none of the Vijayanagara and Nāyaka charters of the Tamil country carry a verse in praise of this much-revered Goddess. On the other hand, while the poets of the earlier inscriptions have not composed any verses on Bhūdevī, the Goddess of the Earth and also a consort of Viṣṇu, the Sanskrit epigraphs of the period of this study have a number of beautiful invocatory verses extolling this Goddess.

The Ālampūṇḍi plates of Virūpākṣa open with a benediction to this Goddess thus: "I perpetually bow to (the Goddess of) the whole earth, who is the consort of Hari (Viṣṇu) who is one of the (eight) bodies of Śiva, who bears the lovely moon on his crest, (and) who has the seven oceans for her girdle!"[216] The Śoraikkāvūr plates of the same ruler also carry a similar verse about this Goddess.[217]

Time and again, in the verses praising the Varāha-*avatāra*, mentioned earlier, the poets of these charters refer to His act of raising the Earth from the depths of the ocean. The Śrīraṅgam plates of Deva Rāya II, in a verse extolling Viṣṇu, mentions that he is attended by the Goddesses Lakṣmī and

215. *TAS*, vol. I, no. I, v. 4, p. 64.
216. Ālāmpūṇḍi plates, *op. cit.*, v. 2, p. 228.
217. Śoraikkāvūr plates, *op. cit.*, v. 2, p. 301.

Bhū (Earth).[218]

Śaiva Mythology

Many of the copper-plate inscriptions of the Vijayanagara kings begin with invocatory verses in praise of Lord Śiva. One particular verse, "Adoration to Śaṁbhu (Śiva) who is adorned as with a *cāmara*, with the moon that kisses his lofty head and who is the principal pillar at the building of the city of the three worlds" is found in a large number of the Vijayanagara copper-plate grants such as the two Śrīraṅgam records of Deva Rāya II,[219] the Nallūr copper-plates of Harihara II,[220] two inscriptions of Vīra-Nṛsiṁha,[221] the Kāñcīpuram,[222] Śrīraṅgam,[223] Udayambākkam[224] inscriptions of Kṛṣṇadeva Rāya, the Ūṇamāñjerī[225] and Kaḍalāḍi[226] plates of Acyuta Rāya, the British Museum plates[227] and Kṛṣṇāpuram[228] plates of Sadāśiva Rāya and the Ariviḷimaṅgalam plates of Śrīraṅga Rāya II.[229]

This same verse is also found in a copper-plate grant dated AD 1710, issued by an emperor of Delhi, probably Bahadūr Shāh gifting money for worship to Lord Candramauḷīśvara

---

218. *EI*, vol. XVIII, no. 17, v. 3, p. 144.
219. *Ibid.*, v. 4, p. 140; *EI*, vol. XVI, no. 8, pp. 112-13.
220. Nallūr plates, *op. cit.*, v. 1, p. 120.
221. *EI*, vol. XVII, v. 1, p. 236 & *CPIK*, v. 1, pp. 38-39.
222. Kāñcīpuram inscription of Kṛṣṇadeva Rāya, *op. cit.*, v. 1, p. 126; *CPIK*, v. 1, p.68.
223. *EI*, vol. XVIII, no. 21A, v. 1, p. 162; *ibid.*, no. 21B, v. 1, p. 166.
224. Udayambākkam plates, *op. cit.*, v. 1., p. 170.
225. Ūṇamāñjerī plates, *op. cit.*, v. 1., p. 316.
226. Kaḍalāḍi plates, *op. cit.*, v. 1, p. 316.
227. British Museum plates of Sadāśiva Rāya, *op. cit.*, v. 1., p. 12.
228. Kṛṣṇāpuram plates, *op. cit.*, v. 1, p. 331.
229. Ariviḷimangalam plates, *op. cit.*, v. 1, p. 350.

who was worshipped by Svāmi Paramahaṁsa Parivrājakācārya of the Maṭha at Kāñcī.[230]

Other beautiful verses in praise of this deity are found in the Kāñcīpuram inscription of Acyuta Rāya[231] and the Śrīraṅgam plates of Mummaḍi Nāyaka.[232]

The copper-plate inscriptions of the later Pāṇḍyan rulers like the Pudukkoṭṭai plates of Śrīvallabha and Varatuṅgarāma Pāṇḍya,[233] the Daḷavāy-agrahāram plates of Varatuṅgarāma Pāṇḍya (AD 1588)[234] and the Daḷavāy-agrahāram plates of Ativīrarāma Pāṇḍya,[235] all contain benedictory stanzas in praise of Śiva. Pārvatī, the consort of Śiva is mentioned in many of the Sanskrit records of the period of this work by names such as Gaurī, Agajā and Umā.

ARDHANĀRĪŚVARA

The Ardhanārīśvara aspect of Śiva in which his left half is represented by Pārvatī rarely finds mention in any of the Sanskrit epigraphs found in the Tamil country till the 14th century AD. However, in the Vijayanagara period, some epigraphs contain verses praising and describing this deity. The Madras Museum plates of Śrīgiribhūpāla record: "I salute him (Śiva), the left half of whose body is the very embodiment of mercy (Pārvatī), who is adorned with good qualities, whose ornament is the moon's digit, and whose eyes are the three lights (viz., sun, moon and fire)!."[236]

---

230. *CPIK*, p. 116.
231. *EI*, vol. XXXIII, no. 39, v. 2, p. 201.
232. *EI*, vol. XIV, no. 3, v. 1, p. 89.
233. *TAS*, vol. I, no. 1, v. 3, p. 64.
234. *TAS*, vol. I, no. XII, v. 4, p. 127.
235. *TAS*, vol. I, no. XIII, v. 1, p. 135.
236. Madras Museum plates of Śrīgiribhūpāla, *op. cit.*, v. 2, p. 309.

ŚĀRADĀ

A beautiful verse in praise of Goddess Śāradā is found in a copper-plate grant which was issued in AD 1710 by an emperor of Delhi, possibly Bahadūr Shāh, and which records a gift of money for worship to Lord Candramauḷīśvara worshipped by Svāmi Parivrājakācārya of the Maṭha at Kāñcī. This verse, couched in beautiful Sanskrit states, "May Śāradā reside in my lotus-like mouth, Śāradā who is, as it were, the stream of honey flowing from the lotus-like face of Brahmā, Śāradā, whose actions (glorious utterances), are praised by the several Vedas and whose lustre equals that of crores of moons shining simultaneously."[237]

GAṆEŚA

It is generally believed that the Gaṇeśa cult was introduced into the Tamil country in the Pallava period after Vātāpi (modern Bādāmi) was captured from the Cāḷukyas in the 7th century AD and the idol of Vātāpi Gaṇapatī was brought to the Tamil country by the Pallava general of Narasiṁhavarman named Parañjoti.

Till the period of the Vijayanagara kings there are hardly any references to Gaṇeśa in the Sanskrit inscriptions of ancient Tamil Nadu, except for one verse in the Kaśākuḍi copper-plate grant of Nandivarman II Pallavamalla (C. AD 753-54) which contains a beautiful invocatory verse to this deity.[238]

However, the copper-plate inscriptions of the Vijayanagara period are replete with references to and descriptions of the elephant-faced deity, called in these epigraphs as Vināyaka, Gaṇādhipati, Ekadanta, Vighneśvara and Gajānana.

---

237. *CPIK*, p. 115.

238. *SII*, vol. II, no. 73, v. 7, p. 346.

The very first line of the Madras Museum plates of Śrīgiribhūpāla contains a sentence "Salutations to Vināyaka" (*vināyakāya namaḥ*).[239] It appears to have become a tradition with the rulers of this dynasty to commence their copper-plate inscriptions with the term *śrī gaṇādhipataye namaḥ*.

Apart from these invocatory sentences, there are also various beautiful verses in different metres about this God at the beginning of the inscriptions. The Madras Museum plates of Śrīgiribhūpāla records: "May that primal one (Vināyaka), increase (our) prosperity, who dispells the darkness of obstacles, who was born of the primal pair (Śiva and Pārvatī) and who is possessed of an unparalleled wealth of kindness to his devotees."[240]

The Śrīraṅgam plates of Mallikārjuna contain a poetic verse in praise of Gaṇeśa as a child.[241] According to the editor of the inscription, this verse is very similar to the first verse of the Tamil work *Naiṣadakāvya* (translation of the Sanskrit work *Naiṣadīya-carita* of Śrī Harṣa) by king Ativīrarāma Pāṇḍya (AD 1563-1583).[242]

Both the Śrīraṅgam charters of Deva Rāya II,[243] the Nallūr plates of Harihara II,[244] two grants of Vīra-Nṛsiṁha,[245] two inscriptions of Kṛṣṇadeva Rāya from Kāñcīpuram,[246] the

239. Madras Museum plates of Śrīgiribhūpāla, *op. cit.*, line 1, p. 309.
240. *Ibid.*, v. 1, p. 309.
241. *EI*, vol. XVI, no. 28, v. 2, pp. 347-48.
242. *Ibid.*, p. 351, no. 17.
243. *Ibid.*, vol. XVI, no. 8, v. 2, p. 113; *EI*, vol. XVIII, no. 17, v. 1, p. 140.
244. Nallūr plates, *op. cit.*, v. 3, p. 120.
245. *EI*, vol. XIV, no. 17, v. 3, p. 236; *CPIK*, v. 3, p. 39.
246. *EI*, vol. XIII, no. 8, v. 3, p. 126; *CPIK*, v. 3, p. 68.

Śrīraṅgam plates[247] and Udayambākkam plates[248] of the same ruler, the Kāñcīpuram,[249] Kaḍalāḍi[250] and Ūṉamāñjerī plates of Acyuta Rāya,[251] the British Museum plates,[252] the Kṛṣṇāpuram plates[253] and the Ariviḷimaṅgalam plates[254] have verses in praise of Gaṇeśa.

In the majority of the above-mentioned inscriptions, one particular verse: "May that lustre (Gaṇeśa), which dispels the darkness of obstacles, and which, though it has an elephant-head (*gaja*), was born of the mountain daughter (Agajā), and is worshipped even by Hari (Viṣṇu) produce happiness" occurs very frequently.

Numerous grants of Veṅkaṭa II such as the Padmaneri,[255] Daḷavāy-agrahāram,[256] two of his inscriptions found in the British Museum[257] and Veḷḷāṅguḍi plates[258] contain verses in praise of Viśvakṣena, in which Lord Gaṇeśa is mentioned as one of the former's attendants. The same verses are also found in some of the charters of Veṅkaṭa III such as the Nīlamaṅgala[259] and the Kūniyūr plates.[260] The Śrīraṅgam plates of Mummaḍi Nāyaka also contain an invocation to Gaṇeśa.

---

247. *EI*, vol. XVIII, no. 21A, v. 3; *Ibid.*, no. 21B, v. 3.
248. Udayambākkam plates, *op. cit.*, v. 3., p. 170.
249. *EI*, vol. XXXIII, no. 39, v. 1, p. 201.
250. Kaḍalāḍi plates, *op. cit.*, v. 3., p. 236.
251. Ūṉamāñjerī plates, *op. cit.*, v. 3., p. 151.
252. British Museum plates of Sadāśiva Rāya, *op. cit.*, v. 3., p. 12.
253. Kṛṣṇāpuram plates, *op. cit.*, v. 3, p. 332.
254. Ariviḷimaṅgalam plates, *op. cit.*, v. 3, p. 350.
255. Padmaneri plates, *op. cit.*, v. 2, p. 292.
256. *EI*, vol. XII, no. 21, v. 2., p. 171.
257. *EI*, vol. XIII, no. 22A, v. 2, p. 226 & *Ibid.*, no. 22B, v. 2.
258. Veḷḷāṅguḍi plates, *op. cit.*, v. 2, p. 313.
259. Nīlamaṅgala plates, *op. cit.*, v. 2., p. 213.
260. Kūniyūr plates, *op. cit.*, v. 2., p. 240.

Some of the copper-plate charters of the later Pāṇḍyas like the Pudukkoṭṭai plates of Śrīvallabha and Varatuṅgarāma Pāṇḍya,[261] the Daḷavāy-agrahāram plates of Varatuṅgarāma Pāṇḍya (AD 1588) [262] and the Daḷavay-agrahāram plates of Ativīrarāma Pāṇḍya[263] also contain invocatory stanzas praising Vināyaka.

MURUGA

Lord Subrahmaṇya, popularly called Muruga in the Tamil country, the son of Śiva and Pārvatī is not mentioned in any of the invocatory verses in the Sanskrit inscriptions of the period of this study. However, the poets do mention him in their compositions, and compare their rulers with this deity. The Nallūr inscription of Harihara II draws a poetic comparison between the birth of Skanda to Lord Śiva and Pārvatī and the birth of Harihara II to Bukka and Gaurī. Harihara is described as a partial incarnation of Skanda (*skandāṁśa*) and as being renowned by his power (*śakti*).[264]

INDRA

Indra, the lord of the celestials (*deva*s), is time and again referred to in the Sanskrit inscriptions of the Tamil country from the time of the Pallavas. In the inscriptions of the Vijayanagara period, this deity is referred to often and is called by many of his names and epithets like Vāsava, Sūtrāman, Mahendra and Jiṣṇu.

The kings of this dynasty are constantly compared to Indra in valour. Prince Śrīgiribhūpāla (Śrīgirīśvara) is described as ruling from the city called Maratakapuri just like Indra rules

261. *TAS*, vol. I, no. I, v. 5, pp. 64-65.
262. *TAS*, vol. I, no. XII, v. 1, pp. 126-27.
263. *TAS*, vol. I, no. XIII, v. 3, p. 135.
264. *EI*, vol. III, no. 19, v. 14, p. 121.

the city of Amarāvatī.[265] The Śrīraṅgam plates of Mallikārjuna mention poetically that Deva Rāya II appeared to be a copy of the king of the gods (Indra).[266]

BRAHMĀ

Invocatory verses in praise of and references to Brahmā, the creator and the first among the Hindu trinity are very rarely found in the epigraphs of the Tamil country, in comparison with those of Viṣṇu and Śiva. Among the Sanskrit epigraphs of the ancient period in Tamil Nadu, only a few records like the Anbil plates of Sundara Coḷa[267] and the Śrīvaramaṅgalam plates of Pāṇḍyan Neḍuñjaḍaiyaṉ[268] contain stanzas praising this deity.

In the inscriptions of the succeeding period, only the copper-plate grants of the later Pāṇḍyas contain invocatory verses extolling this deity. The Pudukkoṭṭai plates of Śrīvallabha and Varatuṅgarāma Pāṇḍya[269] and the Daḷavāy-agrahāram plates of Varatuṅgarāma Pāṇḍya (AD 1588)[270] contain verses in praise of Brahmā.

The poets of the Sanskrit records of the Pallava, Pāṇḍya and Coḷa periods, while repeatedly comparing their rulers with Viṣṇu, Śiva, Indra and Muruga, never draw any comparison with Brahmā. However, the Vijayanagara poets did refer to their kings as being like the Creator himself. A lithic inscription of Virūpākṣa, son of Harihara II records that his maternal grandfather, Rāmadeva was an incarnation of Brahmā.[271]

265. *EI*, vol. VIII, no. 32, v. 11, p. 30.
266. Śrīraṅgam plates of Mallikārjuna, *op. cit.*, v. 9., p. 348.
267. *EI*, vol. XV, no. 5, v. 4, p. 59.
268. *PCP*, v. 1, p. 56.
269. *TAS*, vol. I, no. I, v. 1, p. 64.
270. *TAS*, vol. I, no. XII, v. 1, pp. 126-27.
271. *SII*, vol. XXIV, no. 294, p. 309.

4

Religion

RELIGION played a very important part in the lives of the people in the ancient and medieval days in the Tamil country as was the case in other parts of India also. The literary and epigraphical data of the period of the Pallavas, Pāṇḍyas and the Coḷas reveal that the Vedic religion had gained a firm foothold in the Tamil country and the rulers of these dynasties did their best to disseminate the ancient scriptures by giving grants of land to the learned brāhmaṇas (*brahmadeya*), well-versed in Vedic lore and also building innumerable temples and making numerous benefactions to them in the form of land, gold, jewels and livestock.

The Muslim occupation of south India starting from the 14th century AD, gave a violent setback to the Brāhmanical religion. The Sanskrit poem *Madhurāvijayam* by Gaṅgā Devī gives a graphic description of the havoc caused by the Muslims in the Tamil country and mentions the pathetic condition of holy places like Cidambaram, Śrīraṅgam, Tiruvānnaikāval and Madurai.[1]

It was with the foundation of the Vijayanagara empire that the onslaught of the Muslims was held in check. The Saṅgama brothers dedicated themselves to the task of driving

---

1. S. Tiruvenkatachari, (ed.), *Madhurāvijayam of Gaṅgā Devī*, Annamalainagar, 1957, Canto VIII, pp. 118-19.

out the Muslims from south India. The *Madhurāvijayam* describes in great detail the heroic efforts of Kumāra Kaṁpaṇa, the son of Bukka I, who put an end to the Muslim Sultanate in Madurai.

During the period of the Muslim domination of the south, many of the temples remained closed and the images of the deities were taken away by devotees for safe custody.

The Vijayanagara rulers restored worship in the temples, repaired old temples and towers, settled disputes among temple servants and made extensive endowments in the shape of jewels, lands, taxes and other sources of income.[2] In this chapter, an attempt has been made to trace the contributions of the Vijayanagara, Nāyaka, later Pāṇḍyan, Marāṭha and the other kings, chieftains and officials in the sphere of religion.

The first of the Vijayanagara viceroys in the Tamil country to contribute to the restoration of temples was Kumāra Kaṁpaṇa. One of the earliest Sanskrit inscriptions of the period of this study which deals with the religious activities of the Tamil country is etched on the walls of the Śrī Raṅganāthasvāmi temple at Śrīraṅgam and dated AD 1371.[3] It consists of two Sanskrit verses, one of which is believed to have been composed by the eminent Śrī Vaiṣṇava philosopher and preceptor Vedānta Deśika, and praises the part played by Gopaṇa, a Vijayanagara official of Kumāra Kaṁpaṇa and the Governor of Ginji in restoring the image of Lord Raṅganātha in the Śrīraṅgam temple after the turbulent times of the Muslim sack of Śrīraṅgam. The contents of this record have been dealt with in detail later in this chapter.

---

2. A. Krishnaswami, *The Tamil Country Under Vijayanagara*, Annamalainagar, 1964, p. 42.
3. *EI*, vol. VI, no. 33, pp. 322-30.

Harihara II

Harihara II was a staunch upholder of the Vedic religion. The Nallūr inscription mentions several of his *biruda*s among which one is *vaidika-mārga-sthāpanācārya* (the master in establishing the ordinances prescribed by the Vedas).[4]

A short Sanskrit epigraph of Harihara II, consisting of a Sanskrit verse engraved at the entrance of the inner *prākāra* of the Kāmākṣī Amman temple at Kāñcīpuram dated AD 1393, records that this ruler provided a copper door for the central shrine of the Kāmākṣī Amman temple.[5] Some of the Tamil inscriptions of Harihara II found at the Śrī Varadarājasvāmi temple in Kāñcīpuram mention his benefactions to this temple.[6]

Virūpākṣa

Virūpākṣa, the son of Harihara II who ruled for some time as a viceroy of the Tamil region, continued in the tradition of his forefathers in encouraging the Brāhmanical religion. In his Śoraikkāvūr copper-plate inscription, he is described "as the establisher of the Brāhmanical faith" (*veda-mārga-sthāpana tatparaḥ*).[7] This inscription also mentions some of his religious activities. He weighed himself against gold in the presence of Lord Rāmanātha at Rāmeśvaram. He also gilded the *vimāna* of the temple at Śrīraṅgam and the "Golden Hall" (*kāñcana sabhā*) at Cidambaram.[8]

There are many inscriptions of Virūpākṣa in the temple of Śrī Raṅganāthasvāmi at Śrīraṅgam which speak of the gifts

---

4. *EI*, vol. III, no. 19, p. 122.
5. *EI*, vol. III, no. 32, p. 229.
6. K.V. Raman, *Śrī Varadarājasvāmi Temple, Kāñchī*, New Delhi, 1975, p. 26.
7. *EI*, vol. VIII, no. 31, v. 7, p. 301.
8. *Ibid*.

bestowed on this temple during his reign. An undated Sanskrit epigraph of his, inscribed in the *mukha-maṇḍapa* of the Cakrattāḻvār shrine, states that he constructed the *vimāna*, *gopura* and *maṇḍapa* to Cakrin (i.e. Cakrattāḻvār) and that he made a gift of the village Pāccil to this deity.[9]

According to the *Koiḷ-Oḻugu*, the chronicle of the Śrīraṅgam temple, the *dhvajārohaṇa* (flag-hoisting ceremony) of the Cittirai festival was conducted in the name of Virūpaṇṇa who "enabled the people coming from all parts of the country to visit the long-missed Perumāḷ and to obtain *sevā*."[10] The association of Virūpaṇṇa (Virūpākṣa) with the Cittirai festival has survived and the festival is even today called the Virūppaṇ-tirunāḷ.[11] This work also mentions that he constructed the shrine of Sudarśana Perumāḷ (probably the Cakrattāḻvār shrine) and installed an image of Narasiṁha therein.[12]

Many of the ministers and other officials of his reign gave gifts to this temple as seen from their inscriptions. These records thus reveal that during the time of Virūpākṣa, there was an effort to restore the Śrīraṅgam temple to its days of glory.

Deva Rāya I

There are some Sanskrit inscriptions of Deva Rāya I in the Śrī Raṅganāthasvāmi temple at Śrīraṅgam which indicate that this ruler too evinced interest in restoring the Śrīraṅgam temple to its former glory. Most of his inscriptions mention the gifts made to the temple trustee Uttamanambi for arranging worship in this temple.

---

9. *SII*, vol. XXIV, no. 292, p. 306.
10. V.N. Hari Rao, *History of the Śrīraṅgam Temple*, Tirupati, 1976, pp. 131-32.
11. *Ibid.*
12. K.O., p. 80.

A copper-plate grant from the Śrīraṅgam temple, dated AD 1414 belonging to Harihararāya (III), the son of Deva Rāya I, who probably ruled as a viceroy over the country of the present-day Coimbatore area, mentions a grant of land to the Śrīraṅgam temple to be managed by Uttamanambi.[13] The above-mentioned inscriptions which involve the activities of Uttamanambi have been dealt with in detail later in this chapter.

Deva Rāya II

During the reign of Deva Rāya II, a number of grants were made to the Śrī Raṅganāthasvāmi temple at Śrīraṅgam. A copper-plate grant of this ruler found in this temple dated AD 1427,[14] states that Deva Rāya II gave to God Raṅganātha the village of Pāṇḍamaṅgalam together with the sub-villages of Tirunalūr, Seranaibaṇḍa-perumānallūr and Sunepuha-nallūr. This grant was an auxiliary to the *go-sahasra mahādāna* or "gift of a thousand cows." The income from these villages was meant for the maintenence of lamps in the temple, for the supply of flower-garlands and for the celebration of one festival.

A similar copper-plate grant of this ruler dated AD 1434, also found in this temple, mentions the gift of certain villages to Uttamanambi of the Śrīraṅgam temple for conducting the daily worship of Lord Raṅganātha.[15] There are many more epigraphs in Sanskrit and in Tamil of the reign of Deva Rāya II found in the Śrīraṅgam temple which speak of the contributions of Uttamanambi and his brother Cakrarāya to this temple and which testify to its growing prosperity in this period and discussed later in this chapter.

---

13. *EI*, vol. XVI, no. 15, pp. 224-28.
14. *EI*, vol. XVII, no. 8, vv. 19-21, p. 114.
15. *EI*, vol. XVIII, no. 17, vv. 25-31, pp. 141-42.

Mallikārjuna

During the reign of Mallikārjuna, the son and successor of Deva Rāya II, some more endowments were made to the Śrīraṅgam temple as attested to by the Tamil inscriptions of his reign.

However, there is only one Sanskrit epigraph of this king found in Tamil Nadu. This is a set of copper-plates dated AD 1462 from Śrīraṅgam in which he is called Immaḍi Deva Rāya and Immaḍi Prauḍhabhūpati.[16] This record registers the gift of the village Uttamanceri-kiḷiyūr to Lord Raṅganātha. The income from the village was to be used for making a daily offering of six complete dishes of food for this deity, the maintenance of a watershed permanently in front of the temple, the feeding of sixty Vaiṣṇavas in the Rāmānujakūṭam (choultry) and three grant feasts, one in the month of Phālguna and the other two in Dhanuṣ.

According to the *Koiḷ-Oḻugu*, in AD 1461, Mallikārjuna Rāya removed the bronze flag-staff in the Śrīraṅgam temple courtyard and replaced it with a copper one which was covered with a hundred and two gold plates upon which he erected a gold-plated image of Garuḍa.[17] Mallikārjuna also made many gifts to one of the trustees of the temple named Tirumalainātha Uttamanambi for repairing the Śrīraṅgam temple and making additions to it.

Kṛṣṇadeva Rāya

Kṛṣṇadeva Rāya was a staunch Vaiṣṇava and made numerous benefactions to Viṣṇu temples and greatly encouraged the Śrī Vaiṣṇava scholars of his time. But, at the same time, like his

16. *EI*, vol. XVI, no. 28, vv. 16-37, pp. 349-50.
17. V.N. Hari Rao, *op. cit.*, p. 146.

predecessors, he also showed patronage to the Śaivas of his empire and made many grants to Śiva shrines.

Many of the Sanskrit inscriptions found on the walls of numerous temples in Tamil Nadu mention the benefactions of this king to these shrines. A record found in the shrine of Goddess Vedavallī Thāyār in the Vedanārāyaṇasvāmi temple in Nāgalāpuram (Chengleput district) records that this king gave the village of Devarāyakuppam, renamed as Kṛṣṇarāyapuram as a *sarvamānya* gift to God Kariyamāṇikka Perumāḷ in Arigaṇḍapuram.[18]

This ruler made numerous benefactions to the Varadarājasvāmi temple at Kāñcīpuram. A Sanskrit inscription mentions that this ruler had the *Puṇyakoṭi vimāna* of the shrine of Lord Varadarāja covered with pure gold for the merit of his father Narasanāyaka Uḍaiyār and his mother Nāgājīamman in c. AD 1514.[19]

Many of his Tamil records also speak of his gifts to this temple. This ruler presented five villages yielding an annual income of 1500 *varāhas* as gift to the Varadarājasvāmi temple[20] and also made many other benefactions to this temple as well as to the Ekāmreśvara (Śiva) temple in Kāñcīpuram.[21]

Kṛṣṇadeva Rāya also made numerous endowments to the Raṅganāthasvāmi temple at Śrīraṅgam. One of his records mentions that he caused the two doors of the entrance of the first *prākāra* to be plated with gold.[22] This probably refers to the doors of the sanctum.[23]

---

18. *ARE*, 621 of 1924; *SII*, vol. XVII, no. 677, pp. 309-11.
19. *ARE*, 513 and 478 of 1919.
20. *ARE*, 474 of 1919.
21. *ARE*, 641 of 1919; see K.V. Raman, *op. cit.*, p. 29.
22. *ARE*, 120 of 1937-38; *SII*, vol. XXIV, no. 382, p. 375.
23. V.N. Hari Rao, *op. cit.*, p. 161.

The Śrīraṅgam copper-plate grant of Kṛiṣṇadeva Rāya mentions that he granted the village of Eṇṇakkuḍi under the name Kṛṣṇarāyapuram to a learned brāhmaṇa named Allāḷa Bhaṭṭa, and that this village was situated on the banks of the river Kāverī.[24] The fact that this copper-plate grant was obtained from the Śrīraṅgam temple suggests that the donee or his successors may have gifted away the village to this temple.[25]

Another copper-plate grant of Kṛṣṇadeva Rāya from the Śrīraṅgam temple speaks of the grant of a village named Vaḍambūr-Ekāmbarapuram (which was changed to Kṛṣṇarāyapuram of the time of the grant), situated on the south bank of the Kāverī in the Tiruvālūrsīma (Nāgapaṭṭinam tāluk).[26] The village was divided into thirty-two shares and distributed among learned brāhmaṇas and one share each was given to the Viṣṇu and Śiva temples in that village. It cannot be said with certainty that this village subsequently passed under the control of the Śrīraṅgam temple; the fact that the temple was in possession of this grant might suggest such an inference, but it is clear that, far distant as it was, the village could not have been of any practical use to the temple.[27]

There are also many Tamil inscriptions recording this ruler's contributions to the Śrīraṅgam temple. One of these, dated AD 1516 is important as it mentions that in that year Kṛṣṇadeva Rāya visited Śrīraṅgam and made a gift of five villages for providing offerings and worship to the God.[28]

---

24. *EI*, vol. XVIII, no. 21A, pp. 162-64.
25. V.N. Hari Rao, *op. cit.*, p. 159.
26. *EI*, vol. XVIII, no. 21B, pp. 166-69.
27. V.N. Hari Rao, *op. cit.*, pp. 161-62.
28. *ARE*, 98 of 1938-39.

This ruler's benefactions to the Veṅkaṭeśvara temple at Tirumala are known from his numerous inscriptions found at that shrine. He made about seven visits to this temple and on each these occasions made presentations of valuable jewels, ornaments and other gifts to this deity. He is known to have performed the *kanakābhiṣeka* (bath with gold coins) to Lord Veṅkaṭeśvara and also gilded the *divya-vimāna* (sacred dome) of this shrine.[29]

Despite his Vaiṣṇavite leanings, Kṛṣṇadeva Rāya's benefactions to the Śaiva shrines in the Tamil country were also many. A Sanskrit inscription found in the Ekāmbaranātha (Ekāmreśvara) temple in Kāñcīpuram records the gift of a village by this king for worship and various offerings to Lord Ekāmbaranātha, on the occasion of a festival conducted in the name of this ruler.[30]

Kṛṣṇadeva Rāya also paid a visit to the Naṭarāja temple at Cidambaram (*Ponnambalam*). The north *gopuram* of this temple bears a Tamil inscription of this king which states that after conquering Orissa, he erected a pillar of victory at Siṁhādri Pottanūrū (modern Siṁhāchalam in Andhra Pradesh) and came to visit the Lord of Ponnambalam and built the northern *gopura*.[31] According to B. Natarajan, this should only mean the re-construction in brick and mortar of the seven storeys above the double-storeyed gateway portion as the latter has to be assigned to the days of Kulottuṅga Coḷa II.[32] A beautiful portrait-sculpture of Kṛṣṇadeva Rāya in stone is installed in a western niche in the gateway portion of the northern *gopura*.

---

29. Sadhu Subrahmanya Sastry, *Tirupati Sri Venkatesvara*, Tirupati, 1998, pp. 213-14.
30. *ARE*, 275 of 1955-56.
31. *ARE*, 371 of 1913.
32. B. Natarajan, *Tillai and Nataraja*, Madras, 1994, p. 113.

The Kāñcīpuram inscription of Kṛṣṇadeva Rāya mentions that he made many gifts (*dāna*) for performing rites like the *tulāpuruṣa* at places like Kañcī, Śrīśaila, Śoṇācala (Tiruvaṇṇāmalai), Kanakasabhā (Cidambaram), Veṅkaṭādri (Tirupati) and other places.[33] Kṛṣṇadeva Rāya, thus, did lavish gifts on Śiva *sthala*s like Śrīśaila, Tiruvaṇṇāmalai and Cidambaram also. The Udayambākkam copper-plates of this ruler also list the same details.[34]

An inscription from Madurai dated AD 1516 states that the Saptasāgara-tīrtha was dug in front of the temple of Śokkanātha as a gift of Kṛṣṇadeva Rāya.[35]

Many literary works of the Vijayanagara age speak of Kṛṣṇadeva Rāya's religious disposition and the benefactions made by him to various temples.

Acyuta Rāya

Acyuta Rāya like his brother and predecessor, Kṛṣṇadeva Rāya was also a Vaiṣṇavite. The Kṛṣṇāpuram plates of Sadāśiva Rāya describe him as "a worshipper of Viṣṇu" (*hariceta*).[36] But again, he was not a bigot and made many benefactions to Śiva temples in his empire. The Kaḍalāḍi copper-plate grant of Acyuta Rāya records his benefactions to the holy shrines of Gokarṇa, Saṅgama, Cidambaram, Sonādri (Aruṇācaleśvara temple at Tiruvaṇṇāmalai), Viriñci (Viriñcipuram, South Arcot district), Kāñcī (Kāñcīpuram), Kāḷahasti (in present-day Andhra Pradesh) and Kuṁbakoṇam (near Tañjāvūr).[37]

---

33. *EI*, vol. XIII, no. 8, v. 23, pp. 128-29.
34. *EI*, vol. XIV, no. 12, v. 23, pp. 172-73.
35. *ARE*, 161 of 1937-38.
36. *EI*, vol. IX, no. 52, v. 24, p. 334.
37. *EI*, vol. XIV, no. 22, v. 33, p. 316.

Among these, some of them like Cidambaram, Viriñcipuram, Sonādri and Kāḷahasti are very famous Śaivite centres of pilgrimage, and it is clear that this ruler did not differentiate between Vaiṣṇavite and Śaivite temples when bestowing his benefactions. This inscription as well as the Ūṇamāñjeri plates[38] of this king open with invocations to Gaṇeśa and Śaṁbhu (Śiva).

The attitude of Acyuta Rāya towards Vaiṣṇavism and Śaivism is clearly seen from his benefactions in Cidambaram. Although these epigraphs are in Tamil, it would not be out of place to mention them to reveal the religious catholicity of this ruler. An inscription of Acyuta Rāya (AD 1539) records that he ordered the image of Tillai Govindarāja Perumāḷ in Valudalampaṭṭu be consecrated according to the *Vaikhānasa Sūtra* and granted the income from a few villages for its daily worship.[39] Another inscription of this ruler (AD 1538) records the reconsecration of Govindarājasvāmi (Viṣṇu) at Citrakūṭa (Cidambaram).[40]

An inscription from the Naṭarāja temple at Cidambaram written in Sanskrit and Tamil, records that Acyuta Rāya re-endowed eightly-two villages which had originally been allotted by Kṛṣṇadeva Rāya for the expenses of the car and other festivals and for the repair to the temple of Cidambareśa (Naṭarāja) and this was left in charge of a *tapasvin* named Periyadevar.[41] This inscription also mentions the construction of the north *gopuram* at Cidambaram.

According to B. Natarajan, the reference in the inscription of the construction of the north *gopuram* should refer only to

---

38. *EI*, vol. III, no. 24, line 1 & v. 1, p. 151.
39. *ARE*, 272 of 1913.
40. *ARE*, 1 of 1915.
41. *ARE*, 2 of 1935-36.

the construction of the superstructure over the north *gopuram* over the older stone gateway of Kulottuṅga Coḷa II's days and that perhaps Acyuta Rāya completed what Kṛṣṇadeva Rāya had begun.[42]

Similarly, a record from Kāñcī, dated AD 1533, mentions that this ruler ordered his local agent at this town, Sāḷuva Nāyaka, to distribute his gifts of villages equally between the temples of Varadarāja (Viṣṇu) and Ekāmreśvara (Śiva) in Kāñcīpuram.[43]

Acyuta Rāya's munificient benefactions to the Raṅganāthasvāmi temple, Śrīraṅgam, the Veṅkaṭeśvara temple, Tirumala and the Varadarājasvāmi temple at Kāñcīpuram are known from numerous inscriptions engraved at these places. However, only a few of them are in Sanskrit. One of these, found in the Varadarājasvāmi temple records that Acyuta Rāya performed the *muktā-tulābhāra* ceremony (weighing oneself against an equal weight of pearls) of himself and his queen Varadāmbikā Devī and that his son Cinna-Veṅkaṭādri gave a munificient gift to brāhmaṇas.[44] The Sanskrit work *Acyutarāyābhyudayam* also refers to this event of this king weighing himself against pearls which were distributed for charity.[45]

The same work also states that this ruler, during his expedition to the Tiruvaḍi kingdom, halted at Śrīraṅgam and sent the son of one Sagaḷarāja to conquer the Tiruvaḍi *rājya*.[46]

---

42. B. Natarajan, *op. cit.*, p. 114.
43. *ARE*, 584 of 1919.
44. *ARE*, 511 of 1919.
45. K.V. Raman, *op. cit.*, p. 29.
46. *EI*, vol. IX, p. 330.

Sadāśiva Rāya

Vaiṣṇavism gained a greater footing in the Vijayanagara empire after the accession of Sadāśiva Rāya, the nephew of Acyuta Rāya to the throne. It was a happy combination then that both the *de jure* sovereign Sadāśiva and the *de facto* ruler Rāma Rāja were ardent followers of Vaiṣṇavism in the empire.[47]

Sadāśiva Rāya is described in the British Museum plates as *haribhakti sudhānidhi* (repository of nectar-like devotion to Viṣṇu).[48] This inscription records a grant by this ruler at the instance of Kaṇḍāla Śrīraṅgācārī, a Śrī Vaiṣṇava teacher of that time, of thiry-one villages to the Rāmānuja shrine at Śrīperumbudūr to enable the Vaiṣṇavas to carry on the regular worship of Ananta (Viṣṇu) with incense, lights, oblations of food, flowers, dancing, singing, music, umbrellas, *cāmaras*, etc., to celebrate properly, the annual festival of Viṣṇu. Provision was also made for the distribution of all kinds of food to the Vaiṣṇava brāhmaṇas and their wives, children and aged people at "the extensive hall of the holy Rāmānuja constructed here."

The Kṛṣṇāpuram copper-plate grant of Sadāśiva Rāya, dated AD 1567 states that at the request of Tirumala, who was in turn requested by Kṛṣṇappa Nāyaka I (or Kṛṣṇappa Bhūpati, the Nāyaka of Madurai), Sadāśiva Rāya granted the excellent village of Śrī Kṛṣṇāpuram which included a number of smaller villages to the God Tiruveṅkaṭanātha consecrated at Kṛṣṇāpuram (near Tirunelveli) by Kṛṣṇappa Nāyaka.[49]

An inscription of Sadāśiva Rāya dated AD 1545 in *maṇipravāla* style engraved on a wall in the third *prākāra* of the

---

47. T.V. Mahalingam, *Administration and Social Life Under Vijayanagara*, Madras, 1940, p. 326.
48. *EI*, vol. IV, p. 15.
49. *EI*, vol. IX, no. 52, pp. 331-39.

Śrīraṅgam temple records that a brāhmaṇa named Śrīśailapūrṇa Tātācārya *alias* Avuku Tiruveṅgadayyangār received the village Cintāmaṇi from Ramarāja and Sadāśiva Rāya and in turn, granted the same for the merit of both of the above to the temple of Lord Raṅganātha at Śrīraṅgam for the expenses of offering four dishes of food to this deity as was once arranged by Nalantigaḷ Nārāyaṇa Jīyar, allotting a share of the offerings for himself and his descendents.[50]

Some of the family members and generals of this period were also staunch Vaiṣṇavas. During the reign of Sadāśiva Rāya, Viṭṭhaladeva and Cinna Timma, the cousins of Rāmarāya were despatched to quell the unrest which prevailed in the southern provinces of the Vijayanagara empire. A Sanskrit inscription found in the third *prākāra* of the Raṅganāthasvāmi temple, Śrīraṅgam, mentions the genealogy of Viṭṭhala and his brothers, and states that they defeated all their enemies to the south of their capital.[51] Viṭṭhaladeva made several benefactions to this temple such as the daily *sahasranāma-pūjā* to Lord Raṅganātha and anointing him with the *karpūra-taila* every Friday. He also made a gift of some villages for providing offerings to this deity. His elder brother, Nalla-Timma gifted a *candra-prabhā* made of silver to this God.

The Vijayanagara army also defeated the Travancore forces. A Tamil epigraph with numerous Sanskrit words in it found on the northern doorway of the *gopura* in the Sucīndram temple dated AD 1544, records that the Vijayanagara general, Viṭṭhala Mahārāja built the *gopura* of the temple for Tiruveṅkaṭanātha and also erected the *dhvajasthambha* in front of the Perumāḷ shrine.[52] A Tamil record in the same temple

50. *EI*, vol. XXIX, no. 9, pp. 76-77.

51. *SII*, vol. XXIV, no. 455, p. 437.

52. 5 of 1111-T.A.R.; K.K. Pillai, *The Sucīndram Temple*, Madras, 2002, p. 42.

registers a gift of lands settled by the Travancore king, Bhūtalavīra Vīrakeraḷavarman for offerings to Tiruveṅkaḍa Emberumān on the Rohiṇī nakṣatra, the natal star of Viṭṭhala Mahārāja.[53] According to K.K. Pillai, this general also possibly constructed the Garuḍāḷvār shrine in this temple as he was a great devotee of Viṣṇu.[54]

A Sanskrit epigraph in verse found in the Varadarājasvāmi temple, Kāñcī records that Rāmarāya ordered the repair of the stone steps of the tank called Annantasaras of this temple and also presented gifts to the Varadarājasvāmi and Ekāmranātha temples.[55]

Tirumala I

The kings of the Aravīḍu dynasty were again great devotees of Lord Viṣṇu and Śrī Vaiṣṇavism received a temendrous fillip at the hands of these rulers. Tirumala I, the first ruler of the Aravīḍu line has been described poetically as a "repository of nectar-like devotion to Hari" (*hari-bhakti sudhā-nidhi*)[56] and as "one who sees Hari in his heart" (*hari-gocara-mānasaḥ*).[57] In the Veḷḷāṅguḍi plates of Veṅkaṭa I he is mentioned as frequently performing all the gifts (*dāna*s) mentioned in the *āgama*s such as the *kanakatulāpuruṣa* and the *upadāna*s in many temples at places like Kāñcī and Śrīraṅgam and at sacred *tīrtha*s.[58] He was an ardent devotee of the Lord of Tirupati where his bronze statue is kept.[59] His gifts of *tulāpuruṣa* in gold and other grants

53. 5. of 1111-T.A.R.; K.K. Pillai, *The Sucīndram Temple*, Madras, 2002, p. 42.
54. *Ibid.*, p. 359.
55. *ARE*, 656 of 1919.
56. *EI*, vol. XVI, no. 18, line 95.
57. *Ibid.*, line 82.
58. *EI*, vol. XVI, no. 23, v. 27.
59. K.V. Raman, *op. cit.*, p. 32.

to the temple of Śeṣācala (Tirupati), Kanakasabhā (Cidamabaram) and Ahobala are known from other inscriptions.[60]

Śrīraṅga Rāya

Śrīraṅga Rāya too was a staunch Vaiṣṇava. The Ariviḷimaṅgalam plates describe him as "the worshipper of Viṣṇu" (*śārṅgadharāntaraṅgaḥ*).[61] This ruler also made numerous gifts to the Vaiṣṇava temples at Melkoṭe, Śrīperumbudūr, Śrīmuṣṇam and Tiruvallikeṇi.[62] His benefations to the Varadarājasvāmi temple at Kāñcīpuram are known from numerous Tamil inscriptions at this shrine.[63]

During the reign of this king, there were more Muslim incursions into the Vijayanagara empire. One of his important acts was the restoration of worship in the Viṣṇu temple at Ahobalam since this place and its surrounding areas had been occupied by Ibrāhim Qutab Shah (the Sultān of Golkoṇḍa) and the chiefs of the Haṇḍe family.[64] The military chieftains of Śrīraṅga Rāya named Koṇḍarāju Veṅkaṭarāju and Koṇḍarāju Tirumalarāju conducted this campaign succesfully and also made vast additions and numerous benefactions to this temple for which they and their descendents were granted several rights and privileges in this temple.

Although Śrīraṅga Rāya was a great devotee of Viṣṇu, he had no animosity towards the Śaivite sect, as can be seen from his copper-plate grants which began with invocatory verses

60. *EI*, vol. XII, no. 21, v. 22, p. 173; *EI*, vol. XVI, no. 23, v. 27.
61. *EI*, vol. XII, no. 38, v. 20, p. 352.
62. T.V. Mahalingam, op. cit., p. 327.
63. K.V. Raman, op. cit., p. 32.
64. S.K. Ayyangar, *Sources of Vijayanagara History*, Madras, 1919, pp. 233-34.

in praise of Śiva and Gaṇeśa, apart from Viṣṇu. In fact, the very first verse in the Ariviḻimaṅgalam plates begins with a prayer to Śiva.[65] It ends with the word "Śrī Virūpākṣa," as was the custom with the Vijayanagara inscriptions in the times of his predecessors.

Veṅkaṭa II

Śrīraṅga Rāya's brother, Veṅkaṭa II, who succeeded him to the throne was a very great devotee of Viṣṇu. Till his time the Vijayanagara throne was believed to be under the blessed guardianship of Lord Virūpākṣa.[66] However, this ruler was a great devotee of Lord Veṅkaṭeśvara of Tirupati and his inscriptions instead of bearing the signature "Śrī Virūpākṣa," contain the name "Śrī Veṅkaṭeśvara" at the very end. His copper-plate charters are almost always found to be made in the presence of Lord Veṅkaṭeśvara of Tirupati.[67] Moreover, these inscriptions contain invocatory verses praising Vaiṣṇava deities like Rāma, Viśvakṣena and Viṣṇu only.

The coins of the reign of Veṅkaṭa II also reveal his devotion to Lord Viṣṇu. The gold coin known as Veṅkaṭa *pagoḍā* has a figure of Viṣṇu standing, while the reverse bears the legend *śrī veṅkaṭeśvarāya namaḥ* (adoration to blessed Veṅkaṭeśvara).[68] His coins also bear the figures of Garuḍa and Hanumān.[69]

An interesting inscription discovered near the Jambūkeśvaram temple at Tiruvānnaikkāval (near Śrīraṅgam),

---

65. *EI*, vol. XII, no. 38, v. 1, p. 350.
66. *IA*, vol. XLIV, p. 221.
67. *EI*, vol. XVI, no. 22, p. 206; *EI*, vol. IV, no. 39, v. 278; *EI*, vol. XVI, no. 23, p. 318; *EI*, vol. XIII, no. 22A, p. 321 & no. 22B; p. 235; *EI*, vol. XII, no. 21, p. 185.
68. E. Hultzsch, *The Coins of the Kings of Vijayanagara, IA*, vol. XX, p. 308.
69. R. Nagaswamy, *Tamil Coins — A Study*, Madras 1981, p. 151.

probably belonging to the period of Veṅkaṭa II and written in high-flown *maṇipravāla* style purports to record an order of God Caṇḍeśvara appointing a certain Candraśekharaguru-Uḍaiyār to the post of the trustee of the Tiruvānaikka-Uḍaiyār temple.[70] It appears to be an apologia for the selection of a married person (*gṛhistha*) to the pontificate of the Pāśupata-Maṭha at Tiruvānaikka, which had till then probably been in the keeping of a celibate only. This inscription contains many quotations from several works in support of this transition.[71]

A copper-plate record dated AD 1590 of the reign of Veṅkaṭa II registers the grant by this king of the village of Paḷḷakkāl in Muḷḷināḍu in Tiruvaḍi-rājya for meeting the expenses of worship, offerings and festivals of the deity Prasanna-Veṅkaṭeśa of this place at the request of a chieftain named Kṛṣṇadāsa, the ruler of Tiruvaḍi-rājya.[72]

Veṅkaṭa III

This ruler too was a Vaiṣṇava as can be gleaned from the data found in his inscriptions. The Kūniyūr plates describe him as one "in whose heart Hari (Viṣṇu) takes up his abode" (*hariścittesya datte sthitim*).[73] In another verse in this record he is called as "the favourite of Śārṅgadhara" (Viṣṇu) (*śārṅgadharāntaraṅgaḥ*).[74] Some of his coins depict Lord Veṅkaṭeśvara and His consort.[75]

---

70. *ARE*, 135 of 1936-37.
71. *ARE*, 1936-37, Pt, II, para 79, p. 91.
72. *ARE*, 1962-63, no. A7.
73. *EI*, vol. III, no. 34, v. 30, p. 244.
74. *Ibid.*, v. 34.
75. R. Nagaswamy, *op. cit.*, p. 151.

Nāyaka Rulers of Madurai

The Nāyaka kings of Madurai, starting from the days of Viśvanātha Nāyaka, the founder of the dynasty, did much for the propagation of the Brāhmanical religion by constructing new temples and presenting gifts to the existing temples of the land.

The *Koil-Olugu* states that Viśvanātha Nāyaka gave to Lord Raṅganātha, gifts of several golden vessels, costly ornaments and land. Another work, the *Tiruppaṇi-mālai*, which describes in detail the donations made by various people to the temple of Mīnākṣī and Sundareśvara in Madurai, records that this ruler presented to Lord Sundareśvara of Madurai a valuable necklace and pendant and gifted four villages to that deity. He also covered afresh the old *Indra-vimāna* with gold.[76]

Viśvanātha Nāyaka's acts of generosity were so well-known that the concluding prose section of the Veḷḷāṅguḍi plates mention that the charitable acts performed by his descendent Kṛṣṇappa Nāyaka II were equal to those done by Viśvanātha.[77]

The Kṛṣṇāpuram copper-plate grant of Sadāśiva Rāya dated AD 1567, records that Kṛṣṇappa Nāyaka I, the son of Viśvanātha Nāyaka constructed a temple at Kṛṣṇāpuram (near Tirunelveli).[78] This inscription adds that he built a *prākāra* around it and a tower (*gopura*) over its entrance. In front of the shrine, he erected a *raṅga-maṇḍapa*, standing on pillars containing exquisite sculptures and decorated with rows of beautiful creepers. In this temple, he consecrated the image of Lord Veṅkaṭanātha (Viṣṇu). He built a big chariot (*ratha*) for the deity and surrounded the temple with broad streets for

76. *EI*, vol. XVI, no. 23, p. 305.
77. *Ibid.*, lines 552-54, pp. 317-18.
78. *EI*, vol. IX, no. 52, pp. 331-39.

the procession of the deity. It was at his request that Sadāśiva Rāya granted a number of villages to this temple. The income from these villages was meant for the daily *pūjās*, for offerings, lighting of incense, flower-garlands and for the annual celebration of the chariot and the float festivals.

The Daḷavāy-agrahāram plates mention that prince Vīrabhūpa (Vīrappa Nāyaka), son of Kṛṣṇappa Nāyaka I made many benefactions to the Mīnākṣī temple at Madurai.[79] This record states that this ruler constructed a *maṇḍapa* with finely sculptured pillars in the temple of Sundaranāyaka (Lord Sundareśvara) at Madurai and presented to Goddess Mīnākṣī a golden covering (*kavaca*), studded with gems. This ruler is also praised in this inscription as a devotee of Viṣṇu (*śrimān-upendra-pada-bhakti-viśeṣa-sāndrah*).[80]

The work *Tiruppaṇi-mālai* mentioned earlier states that Kṛṣṇa Vīrappa Nāyaka constructed the Vellambalam, the northern *gopuram*, the shrine called Sevvīśvaram, the kitchen and also the thousand-pillared *maṇḍapa*, the Mūrttiyamman maṇḍapa, the *Śuṟṟu-maṇḍapa* of the second *prākāra* and the Vīrappa *maṇḍapa* with sculptured pillars. He also covered the pillars of a *maṇḍapa* of the temple of Mīnākṣī with gold.[81] The Vīrappa *maṇḍapa* mentioned in this work is probably the one referred to in the above-mentioned inscription.[82]

His son, Kṛṣṇa Mahīpati (Kṛṣṇappa Nāyaka II) is described in this same inscription as being engaged everyday in the performance of one or the other of the sixteen *mahādānas*. He also made many benefactions to the temple of Lord Raṅganātha at Śrīraṅgam. He presented to Lord Raṅganātha,

---

79. *EI*, vol. XII, no. 21, v. 68, p. 177.

80. *Ibid.*, v. 67.

81. *Ibid.*, p. 161.

82. *Ibid.*

a covering (*kavaca*) studded with gems of different kinds, a *uṣṇīśa* (head-dress), yellow silk garments, necklaces, *kirīṭas* (diadems), *kuṇḍalas* (ear-ornaments) and girdles. He also gave to this deity several villages and lands and celebrated the car-festival and the daily services.[83] The Padmaneri copper-plate inscription of Veṅkaṭa II also mentions the same details.[84]

To Lord Sundareśvara (Sundara Nāyaka), he gave several lamp-stands (making provision to burn lights in them), made arrangements for the celebration of the *abhiṣekas* (holy baths) of milk and the car-festival and presented the deity with many rich ornaments. He also constructed a *maṇi-stambha* in front of this deity. This ruler performed the *mahādānas* like *tulā-puruṣa* and *hiraṇya-garbha* and on those occasion made valuable presents to the brāhmaṇas.

The *Koiḷ-Oḷugu* also gives some important information about the gifts given by the Madurai Nāyakas to the temple of Lord Raṅganātha. According to this work, Kṛṣṇappa Nāyaka I gave to this deity a large number of jewels and conducted a number of festivals for this God. He also constructed a bathing *ghāṭ* with steps and a *maṇḍapa* on the banks of the southern Kāverī.[85] This work also states that Kṛṣṇappa Nāyaka II presented to Lord Raṅganātha a diamond shirt and a diamond crown among other gifts worth a lakh and fifty thousand gold pieces.[86]

Cokkanātha Nāyaka was an ardent Śaivite to begin with. The *Koiḷ-Oḷugu* gives a detailed account of his conversion to Vaiṣṇavism. The trustees of the Śrīraṅgam temple invited a Vaiṣṇava named Śrīnivāsa Deśikar to debate with an Advaitin

83. *EI*, vol. XVI, no. 23, p. 316.
84. *EI*, vol. XVI, no. 22, vv. 67-77.
85. *KO*, p. 98.
86. *KO*, pp. 98-99.

named Vajrāṅgi then preaching in Śrīraṅgam. This debate between the two took place with Cokkanātha's brothers, Muttu Alakādri, Acyutappa, Kṛṣṇappa and Vallappa acting as mediators. They tried to favour the Advaitin but could not succeed. When they came to know that the ancestors of Śrīnivāsa Deśikar were the spiritual preceptors of their own forefathers, they renounced Śaivism and made him their spirtitual preceptor. Cokkanātha too become a devout student of this teacher.[87]

Muthuliṅga Nāyaka also called as Muttu Alakādri (or Muddu Alakādri) who become the king in AD 1678, after his elder brother Cokkanātha Nāyaka was deposed, also presented expensive gifts to the Śrīraṅgam temple. An inscription found in the third *prākāra* of this temple dated AD 1679, states that he made a *sūryaprabha* and a *kañcuka* (vest) for God Raṅganātha.[88]

Another undated epigraph of this king found at the same place records that he presented a number of ornaments, a crown and vessels for the deity's bath to Lord Raṅganātha at the request of his teacher, Ācārya Vādhula-Cūḍāmaṇi. He also constructed a *maṇḍapa* and arranged for offerings to the God.[89]

Many Tamil epigraphs reveal that the early Nāyaka kings also made many gifts to the Jaṁbukeśvaram temple at Tiruvānnaikāval near Śrīraṅgam.[90] The Jaṁbukeśvaram grant of Vijayaraṅga Cokkanātha Nāyaka, a later Nāyaka king of Madurai records that this ruler, at the request of the then presiding *guru* (preceptor) of the Śaṅkarācārya Maṭha at

87. *KO*, p. 194.
88. *SII*, vol. XXIV, no. 554, p. 537.
89. *SII*, vol. XXIV, no. 555, p. 537.
90. *ARE*, 138 of 1936-37; *ARE*, no. 1 & 2 of 1938-39; Pt. II of 1938-39, paras 74 and 75.

Jaṁbukeśvaram (Tirvānaikāval), made a grant of lands in certain villages in Tiruchirapalli district and some lands on both sides of the river Kāverī for conducting the worship, offerings and charity of this *maṭha*.[91] He also made grants to *maṭhas* in Tirukkaḻukuṇram and Sosale.[92]

Vijayaraṅga Cokkanātha is known to have been a very religious-minded ruler. The Tamil work *Maduraittala-varalāru* (account of the Sacred City of Madurai), mentions that this king focussed his attention on religious practices and gifts. He is said to have taken the administration of the Devasthānam (temple management) into his own hands and rivalled Tirumala Nāyaka in his arrangements with regard to temple affairs.[93]

Once in two years, he is known to have made pilgrimages to temples in Śrīraṅgam, Jaṁbukeśvaram, Madurai, Tirunelveli, Āḻvār-Tirunagari and Śrī Vaikuṇṭam.[94] He also constructed a number of temples.

Vijayaraṅga Cokkanātha made many munificent donations to the Śrī Raṅganāthasvāmi temple at Śrīraṅgam including the construction of the *vedaparāyaṇa-maṇḍapa*. The life-size statues in ivory of this ruler and his consort kept in the second *prākāra* of this temple are permanent reminders of the great devotion he had for Lord Raṅganātha.[95] Vijayaraṅga Cokkanātha used the sign manuel "Śrī Rāma" in his copper-plate grants.[96]

---

91. *EI*, vol. XVI, no. 12, pp. 95-96.
92. R. Sathyanatha Aiyar, *History of the Nāyakas of Madura*, New Delhi, 1991, pp. 223-24.
93. *Ibid.*, p. 223.
94. *Ibid.*, p. 230.
95. *ARE*, 1936-37, Pt. II, p. 88.
96. *Ibid.*

Nāyaka Rulers of Tañjāvūr

The Nāyaka rulers of Tañjāvūr, like their overlords, the Vijayanagara kings, continued the policy of tolerance and extended their patronage to all religious sects. A few Sanskrit inscriptions speak of the benefactions of the first Nāyaka ruler, Sevappa Nāyaka.

An inscription found in the Aruṇācaleśvara temple, Tiruvaṇṇāmalai records in Sanskrit verse that Sevappa Nāyaka constructed the tall *gopura* of eleven storeys.[97] Some literary sources also mention his contributions to the temple at Tiruvaṇṇāmalai. The *Sāhitya-Ratnākara* by Yajñanārāyaṇa Dīkṣita, son of Govinda Dīkṣita, the chief minister of the Nāyaka rulers, states that Sevappa Nāyaka built a big *gopuram* and a large tank in the temple of Soṇagīriśa (Aruṇācaleśvara).[98] This work also mentions that the tank outside the Tañjāvūr fort which feeds the Śivagaṅgā tank inside it and which bore the name Sevappaneri was constructed by Sevappa Nāyaka.[99]

The *Raghunāthābhyudayam* by the court poetess Rāmabhadrāmbā records that Sevappa Nāyaka constructed the tall *gopura* at Sonādri (Tiruvaṇṇāmalai), the *gopura* and *dhvajastambha* (flag-column) at Vṛddhācalam and the compound-wall and steps leading to the temple of Śrīśailam.[100] The *Raghunāthābhyudayam* of Vijayarāghava Nāyaka, the great-grandson of Sevappa mentions the latter's valuable gifts to the temples of Śrīśailam and Vṛddhācalam.[101]

The religious catholicity of Sevappa Nāyaka can be seen from his numerous benefactions which include grants of lands

97. *ARE*, 419 of 1928-29.
98. S.K. Ayyangar, op. cit., p. 270.
99. *EI*, vol. XII, no. 38, p. 343.
100. *Ibid.*, p. 285.
101. *Ibid.*, p. 255.

in favour of a mosque at Tañjāvūr, his permitting the Christians to come and settle in his country and his grant of lands to the Madhva teacher, Vijayīndra Tīrtha.

Acyutappa Nāyaka, like his father, was religious by nature. He presented gifts to various shrines as seen from epigraphic and literary sources. An inscription of Acyutappa Nāyaka, the son and successor of Sevappa Nāyaka found on the eastern *gopura* of the Aruṇācaleśvara temple, Tiruvaṇṇāmalai, gives details of the date on which the gold finials were installed by Sevappa Acyuta (Acyutappa Nāyaka).[102]

Another epigraph of Acyutappa Nāyaka found in the Sundareśvara temple, Elandurai, near Kuṁbakoṇam records the grant by this king of a village to the temple of Madhyārjuna for the car-festival of the Goddess Perunila-mamulai Ammai.[103]

The devotion which this ruler had for Lord Raṅganātha of Śrīraṅgam is seen from various inscriptions as well as from literary accounts. There are several Sanskrit records of this ruler found in the Śrī Raṅganāthasvāmi temple, Śrīraṅgam. One of these, dated AD 1567, found in the Pagalpattu-maṇḍapam, describes the ten *avatāra*s (*daśāvatāras*) of Lord Viṣṇu in Sanskrit verses and records gifts of lamps for Lord Raṅganātha, Lakṣmī, Viśvaksena, Garutmān and others and also gifts of gold for conducting festivals and offerings to various deities by Kumāra Acyuta (Acyutappa Nāyaka).[104]

An undated record found in the second *prākāra* unfortunately damaged in places, registers a gift of a village to the Śrīraṅgam temple by this ruler.[105] One more Sanskrit inscription of Acyutappa from Tiruvaiyāru near Kuṁbakoṇam

102. *ARE*, 425 of 1928-29.

103. *ARE*, 239 of 1927.

104. *SII*, vol. XXIV, no. 488, pp. 466-67.

105. *SII*, vol. XXIV, no. 487, pp. 465-66.

speaks of several gifts that he made to the temple of Raṅgeśa (Raṅganāthasvāmi) at Śrīraṅgam and that he reconstructed the dam across the river Kāverī which had been breached.[106]

A few epigraphs found at other places also reveal his benefactions to the Śrīraṅgam temple. One of these found at Melūr (Tiruchirapalli district) records the gift of a garden to this temple.[107] Govinda Dīkṣita, the famous minister of the Nāyaka kings in his *Saṅgītasudhā,* his son Yajñanārāyaṇa Dīkṣita in his *Sāhityaratnākara* and Rāmabhadrāmbhā in her *Raghunāthābhyudayam* have described Acyutappa's benefactions to the Śrīraṅgam temple in glowing terms.[108] This ruler is also known to have made annual pilgrimages to Śrīraṅgam and to Rāmeśvaram.[109] He was a broad-minded religious benefactor and gave many gifts to numerous Vaiṣṇava and Śaiva temples and to the Madhva teacher, Vijayīndra-tīrtha.[110]

However, even the literary sources focus on his contributions to the shrine at Śrīraṅgam. Govinda Dīkṣita, in his work *Sāhityasudhā* and Yajñanārāyaṇa Dīkṣita in his *Sāhityaratnākara* have praised Acyutappa's contributions to the Śrīraṅgam temple.[111] The *Raghunāthābhyudayam* by Rāmabhadrāmbhā states that he constructed a beautiful golden *vimāna* at Śrīraṅgam and presented to Lord Raṅganātha a crown (*kirīṭa*) and a throne.[112] He also made extensive additions to this temple by constructing walls to the temple compound and making provisions for gardens.[113]

106. *ARE,* 426 of 1924.
107. *ARE,* 410 of 1924.
108. V.N. Hari Rao, op. cit., p. 175.
109. *Ibid.,* p. 174.
110. *Ibid.,* p. 175.
111. *Ibid.*
112. S.K. Ayyangar, op. cit., p. 285.
113. *Ibid.,* p. 255.

The *Sāhityaratnākara*, *Raghunāthābhyudayam* and the letters of the Jesuit fathers Pimenta, Auquetil du Pirron and Coutinho mention that Acyutappa Nāyaka abdicated the throne in favour of his son Raghunātha in AD 1600.[114] The *Sāhityaratnākara* mentions that after his abdication he spent his time at Śrīraṅgam in the company of *paṇḍits*.[115]

Raghunātha Nāyaka

Although the Sanskrit inscriptions of the Nāyaka period do not provide much data on the religious disposition of Acyutappa's son and successor Raghunātha, copious information on this subject is available from literary sources.

Raghunātha was a great devotee of Lord Rāma. The *Saṅgītasudhā* and the *Tanjavūrī Āndhra Rājula Caritamu* record that this ruler built the Rāmasvāmi temple at Kumbakoṇam.[116] The former work also states that he built temples for Rāma at Rāmeśvaram and Śrīraṅgam with towers, *maṇḍapas* and *prākāras*.[117] An excellent portrait-sculpture of this king is found in the Rāmasvāmi temple at Kuṁbakoṇam.

A copper-plate grant of Raghunātha from Tirukkaṇṇamaṅgai (Tañjāvūr district) reveals this ruler's great devotion to Lord Rāma.[118] This grant mentions that this Nāyaka king, having performed worship on a Rāmanavamī day, made a gift of land to the temple of Viṣṇu at Tirukkaṇṇamaṅgai. This charter begins with the words *śrī rāma nīve gati* (Śrī Rāma, you are the solace) and *śrīrāmajayam* (Victory to Śrī Rāma).

---

114. V.N. Hari Rao, op. cit., p. 175.
115. *Ibid.*
116. V. Vriddhagirisan, *The Nāyakas of Tanjore*, New Delhi, 1995, p. 107.
117. S.K. Ayyangar, op. cit., p. 267.
118. R. Nagaswamy, A Copper-plate of Raghunātha Nāyaka, from *Studies in Ancient Tamil Law and Society*, Madras, 1978, pp. 116-23.

Raghunātha also bore the titles, *anavarata rāmakathāmṛtha sevaka* (one who is ever delighted in listening to the nectar-like story of Rāma) and *kodaṇḍarāma*.[119]

A coin of the Nāyaka dynasty which has been assigned to the reign of this king bears on the obverse, standing figures of Rāma, Lakṣmaṇa, Sītā and Hanumān and on the reverse, a portrait of this king standing in *añjali* pose with a long sword hanging from his waist.[120]

Apart from his devotion to Lord Rāma, this king also made numerous benefactions to other Śiva and Viṣṇu temples. The *gopura* of Lord Kumbakoṇeśvara (Kuṁbeśvara) at Kuṁbakoṇam and a *maṇḍapa* are believed to have been constructed by him.[121] According to the *Saṅgītasudhā*, Raghunātha evinced keen interest in the celebrations of *rathotsvams* (car-festivals) to the Gods Jalpeśa of Tiruvaiyāru and Dhenunātha of Paśupatikoil.[122] The *Sāhityasudhā* by Govinda Dīkṣita mentions that he made additions to the temples of Campeśa (Lord of Mannārguḍi), Pañcanadīśa (Lord of Tiruvaiyāru), Dhenunātha (Paśupatikoil) and Śrīnivāsasthala (Oppiliappan Koil).[123]

Later Pāṇḍyan Kings

The later Pāṇḍyan rulers were also devout followers of the Brāhmanical religion. A number of temples were constructed during this period, the most well-known one being the Vīśvanātha temple which was built by Arikesari Parākrama at the capital Tenkāśī which was founded by him.

---

119. R. Nagaswamy, A Copper-plate of Raghunātha Nāyak, from *Studies in Ancient Tamil Law and Society*, Madras, 1978, pp. 116-23.
120. R. Nagaswamy, *Tamil Coins — A Study*, op. cit., p. 166.
121. V. Vriddhagirisan, op. cit., p. 107.
122. *Ibid.*
123. S.K. Ayyangar, op. cit., p. 267.

According to the Tenkāśī inscription of Parākrama, Lord Viśvanātha of Kāśī appeared in the dream of this ruler and stated that the temple (Śivālaya) at Uttara Kāśī (Varanasi) was in ruins and that a temple should be built under the name Dakṣiṇa Kāśī on the northern bank of the river Citrā. Following this, Parākrama founded the city of Tenkāśī (Dakṣiṇa Kāśī) and built the Viśvanātha temple.[124]

The Tenkāśī inscriptions of Parākrama reveal that many brāhmaṇas from the north migrated to this place. They probably sought asylum in the south when the Benaras temple was destroyed by the Muslims.[125] The construction of this temple was started in AD 1446 and the Śivaliṅga was consecrated in AD 1447. Following Parākrama's death in AD 1463, the rest of the construction was done by his younger brother, Aḷagaṉ Perumāḷ Kulaśekhara. Parākrama also created a large tank called Viśvanāthappereri and constructed *maṇḍapa*s in many Śiva temples in his kingdom.

A number of Tamil inscriptions mention the benefactions made by this ruler and his succesors to the Viśvanātha temple and also to many other temples in the Pāṇḍyan country.

The Sanskrit Daḷavāy-agrahāram plates of Varatuṅgarāma Pāṇḍya (1588 AD) mention clearly that God Viśvanātha appreared in the dream of Parākrama Pāṇḍya and blessed this king to build a temple for Him at Dakṣiṇa-Kāśī.[126]

A Sanskrit inscription dated AD 1615, engraved on the north wall of the *mahā-maṇḍapa* of the Viśvanāthasvāmi temple at Tenkāśī records that king Varaguṇa Śrīvallabha *alias*

---

124. *TAS*, vol. VI, p. 98; N. Sethuraman, *The Later Pāṇḍyas* (1371-1759 AD) Paper presented at the 19th Annual Congress of The Epigraphical Society of India, Tiruchirapalli, 1993, pp. 4-5.

125. N. Sethuraman, op. cit., p. 5.

126. *TAS*, vol. I, no. XII, v. 11, p. 128.

Kulaśekhara set-up on the bank of the river Citrānadī, an image of Gaṇeśa called Yajñeśa (or Yajñeśvara) during a sacrifice.[127] He gave to the sacrificial priests an *agrahāra* named Abhiśekhapura situated in front of the deity. In one or two inscriptions, this king calls himself Varaguṇa Śrīvallabha Dīkṣitar.[128] The Dharma-śāstras permit a kṣatriya to request brāhmaṇas to perform *yāga*s in his name and since Varaguṇa Śrīvallabha got a *yāga* performed, he styled himself a Dīkṣita, a title borne by those who have performed *yāgas*.[129] Many kings of the later Pāṇḍyan dynasty who succeeded this king also adopted this title.

Apart from the Vijayanagara, Nāyaka and the later Pāṇḍya rulers, some of the kings of the Kerala country also made benefactions to the temples in the southern part of the ancient Tamil country and some of these are recorded in the Sanskrit inscriptions found in these shrines.

A record of the Travancore king, Cera Udaya Mārtāṇḍavarma (AD 1410) written in Sanskrit verse found on the north wall of the Vīra-Pāṇḍyan *maṇi-maṇḍapa* and also on a pillar in the *maṇḍapa* south of the Pañcaliṅga shrine in the Sucīndram temple registers that this ruler constructed a hall (*sabhā*) in this temple-complex.

This king, who was closely associated with the activities of this temple is described in this record as Kerala Kṣamāpatīndra (the great emperor of Kerala).[130] This ruler, who had the longest reign in Travancore history (AD 1383-1444), ruled over territories on either side on the Western

127. *TAS*, vol. I, no. XIV, p. 147.

128. *TAS*, vol. I, p. 59.

129. *TAS*, vol. I, no. XIV, p. 147.

130. *TAS*, vol. VIII, p. 28; K.K Pillai, *op. cit.*, p. 37.

Ghats and it was from his time onwards that Venāḍ gradually extended its sway into the interior of the Tirunelveli region.[131]

Another Sanskrit record inscribed in the Cempakarāman *maṇḍapa* dated AD 1478 in the regin of Rāmavarma, records the construction of this huge *maṇḍapa* by this king.[132] It is known from an inscription at Quilon that this king had the surname Cempaka, and this accounts for the name Cempakarāman maṇḍapa given to the pavilion.[133] Rāmavarma is also known to have presented expensive jewels to the Sucīndram temple.[134]

A Sanskrit inscription of Ādityavarman, consisting of a single verse, is found inscribed on a large bell in the Nambi (Viṣṇu) temple at Tirukuranguḍi (Tirunelveli district). This record, datable to C. AD 1468 mentions that Ādityavarma "hung up the bell which adorns the gate of Murāri (Viṣṇu) (*dvārālaṅkṛta ghaṇṭam*) enshrined in the Śrīkuraṅga (Tirukuranguḍi) temple."[135]

A Tamil inscription on a wall inside the temple also records this gift of Ādityavarman. According to an interesting legend, associated with the installation of this bell, this Cera ruler was a great devotee of Lord Nambi of this shrine and decided that even when he was in faraway Kerala, would eat his evening meal only after the food-offering was given to this God at Tirukuranguḍi. So he had the bell installed in this temple and enroute between the temple and Tiruvanantapuram (his capital) had similar bells installed. When the Tirukuranguḍi

131. A. Sreedhara Menon, *A Survey of Kerala History*, Madras, 1998, p. 244.

132. *TAS*, vol. VIII, p. 23.

133. K.K. Pillai, op. cit., p. 127.

134. *Ibid.*, p. 436.

135. *ARE*, 216 of 1905; see also *IA*, vol. II, p. 360.

bell was rung after the evening *pūjā*, the noise would be picked up by the other bells and once it reached Tiruvanantapuram, the king would partake of his evening meal.[136]

The whole of the seventeenth century was an unfortunate period in the history of the Carnatic as it was characterized by political uncertainty, instability and constant breaks in the administration of the land.[137] Immediatley before the Mughul invasion of the south in AD 1688, the authorities of the three prominent temples in Kāñcīpuram (Varadarāja, Ekāmreśvara and Kāmākṣī temples) apprehending desecration at the hands of the invading troops, took the images secretly out of the town. The images of Lord Varadarāja and his consorts were kept in the forests of Uḍayārpāḷayam in Tiruchirapalli district. In AD 1710, when Kāñcī was safe again and arrangements were made to bring the images back, the local chieftain of Uḍayārpāḷayam refused to part with the images as he had become a devotee of Lord Varadarāja. On the request of the Vaiṣṇava ascetic (or *jīyar*) called Śrīmat Paramahaṁsa Parivrājakācārya Āttān Jīyar, his disciple Lāla Toḍarmalla brought the images safely back after threatening the chieftain with a large number of troops. The images were reinstalled in the temple at Kāñcīpuram.

This incident is recorded in a long Sanskrit inscription in the Varadarājasvāmi temple dated AD 1710.[138] Another inscription in this temple records the same details and gives the dates on which these consecrations took place.[139]

Āṭṭān Jīyar *alias* Śrīnivāsadāsa was a relative of Akkaṇṇa and Madaṇṇa, the two influential brāhmaṇa ministers of the

136. M.S. Ramesh, *108 Vaishnava Divya Desams* (vol. IV), Tirupati, 1996.
137. K.V. Raman, *op. cit.*, p. 37.
138. *ARE*, 639 of 1919.
139. *ARE*, 650 of 1919.

Golkoṇḍā kingdom and Rājā Toḍarmalla was a general of Sa-adet-ullā Khān, the Nawāb of Carnatic.[140]

In recognition of his great service, the authorities of the Varadarājasvāmi temple conferred the right of management of the temple on Toḍarmalla, who in turn transferred it to his guru Āṭṭān Jīyar.[141] On the latter's death, Toḍarmalla re-conferred the title of full proprietorship to Āṭṭān Jīyar's son.

Bronze figures of Rājā Toḍarmalla and his family are even today kept at the entrance of the fourth *prākāra* in memory of this chief's services to this temple. His statues are kept in the Śrīraṅgam and Tirupati temples also where he did notable service.[142]

A copper-plate inscription dated AD 1710 records a gift of money annually for purposes of worship (waving lights before the idol), daily offerings of cakes and all other kinds of worship to God Candramauḷīśvara worshipped by His Holiness Svāmi Paramahaṁsa Parivrājakācārya of the *maṭha* in Kāñcī.[143]

This inscription, written in three languages, Sanskrit, Persian and Telugu is a firman and the grantor of the *inām* is described as "an Emperor who is obeyed by all the world, who is a Sultān upon whom all the *mahārāja*s depend and who is the representative of god on earth."[144]

In AD 1707, the Mughal ruler Aurangzeb died and was succeeded by Bahadur Shāh who died in AD 1712. The date of this firman (1088 of the Hijira era) falls within the reign of Bahadur Shāh, who is believed to have been a wise and valiant

140. K.V. Raman, *op. cit.*, p. 38.

141. *Ibid.*, p. 85.

142. *Ibid.*, p. 173.

143. *CPIK*, pp. 115-20.

144. *Ibid.*, p. 113.

prince and as such might very likely have made the grant of the *inām* to the *svāmi* of the *maṭha* at Kāñcī.[145]

Marāṭhas

The Marāṭha rulers also made many donations and benefactions to the temples in the Tamil country. Some of their copper-plate charters and lithic inscriptions mention their works of charity.

A copper-plate grant of Ekojī Mahārāja Sahebu states that he repaired the *maṇḍapa, gopura* and *prākāra* of the temple of Vaidyānāthasvāmi, constructed out of stone the shrine of Goddess Bālāmbikā Amman, performed the *kumbābhiṣekam* and presented lands and gold for special festivals, worship and offerings in this temple.[146]

Another copper-plate grant written in Sanskrit and Marathi, dated AD 1686 of Sāmbhojī from Tiruvārūr (Tañjāvur district) states that a person named Cittambala Yogin renovated the temple of Śiva at Cidambaram and performed the *kumbābhiṣekam* of this shrine, also called Kanaka Sabhā at the request of an officer of the king called Gopāla Dādājī.[147]

Three more copper-plate inscriptions of the same ruler from Tiruvārūr, also composed in Sanskrit and Marathi mention the same facts. One of these states that the *kumbābhiṣekam* was performed by the *kulaguru* of this family named Muttayya Dīkṣita.[148]

One of these copper-plate epigraphs mentions that Cittambalamuni made the golden pots and pillars, wooden

145. *Ibid.*, p. 114.

146. *ARE*, 1945-46, A no. 15.

147. *ARE*, 1946-47, A no. 20.

148. *ARE*, 1946-47, A no. 22.

and copper-plates for the gilded hall at Cidambaram. This inscription also records two consecration ceremonies conducted at Cidambaram by Cittambala Muni, the first on 21st November 1684 and the second on 14th November, 1686.[149]

A lithic inscription found on the wall of the Śivagaṅgā tank in the Naṭarāja temple at Cidambaram is dated AD 1685, of the reign of Chatrapati Sāmbhojī. It states that the tank was repaired by Gopāla Dādājī, the private secretary of Harīśa, whose overlord was Sāmbhojī.[150]

The ruler mentioned in these records was Sāmbhojī, the first son of Chatrapati Śivājī who ruled at Ginji from AD 1680-89.[151] It is known that the frequent conflicts between the Mughal cadres and the Marāṭha chieftains resisting them had disrupted the political, social and religious life in the Coromandal coast.[152] The priests and devotees at Cidambaram must have been apprehensive about the safety of the Naṭarāja image in this temple.[153] The above-mentioned copper-plate inscriptions found at Tiruvārūr reveal that Lord Naṭarāja was taken away from Cidambaram between 24-12-1648 AD and 14-11-1686 AD, the deity having been taken to Kuḍimiyāmalai and later to Madurai. Cidambara Muni helped in bringing Lord Naṭarāja back to Cidambaram. It is possible that the famine of AD 1647 and the threat from the Bījāpur Sultān to the Hindu kingdoms was the reason for Lord Naṭarāja being moved out of Tillai.[154]

---

149. *ARE*, 1946-47, A no. 23.
150. *ARE*, 329 of 1958-59.
151. Se. Rasu, *Tanjai Marāṭṭiyar Ceppetukaḷ-50*, Tañjāvūr, 1983, p. 278.
152. B. Natarajan, op. cit., p. 119.
153. *Ibid*.
154. *Ibid*.

As mentioned earlier, Sāmbhojī was the Marāṭha ruler of Ginji and it was he who entrusted his minister Gopāla Dādājī with the work of renovating the Naṭarāja temple at Cidambaram.[155] The Marāṭhas of Ginji and Tañjāvūr were well-disposed towards each other. Sahājī II, the Marāṭha ruler at Tañjāvūr (AD 1684-1711) was a great devotee of Lord Tyāgarāja of Tiruvārūr and took it upon himself to see the safe return of the deity to Cidambaram.[156]

The Marāṭha kings also performed many ritual sacrifices as can be seen from some of their inscriptions. Two epigraphs composed in Sanskrit verse and Marathi prose found at the village of Oṛattānāḍ near Tañjāvūr dated AD 1809-10, of the reign of Serfojī II (Chatrapati Rājaśrī Sārabhojī Mahārāja) who ruled from AD 1798-1833, mention some of these sacrifices.[157] These records state that this king ordered the construction of two sacrificial halls (*śālā*) at Muktāmbāpura (which was perhaps the original name of Oṛattānāḍ) and in them the Agniṣṭoma (also called *Śomasava*) sacrifice preceded by Ādhāna was performed by Śittapa-Dīkṣita and the same was perfomed by Śeṣajaṭā-vallabha, under the patronage of the king. Similarly, on the same day, *Ādhāna Prathāmatrirātra* preceded by *Cayana* by Veṅkaṭeśvara-Dīkṣita, son of Mṛtyuñjaya-Vājapeyin, Agniṣṭoma (also called *Somayāga*) preceded by Ādhāna by Appāsvāmi Dīkṣita and Ādhāna and *Prathāmatrirātra* preceded by *Cayana* by *Ṛgvedi* Subrahmaṇya-Jaṭāvallabha were also conducted.[158]

An inscription written in the Nāgarī script and Sanskrit language dated AD 1884, is inscribed on the pedestal of an

155. Se. Rasu, *op. cit.*, p. 228.

156. *Ibid.*, pp. 228-29.

157. *ARE*, 166 and 167 of 1911.

158. *ARE*, 1911, Pt. II, p. 90.

image of Naṭarāja in the Bṛhadīśvara temple at Tañjāvūr.[159] This inscription records in verse in Śragdhārā metre, the repair and consecration of the image of Naṭarāja (Nāṭyarāja) by a person named Nāgarāja under the orders of Kāmākṣī (Kāmākṣīamba Bāyi) who was the dowager queen of the last Marāṭha ruler, Śivājī II (AD 1832-55).

There were two images of Naṭarāja (Āḍavallān) in the Bṛhadīśvara temple, Tañjavūr as referred to in the Tamil lithic inscriptions of this temple. One of these was set-up by Rājarāja Coḷa I and the other by his queen Coḷa Mahādevī.[160] According to R. Nagaswamy, this image which was repaired by the Marāṭha queen was the icon of Āḍavallān set-up by Rājarāja Coḷa I, since the detailed measurements given in the Tañjāvūr inscriptions for the image set-up by Coḷa Mahādevī do not tally with the present figure, which is a much larger one.[161] It is therefore clear that this is the Āḍavallān image set-up by Rājarāja I to whose reign it can be ascribed on grounds of style also.[162] This old, damaged Naṭarāja image in the Tañjāvūr temple, requiring repairs, must have been repaired and reconsecrated by queen Kāmākṣī as the epigraph etched on the original portion of the pedestal, which has been repaired on either side, reveals.[163] This queen was also responsible for carrying out extensive renovations to temples in and around Tañjāvūr.[164]

---

159. *ARE*, 248 of 1971-72.
160. R. Nagaswamy, Āḍavallān and Dakṣiṇameruviṭaṅkar of the Tanjore Temple, from *Lalit Kalā*, no. 12, October 1962, p. 37, Lalit Kala Akademi, New Delhi.
161. *Ibid.*
162. *Ibid.*
163. *Ibid.*, p. 36.
164. *Ibid.*

Vassal Chieftains, Ministers and Officials

In addition to the rulers, many of their vassal chiefs, ministers and other officials and also the common folk presented many gifts to the temples.

One of the greatest services rendered to the Śrī Raṅganāthasvāmi temple, Śrīraṅgam was by Gopaṇa or Gopaṇa-uḍaiyār (also called Gopaṇārya), an official of Kumāra Kaṁpaṇa who resided at Ginji.

The Tamil work, *Guruparamparaprabhāvam*[165] states that when the Muslims captured Tiruchirapalli, the authorities of the Śrī Raṅganāthasvāmi temple at Śrīraṅgam secretly removed the image of Aḻagiyamanavāḷan (Raṅganātha) to Tirumalai (Tirupati). Subsequently, Gopaṇārya brought this image from Tirumalai to Śiṅgapuram near Senji (Ginji) and then later to the temple at Śrīraṅgam where he reconsecrated the God and his two consorts (Śrī Devī and Bhū Devī). On this occasion, the eminent Śrī Vaiṣṇava preceptor, Vedānta Deśika is said to have praised him in a Sanskrit verse.

In a similar manner, the *Koiḷ-Oḻugu* also speaks of the same events, but in greater detail.[166] It states that when the authorities of the Śrī Raṅganātha temple heard that the Muslim forces had reached Samayapuram near Tiruchirapalli, they removed the image of Aḻagiyamanavāḷa Perumāḷ to Tirunārāyaṇapuram (Melkote, near Mysore in Karnataka) and later took it to Tirumalai where the image was worshipped for a long time. When the Vijayanagara ruler Harihara Rāya II conquered Toṇḍaimaṇḍalam, one of his officials, Gopaṇa-Uḍaiyār who resided at Ginji took this image from Tirumalai to Śiṅgapuram where worship was offered to this idol daily.

165. *EI*, vol. VI, no. 33, p. 322.

166. *Ibid.*, pp. 322-23.

With the help of a strong force, he defeated the Muslims and reconsecrated the Lord with the two consorts at Śrīraṅgam. He engraved on the wall of this temple, the verse of Vedānta Deśika mentioned earlier.

The *Koiḷ-Oḻugu* further states that he granted fifty-two villages to the Raṅganātha temple and that his king Harihara Rāya II and Virūpaṇa, his son performed the *tulāpuruṣa* ceremony at this temple.[167]

In the Śrīraṅgam temple, till today can be found this Sanskrit verse together with another similar Sanskrit verse which make up a subjoined inscription engraved on the east wall of the second *prākāra* of the Śrī Raṅganāthasvāmi temple.[168] They are in praise of the achivements of Gopaṇārya who heroically defeated the Muslims and brought back the image of Lord Raṅganātha safely to Śrīraṅgam.

Gopaṇārya, who was a brāhmaṇa, was initially an officer under Kumāra Kaṁpaṇa, the son of Bukka I. Many Tamil inscriptions reveal the part played by Gopaṇa as the general supervisor of temples in the Tamil country. He was later appointed Governor of Ginji by Kumāra Kaṁpaṇa.[169]

Another minister of Kumāra Kaṁpaṇa is mentioned in a bilingual record in Sanskrit and Tamil found in Olagampaṭṭu in North Arcot district dated AD 1396.[170] His minister (*mahāpradhāna*) Duggaṇa granted the village Ulagalpaṭṭu *alias* Śrī Aḷagar-Cakravartī Caturvedimaṅgalam to the Vaiṣṇava Ācārya, Periya-Nallāncakravarti.

---

167. *EI*, vol. VI, no. 33, p. 323.
168. *Ibid.*, p. 330.
169. A. Krishnaswami, *op. cit.*, pp. 55-56.
170. *ARE*, 166 of 1941-42.

A record from the Śrī Raṅganāthasvāmi temple, Śrīraṅgam, also of the time of Kumāra Kaṁpaṇa, states that Viṭṭhapa, a *mahāmantri* (of the king) formed a pasture of land for the temple near the Yoga-Narasiṁhạ temple.[171]

A number of chiefs of the Telugu country presented gifts to the Śrī Raṅganāthasvāmi temple at Śrīraṅgam during this period as seen from their copper-plate grants preserved in this shrine.

A copper-plate epigraph dated AD 1358 of Mummaḍi Nāyaka, a king of the Teliṅgāna country records that this ruler granted to Bhaṭṭa Parāśara VII, the village of Kottallapaṟṟu, which the donee's mother regranted to Lord Raṅganātha of the Śrīraṅgam temple.[172] Mummaḍi Nāyaka was a disciple of Parāśara Bhaṭṭa VII (i.e. the seventh in descent from Parāśara Bhaṭṭa I, the well-known Śrī Vaiṣṇava preceptor).[173]

One more copper-plate grant from the Śrīraṅgam temple dated AD 1411 of the reign of Mādhava Nāyaka, a king of the Telugu country, mentions that this ruler, also known as Rājarāja Mādhava-Bhūpāla, granted the *agrahāra* of Torluri under the name Śrīraṅgapura to Lord Raṅganātha of Śrīraṅgam.[174] The income from this village was meant for providing the daily offerings to this deity, repairs to the dilapidated temple and *gopura*, for the garden and many other works.

A Sanskrit epigraph found in the *candana-maṇḍapa* in the Śrī Raṅganāthasvāmi temple, Śrīraṅgam, dated AD 1383, records in verse, that Muddarasa, a minister of Virūpākṣa II gifted twenty cows for maintaining a perpetual lamp in this temple.[175] Another record found at the same place, speaks of a gift of

---

171. *SII*, vol. XXIV, no. 288.
172. *EI*, vol. XIV, no. 3, pp. 83-86.
173. *Ibid.*, p. 85.
174. *EI*, vol. XIII, no. 21, pp. 220-25.
175. *SII*, vol. XXIV, no. 296, p. 310.

land by the same minister of Virūpākṣa for maintaining a flower-garden for supplying flowers to Lord Śrī Raṅganātha.[176]

A damaged Sanskrit inscription found in the *Veḷḷai-gopuram* in the same temple, refers to the construction of a bridge over the river Sahyātmajā (Kāverī) by this minister Muddapa-mantri here mentioned as belonging to the Kāśyapa *gotra*.[177]

Yet another epigraph found in the *candana-maṇḍapa* of this temple dated AD 1385 registers a gift of twenty cows for supplying milk to the temple by Devarāja, a *pradhāni* of Virūpaṇa and son of Saṅgamāmātya.[178] A Tamil inscription of this *pradhāni*, found at the same place, records the gift of a perpetual lamp to Śrī Raṅganātha on the occasion of a lunar eclipse.[179]

Uttamanambi Family

The Uttamanambi family which belonged to the Kāśyapa *gotra* and to the *pūrvaśikhā* sect of brāhmaṇas are believed to have migrated to Śrīraṅgam along with the Vaiṣṇava saint, Periāḻvār and his daughter Āṇḍāḷ from Śrīvilliputtūr.[180] They became one of the most important families of Śrīraṅgam.

Garuḍavāhana Paṇḍita, the contemporary of the Vaiṣṇava preceptor and philosopher, Śrī Rāmānuja, who is stated to have been in charge of a hospital in the Śrī Raṅganāthasvāmi temple at Śrīraṅgam is said to have belonged to the Uttamanambi family.[181] Periya Kṛṣṇarāyar Uttamanambi is believed to have invited Kumāra Kaṁpaṇa, the son of Bukka I to pay a visit to the Śrī Raṅganātha temple.

---

176. *SII*, vol. XXIV, no. 297, p. 311.
177. *SII*, vol. XXIV, no. 299, p. 312.
178. *SII*, vol. XXIV, no. 300, p. 312.
179. *SII*, vol. XXIV, no. 298, p. 311.
180. *ARE*, 1937-38, Pt. II, p. 102.
181. *Ibid*.

The two famous brothers, Uttamanambi and Cakrarāya, the trustees of the temple, figure in the inscriptions of Deva Rāya I and Deva Rāya II inscribed in the Śrīraṅgam temple. The Śrīraṅgam copper-plate grant of Harihara Uḍaiyār (III), dated AD 1414, records the grant of village Naruvūru (Nerūr in Karūr taluk, Tiruchirapalli district) to Uttamanambi, the *sthānika* of Śrī Raṅganāthasvāmi temple by Harihararāya Oḍeya (the son of Vīrapratāpa Deva Rāya I) who was the viceroy of a part of present-day Coimbatore area with headquarters at Cevūrakoṭe (Sevūr in Palladam taluk, Coimbatore district).[182] The inscription states that this village was originally granted to Appaṇṇaṅgaḷu by Harihara Rāya at Cevūrakoṭe on the banks of the river Bhavānī. It is possible that this gift changed hands because Appaṇṇaṅgaḷu could not manage the charity at that distance as effectively as a native of that place and therefore handed over the management of the charity to Uttamanambi.[183] It was stipulated that Uttamanambi was to hold a subordinate position to Appaṇṇaṅgaḷu with reference to this grant.

The deed of gift to Uttamanambi stipulated that the village of Naruvūru should be renamed Raṅganāthapura; that a daily service with every detail of offerings to God Raṅganātha should be maintained; a flower garden was to be cultivated and garlands supplied to the God on the occasion of the service called Padineṭṭāmpaḍi-sevai; a choultry or *chatra* was to be constructed within the enclosure of the Śrīraṅgam temple and twelve brāhmaṇas were to be fed there with rice, *dāl*, ghee, vegetables, butter-milk, betel-leaves and nuts and eight brāhmaṇas in the village were to be given each four *mā* of wet-land rent-free.

---

182. *EI*, vol. XVI, no. 15, pp. 224-28.

183. *Ibid.*, p. 223.

The Uttamanambi of this record is undoubtedly the same as Vaḻiyaḍimai-nilaiyiṭṭa Perumāḷ Uttamanambi who was the warden of the Śrīraṅgam temple between the years AD 1407-50.[184]

A Sanskrit record of Deva Rāya I, dated AD 1415, records that Uttamanambi was the recipient of several honours such as parasol, etc., from this king.[185] Another Sanskrit inscription in this temple mentions that Uttamanambi, the brother of Cakrarāya obtained from Deva Rāya I several honours such as the royal umbrella, ornaments and vehicles and the proprietary rights of administration in this temple.[186] Two other inscriptions consisting of only one Sanskrit verse each in praise of Uttamanambi are found in the Śrīraṅgam temple.[187]

There are many inscriptions at this shrine of the period of Deva Rāya II mentioning Uttamanambi and Cakrarāya. The Śrīraṅgam copper-plate grant of this ruler dated AD 1434 states that Deva Rāya II granted the villages of Nācchikurucci, Tiruvaraṅganallūr, Rāmanārāyaṇanallūr, Kumārakkūḍi and Rājanārāyaṇanallūr to Vaḻiyaḍimai-nilaiyiṭṭa Perumāḷ Uttamanambi, the *sthānapati* of the Śrīraṅgam temple. He was to conduct the daily worship of Śrī Raṅganātha with the income from these five villages.[188]

The literary works like the *Koiḷ-Oḻugu* and the *Lakṣmīkāvyam* mention Uttamanambi. He was called Vaḻiyaḍimai-Nilaiyiṭṭa, meaning "he who established his title as the hereditary servant of God" — a rendering in Tamil of the Sanskrit *vaṁśa-krama*

---

184. V.N. Hari Rao, *op. cit.*, p. 134.
185. *ARE*, 60 of 1938-39; *SII*, vol. XXIV, no. 307, p. 319.
186. *ARE*, 84 of 1937-38; *SII*, vol. XXIV, no. 311, p. 322.
187. *ARE*, 90 of 1937-38; *SII*, vol. XXIV, no. 308, p. 319 and *ARE*, 85 of 1937-38; *SII*, vol. XXIV, no. 312, p. 323.
188. *EI*, vol. XVIII, no. 17, p. 140-44.

mūlabhṛtya which occurs in the *Lakṣmīkāvyam*.[189] According to this work, Uttamanambi possessed royal insignia and managed the affairs of the temple and this is in agreement with the data supplied by the Sanskrit inscriptions seen above. The *Koiḷ-Oḻugu* also credits Uttamanambi with some repairs of damages to the temple caused by the Muslim occupation.[190]

According to the *Koiḷ-Oḻugu*, Tirumalainātha Uttamanambi, the author of the work *Lakṣmīkāvyam* and grandson of Vaḻiyaḍimai Nilaiyiṭṭa Uttamanambi went to Vijayanagara and stayed at the court of the king from AD 1444 to 1451.[191] During this period he received many endowments in cash and also twenty-two villages as benefactions to the Śrīraṅgam temple from Praudha Deva Rāya, Mallikārjuna and others. On his return to Śrīraṅgam, he made many additions and repairs to this temple. He constructed the hundred-pillared *maṇḍapa* to the east of the *Periatirumaṇḍapa* and performed there the *Sahasrakalāśābhiṣeka* for the God.

Similarly, Vaḻiyaḍimai Nilaiyiṭṭa Uttamanambi's brother, Cakrarāya also made many gifts to the Śrīraṅgam temple as mentioned by the Sanskrit inscriptions. One of the epigraphs of the reign of Deva Rāya I mentioned earlier, refers to the consecration of an image of Garuḍa by Cakrarāya in Manmatha year, corresponding to AD 1415.[192]

The consecration of this image is also mentioned in the *Koiḷ-Oḻugu* where it is stated that the copper-image of this deity which had been endowed by a Coḷa king had become mutilated in the troubled times that followed and was recast and set-up in the Manavāḷaperumāḷ Tirumaṇḍapa by Cakrarāya

189. V.N. Hari Rao, *op. cit.*, p. 136.

190. *KO*, p. 79.

191. *KO*, p. 87.

192. *ARE*, 60 of 1938-39; *SII*, vol. XXIV, no. 307, p. 319.

in the cyclic year Manmatha.[193]

Another Sanskrit record in the Śrīraṅgam temple speaks of the structural improvements made by Cakrarāya to the Annadi-Emberumān and the Māruti shrines and to the kitchen in the Śrī Raṅganātha temple and the establishment of a colony in the precincts of the shrine of Aḻagiyasiṅga (Kāṭṭaḻagiyasiṅgar) at Śrīraṅgam. The Tamil part of this inscription states that he made many more additions to this temple such as the consecration of an image of Hanumān and an image of Goddess Lakṣmī.[194]

A Sanskrit record of the reign of Deva Rāya II speaks of the gift of a golden *kuṁbha* (pot) to Lord Śrī Raṅganātha by Cakrarāya.[195] Another Sanskrit record in this temple states that Cakrarāya installed the *daśāvatāra* images in a temple on the southern bank of the river Kāverī (Sahajā) at Śrīraṅgam.[196]

According to the *Koiḷ-Oḻugu,* Cakrarāya was responsible for most of the repairs of the damages caused to various parts of the temple as a consequence of the Muslim raids and occupation like the shrines of Nammāḻvār, Śrīvarāha Nainār and the Āryabhaṭṭāl gateway.[197]

Another Sanskrit lithic inscription of the reign of Deva Rāya II, dated AD 1428, from the Śrīraṅgam temple registers some structural changes made here by the chief minister of this king named Śrīpati.[198]

Many inscriptions speak of the benefactions to this temple by other people. An epigraph of the reign of Acyutadeva (Acyuta

193. *ARE,* 1938-39, Pt. II, p. 86; *KO,* p. 85.
194. *ARE,* 82 of 1937-38; *SII,* vol. XXIV, no. 313, pp. 323-24.
195. *ARE,* 337 of 1950-51; *SII,* vol. XXIV, no. 325, p. 330.
196. *ARE,* 83 of 1937-38; *SII,* vol. XXIV, no. 333, p. 336.
197. *KO,* pp. 85-86.
198. *SII,* vol. XXIV, no. 321, p. 328.

Rāya) dated AD 1531, from the Śrīraṅgam temple records a gift of gold and land for offerings to Lord Raṅganātha on the second day of the festival called Bhūpati-Uḍaiyār-tirunāḷ by Ellamarasaru, son of Anantayyar, the mace-bearer to the God.[199]

A bi-lingual inscription in this temple, dated AD 1535, also of the reign of Acyuta Rāya mentions a benefaction to this temple by a chieftain, probably a vassal of this king, called Oṁkārāja Cennaya Bāladeva Mahārāja. The Tamil portion of this inscription registers a gift of a village for daily offerings of curd-rice (*dadhyodna*) to Goddess Uraiyūr-valli and for offerings to God Raṅganātha during the Śrī Rāmanavamī festival. The Sanskrit verses mention the gift of a jewelled gold garland with a pendant by the same chief.[200]

A copper-plate record dated AD 1590, of the reign of Veṅkaṭa II mentions the grant by this king of the village of Pallakkal in Mullināḍu in Tiruvaḍī-rājya for meeting the expenses of worship, offerings and festivals of God Prasanna Veṅkaṭeśa of this place at the request of a chieftain of Tiruvaḍi-rājya named Kṛṣṇadāsa, son of Koneribhūpāla. This chief had built the *prākāra, raṅga-maṇḍapa, gopura* and other structures of this temple and approached the king for securing the grant of the village.[201]

Tātācārya

Just as Uttamanambi was the manager of the Śrī Raṅganāthasvāmi temple at Śrīraṅgam, Lakṣmīkumāra Tātācārya, the preceptor of Veṅkaṭa II, managed the affairs of the Śrī Varadarājasvāmi temple at Kāñcīpuram during his reign. Tātācārya presented numerous gifts to this temple and these are recorded in many Sanskrit epigraphs etched on the walls of this temple.

199. *SII*, vol. XXIV, no. 405, p. 391-92.
200. *SII*, vol. XXIV, no. 421, pp. 406-07.
201. *ARE*, 1962-63, no. A7.

One of these inscriptions found on the south wall of the shrine of the Goddess (*Tāyār*) in the Varadarājasvāmi temple records that the high *vimāna* of this temple known as Kalyāṇakoṭi was erected by him to Goddess Lakṣmī in emulation of the *vimāna* known as Puṇyakoṭi of Lord Varadarāja in AD 1614. The *vimāna* was named Kalyāṇakoṭi probably as a remembrance of Tātācārya's title "Koṭikanyādānam."[202]

Another record praises Tātācārya as a great scholar, an emperor among muses who was worshipped by the king of the Karnāṭa country "whose crowns were worn as a garland at the feet of this scholar" and that his fame had spread far and wide.[203] The statement was not an empty boast as it is learnt from the literary work *Prapannāmṛtam* that Lakṣmī Kumāra Tātācārya performed the coronation of Veṅkaṭa II and that the king "entrusted the whole kingdom to his preceptor and himself led a life of retirement."[204] Eṭṭūr Kumāra Tātācārya had many eloquent titles like *Vedamārga-pratiṣṭhācārya* and *Ubhayavedānta Sthāpanācārya*. He was the manager of the temple affairs (*śrī-kārya-dhurandhara*) with a staff of subordinates under him. He lived in kingly splendour at Kāñcīpuram in the later part of his life.[205]

One more record consisting of two Sanskrit verses states that Tātācārya constructed all the necessary *vāhana*s (vehicles) for Lord Varadarāja, covered the Kalyāṇakoṭi and the Puṇyakoṭi *vimāna*s with thick gold plates and that he dug a tank called Devarājārṇavam for the God's delight. The vehicles made by him were the elephant, horse, serpent, Garuḍa,

202. *SITI*, vol. III, Pt. II, p. 1353.

203. *SITI*, vol. III, Pt. II, pp. 1354-55.

204. *Ibid.*, p. 1354.

205. *Ibid.*

Āñjaneya, the *bimbas* of the sun and the moon, the palanquin, swing, swan and lion all covered with silver and gold. He also constructed the *bali-pīṭha* for receiving the offerings and also made a *kirīṭa* (crown) set with precious stones. He endowed a rich village and made arrangements for the celebration of festivals.[206]

Another record in the Śrī Varadarājasvāmi temple states that Tātācārya celebrated eleven *tulābhāras* and distributed the gold to many learned men.[207] He also weighed himself separately against gold and silver and used all that wealth in the service of Varadarāja in erecting the Kalyāṇakoṭi *vimāna*.

Another epigraph in the Śrī Varadarājasvāmi temple states that Tātācārya constructed the *vimāna* of the temple of Veṅkaṭapati at Phanipatigiri (i.e. Tirupati) in the year Pramodūta.[208] The cyclic year should be either the one which coincided with Śaka 1552 (AD 1630-31) or the previous one in Śaka 1492 (AD 1570-71). It was more likely the later date.[209]

Govinda Dīkṣita

The famous minister of the Tañjāvūr Nāyaka rulers, Govinda Dīkṣita who was a great administrator and profound Sanskrit scholar, was also very well-known for his activities in the religious sphere. Although only one Sanskrit inscription of his is found in the temple at Tiruvaṇṇāmalai,[210] his gifts and benefactions are known through many Tamil epigraphs, literary sources and traditional accounts.

Govinda Dīkṣita, an orthodox Kannaḍa brāhmaṇa who performed the Agnihotra (daily fire-worship) is spoken of by

206. *ARE*, 475 of 1919; *SITI*, vol. III, Pt. II, pp. 1356-57.
207. *ARE*, 363 of 1919.
208. *ARE*, 354 of 1919.
209. *SITI*, vol. III, Pt. II, p. 1354.
210. *ARE*, 422 of 1928-29.

his scholarly son, Yajñanārāyaṇa Dīkṣita as the performer of various sacrifices such as the *Sāgnicitya, Vājapeya* and the *Sarvatomukha* sacrifices.[211] He is also believed to have made numerous gifts and benefactions on the completion of these sacrifices. He is credited with the repair and construction of the sixteen *maṇḍapas* on the banks of the Mahāmagam tank in the Kuṁbeśvara temple at Kuṁbakoṇam.[212]

Govinda Dīkṣita is believed to be responsible for the construction of many *Puṣyamaṇḍapas* at places like Tiruvaiyāru, Kuṁbakoṇam, Tiruviḍaimarudūr, Tiruvalañjūḷi and Vṛddhācalam. The Rāmasvāmi temples in Kuṁbakoṇam, Vijayarāghavapuram and Śrīraṅgam were constructed during his time.[213] He gave many gifts to the Paṭṭiśvaram temple and also made additions to it. The Ācāravāśal and the Anantakalyāṇa maṇḍapa of the Śārṅgasvāmi Maṭha at Kuṁbhakoṇam[214] and the Turaikkāṭṭuvār maṇḍapa at the Viḷanagar temple near Māyavaram[215] were built by Govinda Dīkṣita.

A bi-lingual epigraph engraved in the Vaikuṇṭhanārāyaṇa Perumāḷ temple at Ākkūr belonging to the period of Perumāḷ Kulaśekhara of the later Pāṇḍyan dynasty records that this temple was constructed for the welfare of the king by Uḍaiyapiḷḷai *alias* Vāṇadarāyar of Kappalūr who was this king's minister.[216]

Spiritual Preceptors

The kings of ancient and medieval India almost always appointed a learned and religious teacher as a royal preceptor

211. V. Vriddhagırisan, *op. cit.*, p. 120.
212. *ARE*, 1926-27, p. 117.
213. V. Vriddhagirisan, *op. cit.*
214. *ARE*, 270 of 1927.
215. *ARE*, 164 of 1925.
216. *ARE*, 230 of 1925.

to help them in various affairs of the state and also as a personal guru. The inscriptions of the Coḷa age speak of a number of such spiritual preceptors like Īśānaśiva Paṇḍita, Sarvaśiva Paṇḍita and Īśvaraśiva. Karuvūr Devar, the preceptor of Rājarāja Coḷa I is depicted in a beautiful fresco in the Bṛhadīśvara temple at Tañjāvūr.

The Vijayanagara rulers likewise also depended on their religious teachers on matters both spiritual and temporal. The members of the early Saṅgama dynasty were followers of the Kashmir school of Śaivism and Kriyāśakti Paṇḍita was their *guru*.[217]

In the poem *Madhurāvijayaṃ* the poetess Gaṅgā Devī, wife of Kumāra Kaṁpaṇa, after invoking the blessings of Gaṇeśa, Śiva, Pārvatī and Sarasvatī, has composed a verse revealing her reverence to Guru Kriyāśakti whom she describes as "unparalleled in wisdom and resplendent with auspiciousness like another Trilocana (Śiva) with Sarvamaṅgaḷā (Pārvatī) shining (by his side)."[218] The fact that this poetess-princess makes her obeisance to Kriyāśakti immediately after the invocatory verses addressed to the Gods, reveals the exalted position which he enjoyed in the realm.

Vidyāraṇya

The most famous of these spiritual preceptors of the Vijayanagara kings was Vidyāraṇya a renowned scholar and Advaita teacher who aided the five brothers, Harihara, Kampa, Bukka, Māra and Mudda, the sons of a chieftain named Saṅgama in founding the city of Vijayanagara or Vidyānagara. He was a great ascetic and head of the Śṛṅgerī Maṭha and was held in very high esteem by the rulers of the Vijayanagara

217. T.V. Mahalingam, *op. cit.*, p. 321.

218. *Madhurāvijayam, op. cit.*, v. 4, p. 73.

empire and advised them on spiritual and temporal affairs. He is believed to have been born in AD 1267, thus living for hundred and nineteen years.[219]

The association of the two brothers, Harihara and Bukka with Vidyāraṇya starts, according to tradition, when the two who were ministers in the Hindu kingdom of Kampili were taken captive by Muhammad Tughlaq and embraced Islam, and were again sent to Kampili to take over the administration and to quell the revolt of the Hindu subjects and came under the influence of this great sage.[220] The brothers decided to abandon Islam and take up the cause of Hindu *dharma* and accepted Vidyāraṇya as their preceptor.[221] The latter, with the approval of his own teacher, Vidyātīrtha, the head of the Advaita Maṭha at Śṛṅgerī, arranged for Harihara and Bukka to be reconverted to Hinduism.[222]

Harihara, who wanted to shift his capital from Anegondi which was on the northern bank of the Tuṅgabhadrā, as it was susceptible to enemy attacks, acted upon the advice of Vidyāraṇya and selected the opposite bank of the river, in the neighbourhood of the Virūpākṣa temple.[223] There, the two Saṅgama brothers laid the foundations of the new capital to which they gave the significant names Vijayanagara (city of victory) and Vidyānagara (city of learning), the second name commemorating the role of Vidyāraṇya in these momentous events.[224]

---

219. *USVAE*, vol. II, p. 20.
220. R.C. Majumdar, ed., *The History and Culture of the Indian People* (vol. VI — The Delhi Sultanate), Bombay, 1990, p, 271.
221. *Ibid.*
222. *Ibid.*
223. *Ibid.*, p. 273.
224. K.A. Nilakanta Sastri, *A History of South India*, Madras, 1988, p. 239.

An undated Sanskriṭ epigraph found in the Śrī Varadarājasvāmi temple at Kāñcīpuram mentions Vidyāraṇya and his brothers.[225] It speaks of Mādhava, (who was to be known as Vidyāraṇya after he became an ascetic) as the eldest, Sāyaṇa, his younger brother (who was to be known as Bhāratītīrtha after he became an ascetic) and Bhoganātha, the youngest brother. All three brothers, at one time or another were to be counsellors of emperors and kings; Mādhava and Sāyaṇa to the Vijayanagara emperors and Bhoganātha to king Saṅgama II.[226] This record mentions the name of Vidyāraṇya's mother as Śrīmāyī and his father as Māyaṇa. The reference found in this inscription of this family belonging to the Bhāradvāja-*gotra* is specially important as it helps in distinguishing Mādhava (who was later Vidyāraṇya, and who was sometimes called Mādhavamantri) from another Mādhava belonging to the Aṅgīrasa-*gotra* who was also an erudite scholar and who served the early Vijayanagara emperors as *mantri* in the capacity of provincial governor of the area of modern Goa.[227]

A lithic inscription of Virūpākṣa found in the Śrī Raṅganāthasvāmi temple, Śrīraṅgam mentions this king's disenchantment with wordly life and his visit to Vidyāraṇya.[228] The composer of this epigraph presents the turmoil in the mind of this noble king as follows: "At one time, seeing the grave troubles and torments undergone by beings passing everlastingly through the cycle of birth, death and rebirth, and moved by the deepest compassion for them, approached and prostrated himself before his own preceptor and the

225. *USVAE*, vol. I, p. 34.

226. *Ibid.*, p. 33.

227. *Ibid.*

228. *SII*, vol. XXIV, no. 294, p. 304.

refuge of the whole world, namely, Paramahaṁsa, Parivrājakācārya Vidyāraṇya Śrīpāda, who was the most distinguished of all ascetics, vision of whom was easy to the virtuous, whose mind was always engaged in meditation involving the self and the soul and who was like Śaṅkarācārya incarnate. He then realized that without serving at the holy feet of this enlightened soul, he could not hope to get rid of hauteur born of shortcomings attributable to the body, the mind and speech, that he could not hope to see the dispelling of darkness (spiritual ignorance) and that he could not hope to achieve that spiritual height that would yeild him the fruit of the four requisites of human existence (righteousness, wealth, fulfilment of desire and salvation)."[229]

It is known that Virūpākṣa crowned himself immediately after the death of Harihara II, but was displaced after a short period by Bukka II. The spirit of disenchantment and his realization that salvation lay only in the service of sage Vidyāraṇya, as revealed by this inscription may have made Virūpākṣa's exit from the throne not wholly involuntary.[230]

An inscription from outside Tamil Nadu, the Śṛṅgerī plates of Harihara II mentions a grant of land made by this king on the solemn occasion of the ceremonies attendant on sage Vidyāraṇya becoming one with Divinity.[231] This record too speaks with great reverence about the greatness of this ascetic.

In the reign of Kṛṣṇadeva Rāya, who, as has been stated earlier, was a staunch Vaiṣṇava, an eminent Śrī-Vaiṣṇava teacher named Veṅkaṭa Tātārya was greatly honoured by this king, was made the head of all the Śrī-Vaiṣṇavas in the empire, and Kṛṣṇadeva Rāya in AD 1523, ordered that he was to be

229. *USVAE*, vol. I, p. 124.

230. *Ibid.*, p. 121.

231. *USVAE*, vol. I, pp. 112-13.

shown the first honours in every public assembly and a charter was issued to that effect.[232]

During the later days of the Vijayanagara dynasty, rulers like Sadāśiva Rāya and Rāma Rāya were more inclined towards Vaiṣṇavism and Śrī Vaiṣṇava teachers were patronized. Rāma Rāya appointed the famous Śrī Vaiṣṇava preceptor, Tātācārya in place of Govinda Deśika, the royal preceptor of Kṛṣṇadeva Rāya.[233]

Tātācārya, who was the spiritual preceptor of Rāma Rāya lived with him for some time at Candragiri and later settled down at Kāñcī. He was the author of the famous work *Pañcamata-bhañjanam* and was therefore called Pañcamata-bhañjanam Tātācārya.[234] According to the Sanskrit work *Prapannāmṛtam* written by Anantācārya, a disciple of Tātācārya, the Tātācāryas were the descendents of Śrī Śailanātha or Tirumalai Nambi, uncle and teacher of Rāmānuja. Two early members of this family who were proficient in the exposition of the *Rāmāyaṇa,* migrated from Tirupati to Eṭṭūr and from there to Hampi, the capital of the Vijayanagara kings and were highly respected by these monarchs.[235] A descendent of this family was Pañcamata-bañjanam Tātācārya, who was a contemporary of Doḍḍācārya of Coḷaśiṁhapuram (Shoḷiṅgūr) who wrote the renowned work *Caṇḍamārutam* in refutation of Appaya Dīkṣita's *Advaita Dīpikā.* Tātācārya's son was the famous Śrīnivāsārya, better known by the names Lakṣmīkumāra Tātācārya and Koṭikanyādānam Tātācārya who was the *guru* of Veṅkaṭa II.[236]

232. T.V. Mahalingam, *op. cit.*, p. 324.
233. *MER*, 1906-07, para 53; T.V. Mahalingam, *op. cit.*, p. 326.
234. *EI*, vol. XII, no. 38, p. 347.
235. K.V. Raman, *op. cit.*, p. 82.
236. *EI*, vol. XII, no. 38, p. 347.

There are many inscriptions of Veṅkaṭa II in the Śrī Varadarājasvāmi temple, Kāñcīpuram and elsewhere, which mention the benefactions and other acts of Lakṣmīkumāra Tātācārya and they are dated between AD 1587 and 1614, till almost the end of Veṅkaṭa's reign[237] as has been mentioned earlier in this chapter. He was the manager of the Śrī Varadarājasvāmi temple.[238]

During the reign of Sadāśiva Rāya, the cousins of Rāmarāya named Viṭṭhaladeva and Cinna Timma, mentioned earlier in this chapter, appear to have revered Ahobala Dīkṣita of Kṛṣṇāpuram as their preceptor (*guru*). In an inscription from Śrīraṅgam which mentions the benefactions of Viṭṭhaladeva to the temple of Raṅganātha, Ahobala Dīkṣita is mentioned as having presented a golden *Sūryaprabhā* to this deity to be used during the festival processions.[239] This Ahobala Dīkṣita also figures in an inscription from Kāñcīpuram.[240]

A spiritual preceptor of Tirumala Nāyaka of Madurai is mentioned in one of his bi-lingual copper-plate inscriptions composed in Sanskrit and Telugu.[241] This record registers a gift of land in several villages to Mahādeva Dīkṣitulu of the Kauṇḍinya *gotra* and of the lineage of Śrīkaṇṭha-Ākāśavāsi, the *guru* of the king, together with certain privileges and honours in the four temples of Jaṁbukeśvaram, Mātṛbhūteśvaram, Rāmeśvaram and Cokkanāthapuram.

This record also states that the members of the Ākāśavāsi family were the *kulagurus* (family preceptors) of the earlier Madurai Nāyakas and a certain Śrīkaṇṭhākāśavāsi is said to

237. K.V. Raman, *op. cit.*, p. 83.

238. *ARE*, 421, 381 & 382 of 1919; K.V. Raman, *op. cit.*, p. 33.

239. *SII*, vol. XXIV, no. 455, p. 437.

240. *ARE*, 656 of 1919.

241. *ARE*, 1937-38, no. A25.

have been the recipent of five villages from his disciple, Viśvanātha Nāyaka.[242] Another inscription mentions that he died in AD 1665-66.[243]

The date given in this copper-plate grant is Śaka 1584 or AD 1662. Since Tirumala Nāyaka passed away in AD 1659 and since this record purports to have been issued in AD 1662 "while Tirumala Nāyaka was ruling," it is possible that it had been issued earlier during the lifetime of the Nāyaka ruler and was actually engraved and granted to the donee later on the date specified in the copper-plate.[244]

Although the rulers made many gifts to the learned brāhmaṇas of their land on a regular basis, certain special days were sometimes chosen for making these gifts. The Dharmaśāstras have decreed that grants made on the occasions such as eclipses, new moon and full-moon days and the first day of each *ayana* (the passage of the sun to the north or south) like *uttarāyana* and *dakṣiṇāyana* would be specially meritorious.

The Sanskrit inscriptions of the ancient period belonging to the Pallava, Pāṇḍya and Coḷa dynasties repeatedly mention the gifts made by these rulers on such special days. Similarly, many of the gifts of the Vijayanagara, Nāyaka and later Pāṇḍyan rulers discovered in the Tamil country also speak of many presents gifted on such occasions.

The Ālampūṇḍi plates of Virūpākṣa I state that on the Puṣya-Saṁkrānti day in AD 1383, this king granted to certain brāhmaṇas of various *gotras*, the village of Ālampūṇḍi.[245]

The Tamil section of the bi-lingual Śoraikkāvūr copper-plate grant of Virūpākṣa I states that on a new-moon day

242. *ARE*, 1937-38, Pt. II, p. 108.

243. *Ibid*.

244. *Ibid*.

245. *EI*, vol. III, no. 32, v. 8, p. 227.

(*amāvasyā*), in the month of Phāngunī in AD 1386, this king gave to a number of *bhaṭṭas* (brāhmaṇas), gifts of land in order to propitiate (the bad influence) of Rāhu.[246]

Similarly, the Satyamaṅgalam plates of Deva Rāya II also mention a grant of land on a new-moon day.[247] The Kṛṣṇāpuram plates of Sadāśiva Rāya dated AD 1567 state that this ruler gave a number of villages to the God Tiruveṅkaṭanātha at Kṛṣṇāpuram on the new-moon *tithi* in the month of Pauṣa during the *makara-saṁkramaṇa*.[248]

A later Pāṇḍyan inscription, the Śrīvilliputtūr plates of Abhirāma Pāṇḍya dated AD 1552 records that this ruler made a grant of land to brāhmaṇas during the *uttarāyaṇa* in the Hemanta-*ṛtu* on a new-moon *tithi* when the moon was in the constellation of Śrāvaṇa on the auspicious occasion of a solar eclipse.[249]

Similarly, some donations were also made on the occasion of lunar eclipses. An inscription found in the *candana-maṇḍapa* of the Śrī Raṅganāthasvāmi temple, Śrīraṅgam, dated AD 1384, records the gift of a perpetual lamp to Lord Śrī Raṅganātha by Devarasar on the occasion of a lunar-eclipse in that year.[250]

A long inscription dated AD 1567 in the Pagalpattu-*maṇḍapam* in the same temple mentions the gifts of lamps and gold to various deities in this temple by Kumāra Acyuta (Acyutappa Nāyaka) on a full-moon day (*pūrṇimā*) during which there was an eclipse of the moon.[251]

---

246. *EI*, vol. VIII, no. 31, p. 302.
247. *EI*, vol. III, no. 5, v. 24, p. 38.
248. *EI*, vol. IX, no. 52, vv. 44-45, p. 335.
249. *T.A.S.* vol. I, no. IX, v. 16, pp. 109-10.
250. *SII*, vol. XXIV, no. 298, p. 311.
251. *SII*, vol. XXIV, no. 488, pp. 466-67.

Similarly, many donations and other auspicious events were performed on full-moon days. An inscription in this temple states that Cakrarāya installed the *daśāvatāra* images in a temple on the southern bank of the Kāverī at Śrīraṅgam on a *paurṇamī* day in AD 1439.[252]

The Śrīraṅgam copper-plate inscription of Deva Rāya II dated AD 1434, records that on the full-moon day of the month of Vaiśākha, this ruler made the celebrated *mahādāna* gift called *Hemāśvaratha* to a brāhmaṇa named Uttamanambi, the *sthānapati* of the Śrīraṅgam temple.[253]

The Śrīraṅgam copper-plate epigraphs of Mallikārjana dated AD 1462, speaks of the gift of a village for offerings and other kinds of worship to Lord Śrī Raṅganātha of Śrīraṅgam on the full-moon day (*paurṇamī tithi*) of the month of Vaiśākha on the auspicious occasion of *vyatipāta* to ensure for himself victory (over his enemies), protection from their violence and for longevity.[254]

The village of Udayambākkam was presented to the pontiff of the Śaṅkarācārya Maṭha at Kāñcīpuram named Sadāśiva Sarasvatī in AD 1527, by Kṛṣṇadeva Rāya on *pūrṇimā tithi* in the month of Vaiśākha.[255]

Mahādānās

The kings of south India in the ancient and medieval periods periodically presented gifts (*dāna*) to temples and to scholars of their land. The gift of certain items was known as *mahādāna*. The sixteen *mahādāna*s traditionally known are the *tulāpuruṣa*, *hiraṇyagarbha*, *brahmāṇḍa*, *kalpavṛkṣa*, *gosahasra*, *kāmadhenu*,

---

252. *SII*, vol. XXIV, no. 333, p. 336.
253. *EI*, vol. XVIII, no. 17, vv. 32-35, pp. 141-42.
254. *EI*, vol. XVI, no. 28, vv. 16-37, pp. 349-50.
255. *EI*, vol. XIV, no. 12, vv. 29-43, pp. 173-74.

hiraṇyāśva, hiraṇyāśvaratha, hemnastiratha, pañcalaṅga, dharādāna, viśvacakra, kalpalatā, saptasāgara, ratnadhenu and *mahābhūtagata.*

Numerous Sanskrit inscriptions of the Vijayanagara period refer to the *mahādāna*s given by the kings, especially Harihara II who is repeatedly spoken of in the inscriptions of his successors as the "performer of *mahādāna*s." The Ālampūṇḍi plates of Virūpākṣa speak of Harihara II as one "who being devoted to (the performance of) the sixteen great gifts (*ṣoḍaśa-mahādāna-dīkṣitaḥ*) has destroyed the sins of the Kali age."[256] This is also mentioned in the Śoraikkāvūr plates of Virūpākṣa.[257] The same record states that Virūpākṣa was the donor of a thousand cows (*gosahasra*).[258]

The Satyamaṅgalam record of Deva Rāya II states poetically of Harihara II that "by erecting spacious halls (for the performance) of the sixteen great gifts (*ṣoḍaśa-mahāmaṇḍapa*), he made the whole world (*bhuvana*), the dwelling (*bhavana*) of his wife-the Goddess of Fame."[259]

Again, a copper-plate record of the period of Deva Rāya II from Śrīraṅgam (AD 1428), while speaking of Harihara II, states that "the renown of his making the sixteen great gifts (*mahādāna*) redounded even beyond the fourteen worlds."[260] The Kannaḍa portion of this record states that Deva Rāya II granted to Śrī Raṅganātha a village along with some sub-villages and that this grant was made as an auxiliary to the *gosahasra mahādāna* performed by the king on the auspicious occasion of *Uttānadvādaśī.*[261]

---

256. *EI*, vol. III, no. 32, v. 4, p. 227.
257. *EI*, vol. VIII, no. 31, v. 4, p. 301.
258. *Ibid.*
259. *EI*, vol. III, no. 5, v. 8, p. 37.
260. *EI*, vol. XVI, no. 8, v. 9, p. 113.
261. *EI*, vol. XVI, no. 8, p. 115.

Deva Rāya II is described in his Śrīraṅgam copper-plate inscription (AD 1434) as having made the celebrated *mahādāna* gift called *Hemāśvaratha* to Vaḻiyaḍimai-nilayiṭṭa-Perumāḷ Uttamanambi, the *sthānapati* of the Śrīraṅgam temple.[262]

Vīra-Nṛsiṁha, the elder brother of Kṛṣṇadeva Rāya, according to his Kuḍiyantaṇḍal copper-plate grant, presented many gifts at holy places like Cidambaram, Kāḷahasti, Tirupati, Śrīraṅgam, Kuṁbhakoṇam, Kāñcī, Ahobalam, Gokarṇa and Rāmeśvaram.[263] The same facts are repeated in Kṛṣṇadeva Rāya's inscriptions like his Kāñcīpuram and Udayambākkam plates.[264]

A copper-plate record of this ruler from Śrīraṅgam states that he granted a village to a brāhmaṇa named Allāla Bhaṭṭa who officiated as a priest during the *gosahasra mahādāna* of this king.[265]

The Kaḍalāḍi plates of Acyuta Rāya mention that this ruler also presented many gifts at several holy places.[266] In a lithic inscription found in Śrīraṅgam, composed by Acyuta Rāya's queen Oḍuva Tirumalaidevī Ammanavargal, this king bestowed the gift of *Ānandanidhi* on brāhmaṇas.[267] According to Hemādri, who describes this gift in some detail in the Dānakhāṇḍa of his *Caturvarga-Cintāmaṇi*, the *Ānandhanidhi-dāna* consists of presenting to learned brāhmaṇas, after some ceremonial preliminaries, pots made of *uḍumbara* wood (*auḍumbarām ghaṭam*), filled with precious stones and coins of

262. *EI*, vol. XVIII, no. 17, vv. 32-34, p. 143.

263. *EI*, vol. XIV, no. 17, vv. 15-16, p. 238.

264. *EI*, vol. XIII, no. 8, vv. 15-16, pp. 127-28; *EI*, vol. XIV, no. 12, vv. 14-17, pp. 171-72.

265. *EI*, vol. XVIII, no. 21A, v. 34, p. 163.

266. *EI*, vol. XIV, no. 22, v. 33, p. 323.

267. *EI*, vol. XXIV, no. 41, pp. 289-90.

gold, silver or copper and the merit accruing from this ceremony was believed to be longevity, perfect health and imperial sovereignty.[268]

The Veḷḷāṅguḍi plates of Veṅkaṭa II state poetically that Śrīraṅga, the son of Tirumala Rāya presented so many gifts during the time of his coronation that "poverty was completely wiped out for good men."[269]

The Veḷḷāṅguḍi copper-plates also add that Vīrappa Nāyaka performed the gifts called *hemāśva, hemagarbha, tulāpuruṣa, viśvacakra, brahmāṇḍa, gosahasra, saptāmbodhi, mahābhūtaghaṭa, svarṇakṣma* and *ratnadhenu.*[270]

Tulāpuruṣa

One of the sixteen *mahādānas* was *tulāpuruṣa* in which a person was weighed against an equal amount of gold, precious gems or other items which were then given away to temples or to learned brāhmaṇas. The Sanskrit inscriptions of the Pāṇḍyas and the Coḷas point to numerous occasions when this *mahādāna* was performed by the kings of these dynasties.[271]

The Sanskrit epigraphs of the Vijayanagara rulers also repeatedly refer to the *tulābhāra mahādāna* performed by these kings. The Śoraikkāvūr copper-plate inscription of Virūpākṣa states that this ruler weighed himself against gold in the presence of Lord Rāmanātha (of Rāmeśvaram).[272]

---

268. *Ibid.*, p. 288.
269. *EI,* vol. XVI, no. 23, vv. 28-30.
270. *Ibid.*, v. 77, p. 315.
271. Chithra Madhavan, *History and Culture of Tamil Nadu – vol. I* (up to c. AD 1310), New Delhi, pp. 257-59.
272. *EI,* vol. VIII, no. 31, v. 6, p. 301.

According to the Kāñcīpuram[273] and Udayambākkam[274] copper-plate inscriptions of Kṛṣṇadeva Rāya, this ruler made many gifts after performing rites like the *kanaka-tulāpuruṣa* at places like Kanaka-sadas (Cidambaram), Kāḷahasti, Veṅkaṭādri (Tirupati), Kāñcī, Śrīśaila, Sonachala (Aruṇagiri), Ahobala, Saṅgama, Śrīraṅga, Kuṁbakoṇam, Mahānanditīrtha, Gokarṇa, Rāmeśvaram and other holy places.

Acyuta Rāya performed the *tulābhāra* ceremony at many places as can be seen from his Sanskrit epigraphs. An inscription found on the east wall of the second *prākāra* of the Śrīraṅgam temple, composed in Tamil and Sanskrit and dated AD 1539, records that on the occasion of Acyuta Rāya performing the *tulābhāra* ceremony, his *rājamahiṣī* (queen), Oḍuva Tirumalādevī Ammanavargaḷ composed two Sanskrit *śloka*s. While the performance of the *tulābhāra* is mentioned in the Tamil section, the *Ānandanidhi* gift presented by Acyuta Rāya is recorded in the Sanskrit verses.[275]

This ruler also performed the *tulābhāra* ceremony at Kāñcīpuram. A Sanskrit inscription found in the Śrī Varadarājasvāmi temple in Kāñcīpuram dated AD 1533, records that this king performed the *muktā-tulābhāra* (weighing oneself against pearls) of himself and his queen Varadāmbikā at Kāñcī and that his son Cinna-Veṅkaṭādri gave munificent gifts to brāhmaṇas on this occasion. The same verses are re-engraved in Tamil, Telugu and Kannaḍa.[276] The Sanskrit historical poem *Acyutarāyābhyudayam* also refers to this event.[277]

---

273. *EI*, vol. XIII, no. 8, v. 23, pp. 128-29.
274. *EI*, vol. XIV, no. 12, v. 23, pp. 172-73.
275. *EI*, vol. XXIV, no. 41, pp. 289-90.
276. *ARE*, 546, 543 & 511 of 1919.
277. K.V. Raman, *op. cit.*, p. 29.

In the Śrī Varadarājasvāmi temple are two small four-pillared *maṇḍapa*s called *tulāpuruṣa maṇḍapas*, probably because they were built on the occasion of the *tulābhāra* ceremony of Acyuta Rāya.[278] There is a specific reference to the *tulābhāra maṇḍapa* in his inscription dated AD 1533.[279]

The Daḷavāy-agrahāram plates of Veṅkaṭa II record that his father Tirumala Rāya made large gifts of *tulāpuruṣa* in gold and other gifts to the temples at Kāñcī, Śrīraṅgam, Śeṣācala (Tirupati), Kanakasabhā (Cidambaram), Ahobala and other places.[280]

The Veḷḷāṅguḍi plates also of the reign of Veṅkaṭa II praise Tirumala Rāya and state that he frequently performed all the *dāna*s mentioned in the Āgamās such as the *kanaka-tulāpuruṣa* and the *upadāna*s in the temples at Kāñcī, Śrīraṅgam and others and at the sacred *tīrtha*s.[281]

From the data supplied by the inscriptions it is seen that the *tulāpuruṣa* ceremony was perfomed not only by kings but also by brāhmaṇas. A Sanskrit inscription found in the Śrī Varadarājasvāmi temple mentioned earlier in this chapter, records that Tātācārya, the spiritual preceptor of Veṅkaṭa II performed eleven *tulābhāra*s with his eleven wives and distributed the gold to scholars.[282] He also weighed himself separately against gold and silver and utilized these in constructing the Kalyāṇakoṭi vimāna over the shrine of the Goddess in this temple.

---

278. *Ibid.*, p. 50.
279. *SITI*, vol. I, no. 406, p. 365.
280. *EI*, vol. XII, no. 21, v. 22, p. 173.
281. *EI*, vol. XVI, no. 23, v. 27.
282. *ARE*, 363 of 1919.

The fact that even minor rulers like the Setupati kings of the Rāmanāthapuram area in south Tamil Nadu also performed some of these *mahādāna*s even up to the eighteenth century AD, is seen from a few of their copper-plate charters. The emergence of the Setupati rulers to power can be traced to the reign of the Madurai Nāyaka king, Muthu Kṛṣṇappa Nāyaka (AD 1601-09), who had to deal with problems on several fronts such as the suppression of turbulent chieftains, the collection of revenue from the coastal regions of Rāmeśvaram where the Portuguese had settled and to ensure the safety of pilgrims to Rāmeśvaram.

Many of the Setupati kings were great devotees of Rāmanāthasvāmi at Rāmeśvaram and contributed to the architectural expansion of this temple. They were also noted for their charity and patronage of literary men. The *mahādāna*s like *hiraṇyagarbha* and *tulāpuruṣa* seem to have been perfomed by them often. A copper-plate inscription of the time of Tirumalai Raghunātha Setupati Kāṭṭadevar, mentions that he bore the title *hiraṇyagarbhayāji* (performer of the *hiraṇyagarbha* sacrifice).[283]

Another king who held this title was Muddu Vijayaraghunātha Setupati Kāṭṭadevar, who was ruling in AD 1713-14.[284] Yet another scion of this dynasty was Muddu Rāmaliṅga Vijayaraghunātha Setupati Kāṭṭadevar, whose copper-plate record dated AD 1770-71 eulogizes him as *hiraṇyagarbhayāji* and states that he perfomed the sixteen great gifts, commencing with the *tulāpuruṣa*.[285]

---

283. *ARE*, 10 of 1911.
284. *ARE*, 9 of 1911.
285. *ARE*, 7 of 1911.

Ālampūṇḍi copper-plate inscription of Virūpākṣa (1383 AD)

(Grantha script)

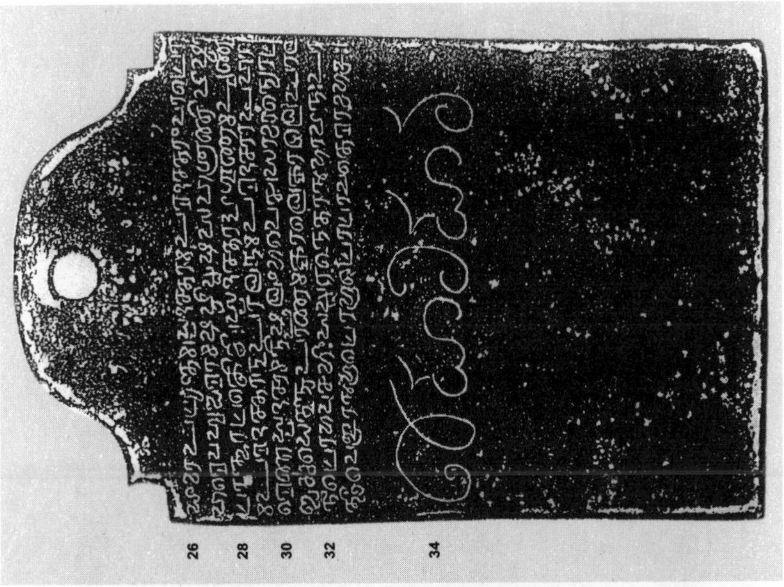

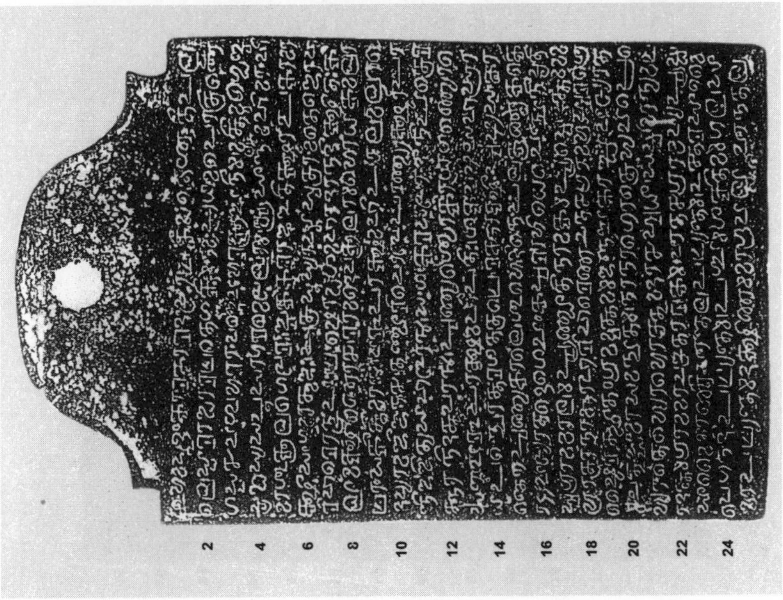

(Source: *E.I.*, Vol. III; Courtesy: Archaeological Survey of India)

Madras Museum Plates of Śrīgiribhūpāla (1424 AD)

(Grantha script)

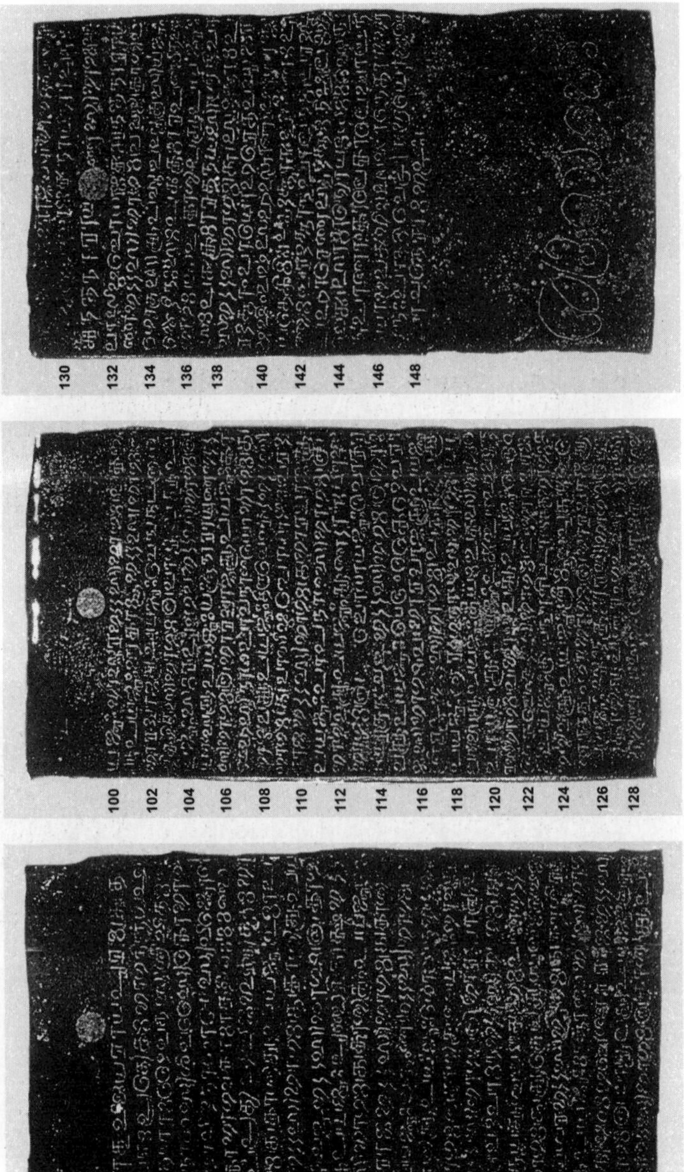

(Source: *E.I.*, Vol. VIII; Courtesy: Archaeological Survey of India)

Kāñcīpuram copper-plate inscription of Kṛṣṇadeva Rāya (1521 AD)

(Nandināgari script)

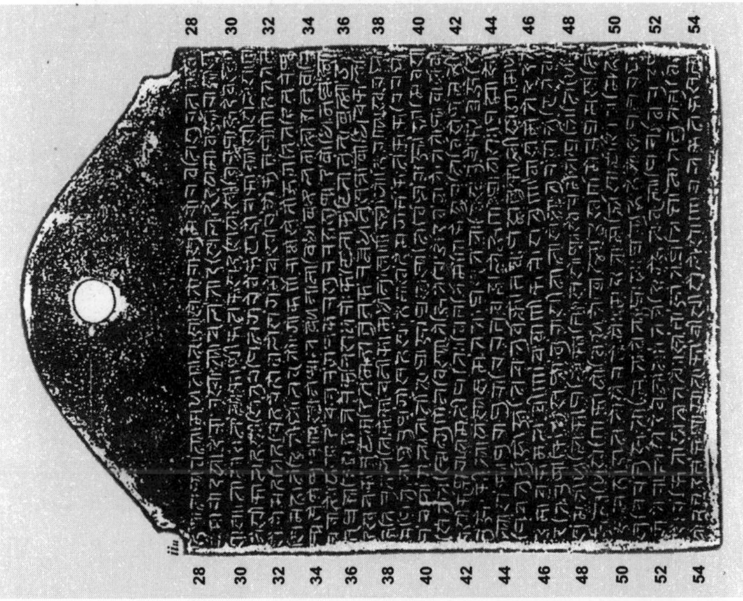

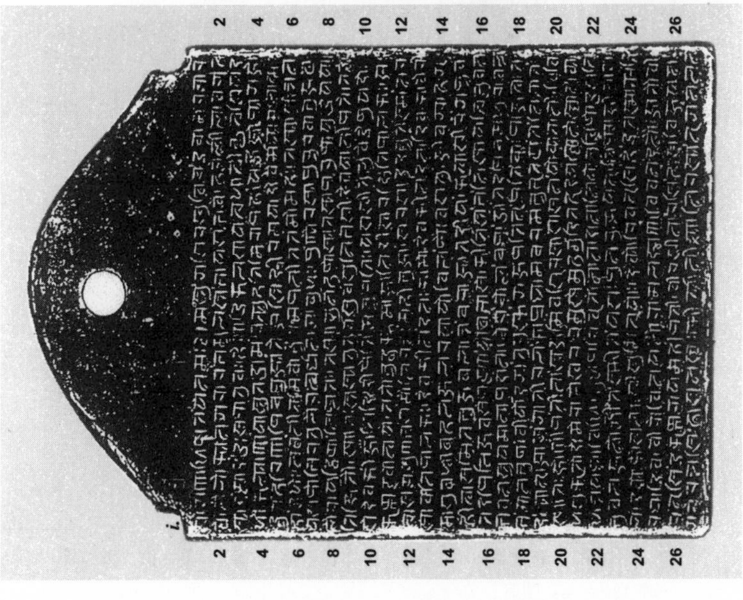

(Source *E.I.*, XIII; Courtesy: Archaeological Survey of India)

Ūṇamāñjeri copper-plate inscription of Acyuta Rāya (1540 AD)

(Nandināgari script)

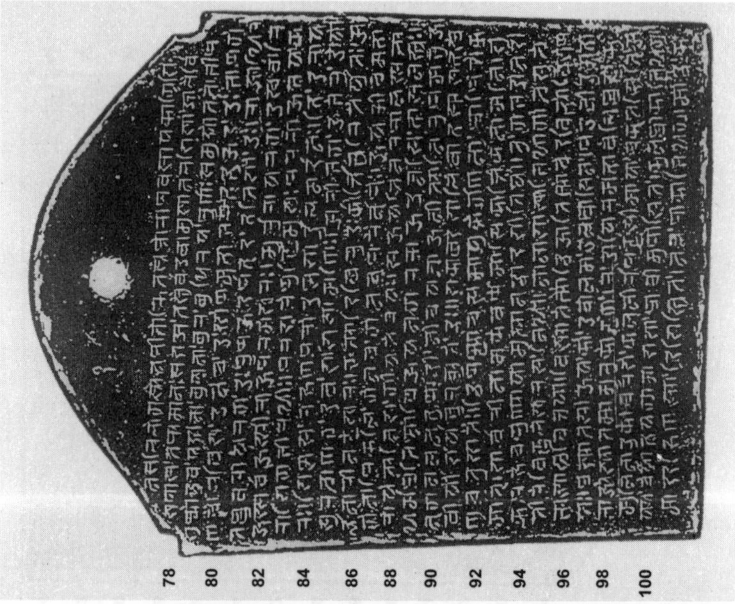

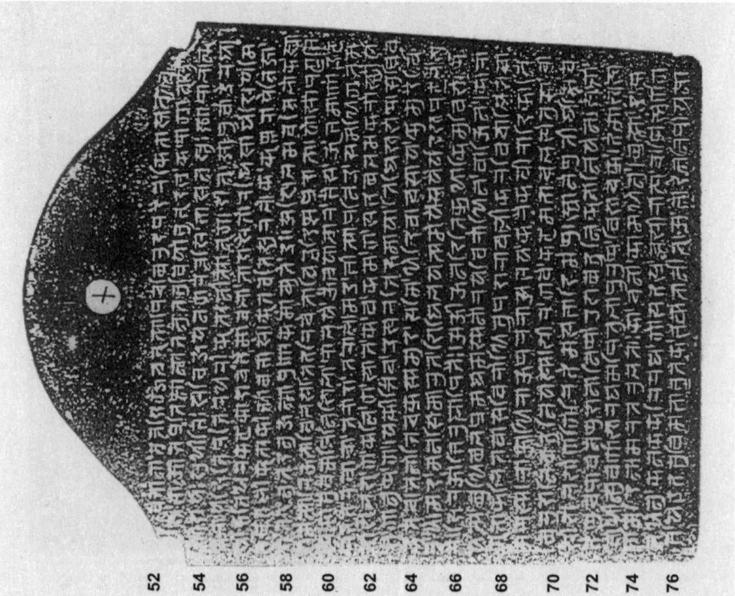

(Source: *E.I.*, Vol. III; Courtesy: Archaeological Survey of India)

Pudukkoṭṭai copper-plate inscription of Śrīvallabha and Varatuṅgarāma Pāṇḍya (1583 AD)

(Grantha Script)

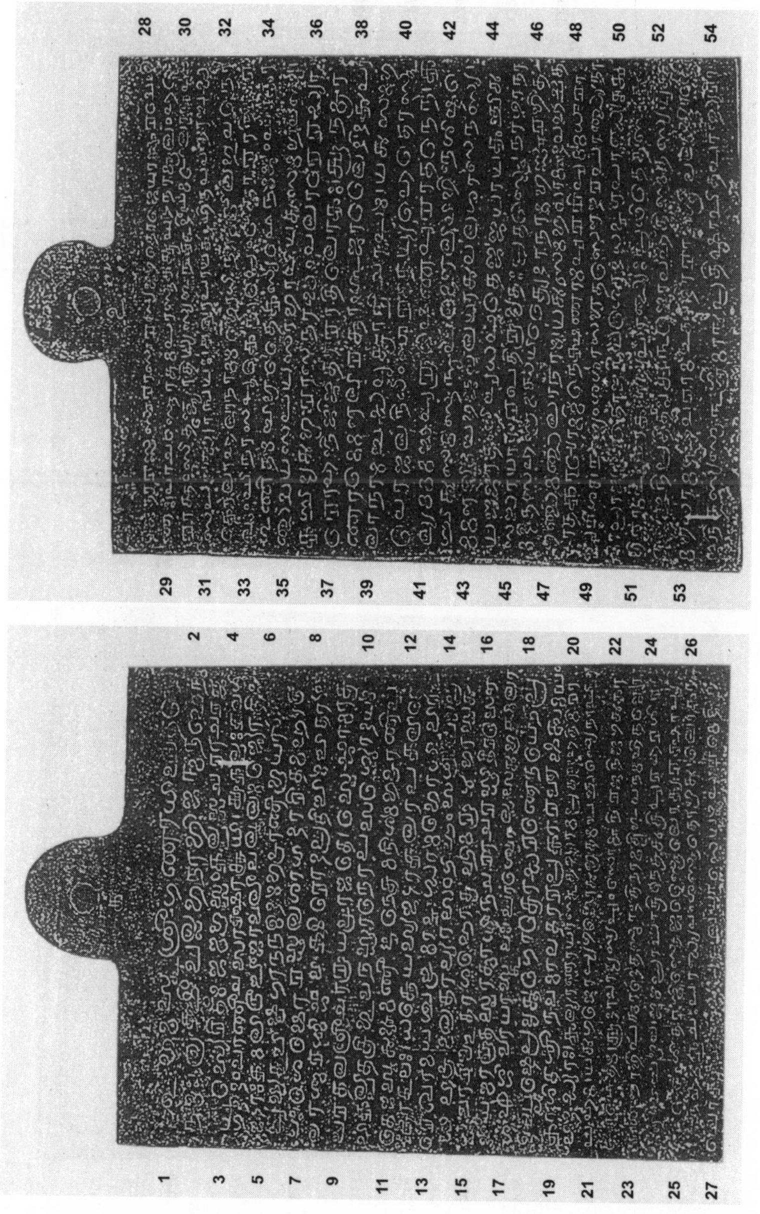

(Source: *T.A.S.*, Vol. I; Courtesy: Travancore Archaeological Series)

Daḷavāy-Agrahāram Plates of Veṅkaṭapatideva (1586 AD)

(Nandināgari script)

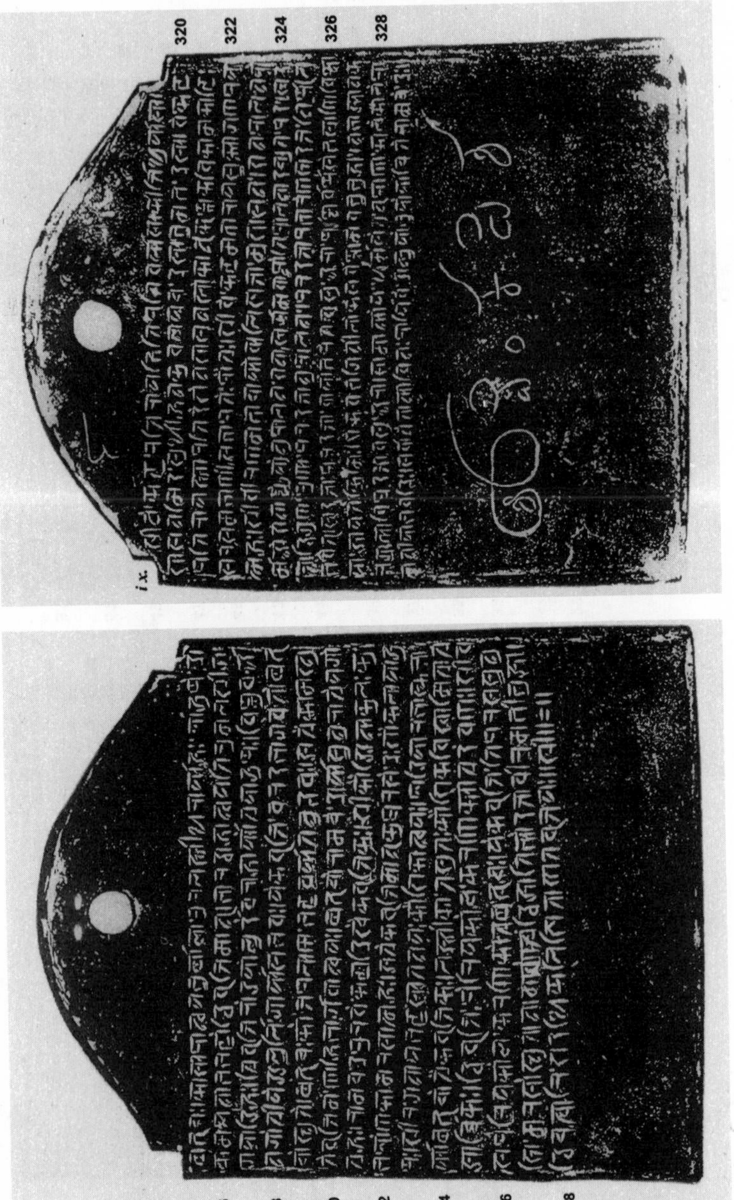

(Source: *E.I.*, Vol. XII; Courtesy: Archaeological Survey of India)

Daḷavāy-Agrahāram Plates of Varatuṅgarāma Pāṇḍya (1588 AD)

(Grantha script)

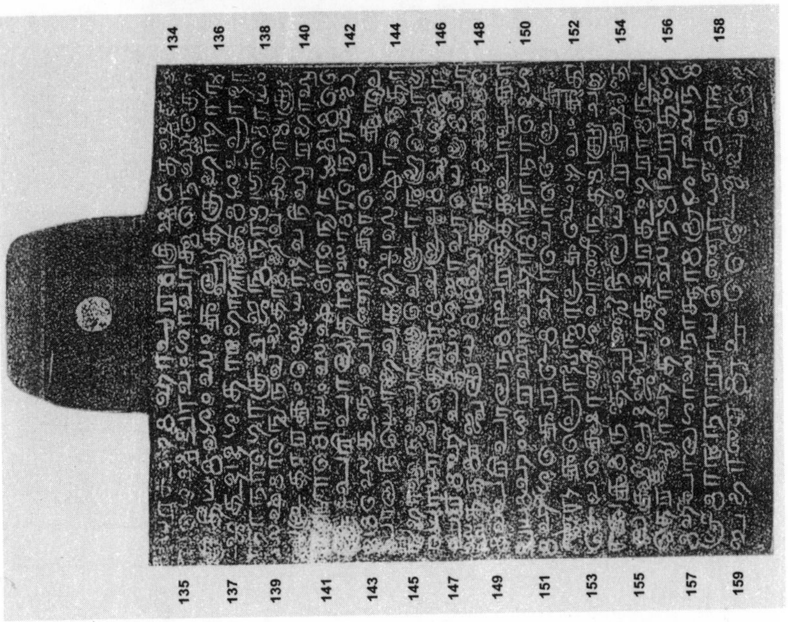

(Source: *T.A.S.*, Vol. I; Courtesy: Travancore Archaeological Series)

Daḷavāy-Agrahāram Plates of Varatuṅgarāma Pāṇḍya (1588 AD)

(Grantha script)

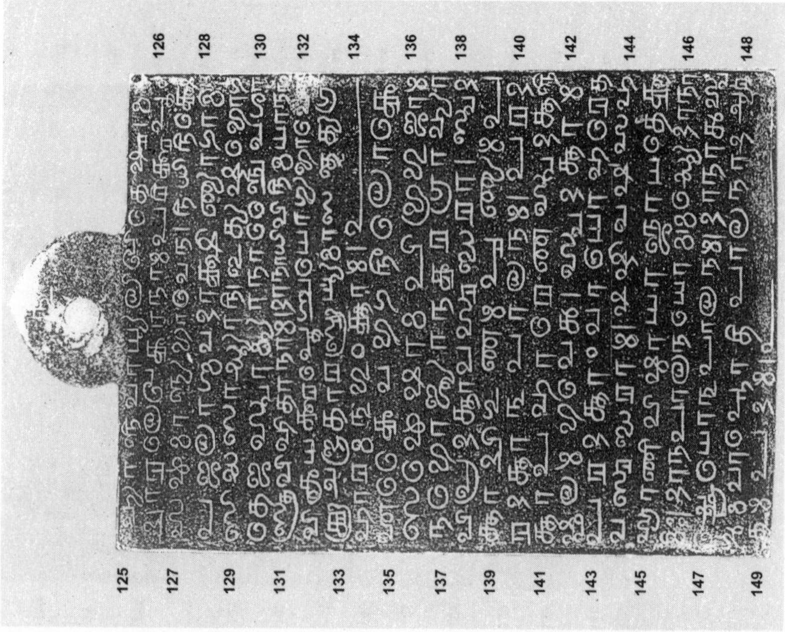

(Source: *T.A.S.*, Vol. I: Courtesy: Travancore Archaeological Series)

Daḷavāy-Agrahāram Plates of Ativīrarāma Pāṇḍya (1595 AD)

(Grantha script)

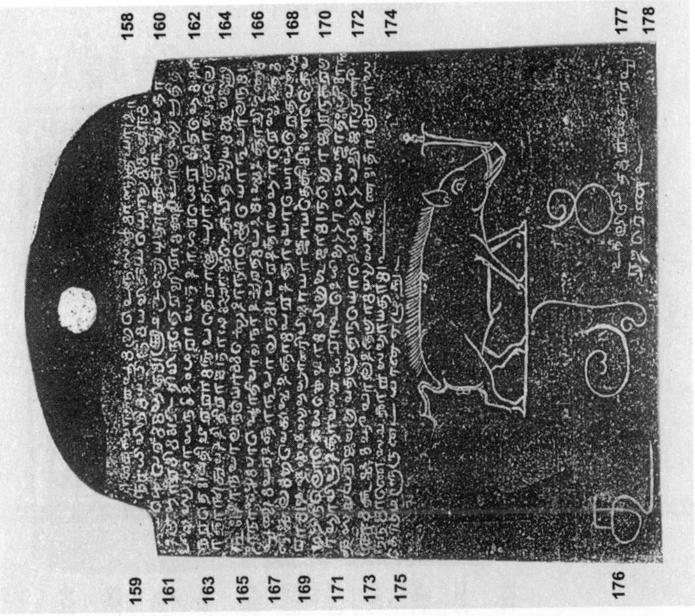

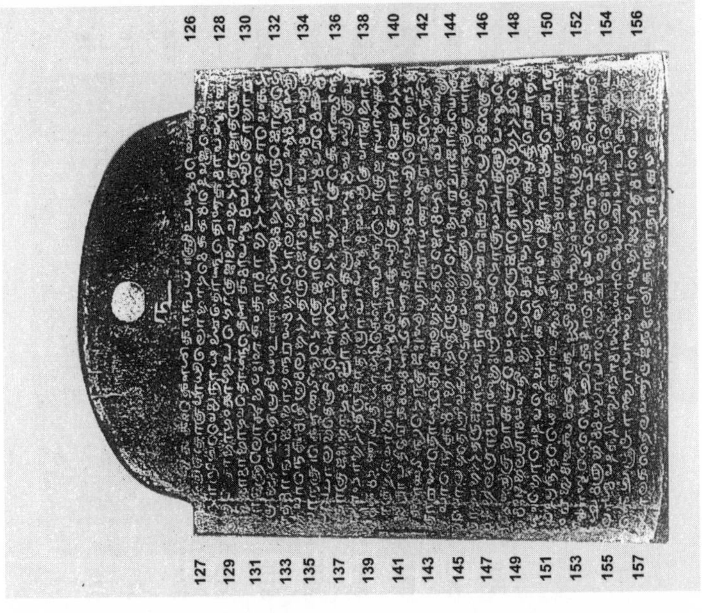

(Source: *T.A.S.*, Vol. I; Courtesy: Travancore Archaeological Series)

Veḷḷānguḍi copper-plate inscription of Veṅkaṭapatideva (1598 AD)

(Nandināgari script)

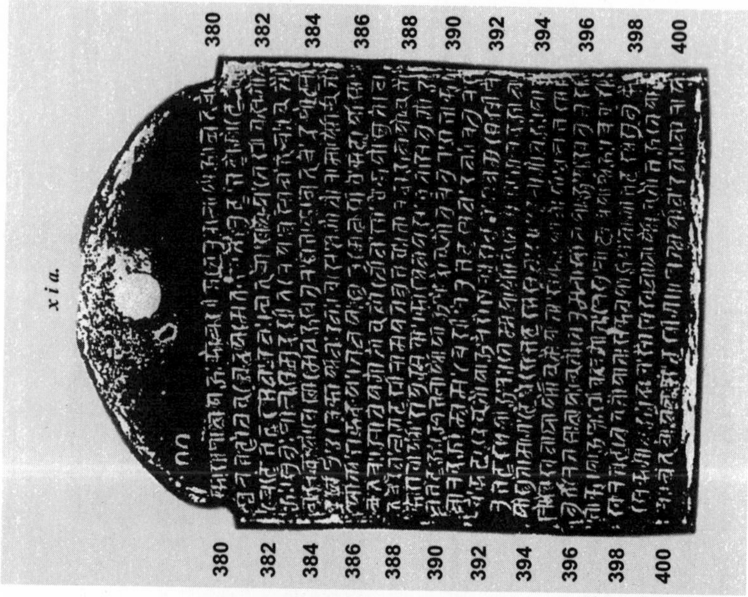

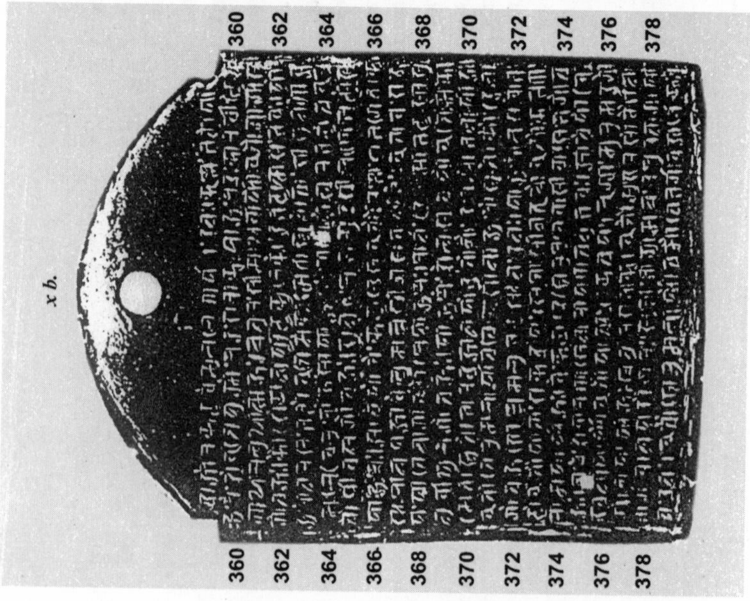

(Source: *E.I.*, Vol. XVI; Courtesy: Archaeological Survey of India)

Tiruvārūr copper-plate inscription of Marāṭhā King Sāmbhojī (1686 AD)
(Grantha script)

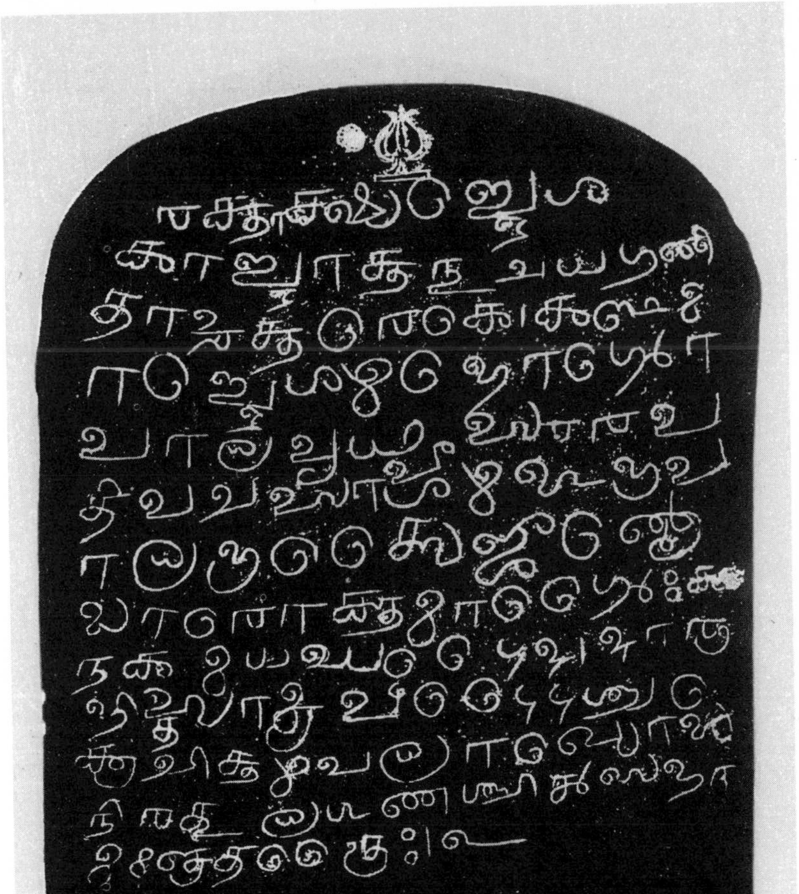

Courtesy: Se. Rasu, *Tanjai Marattiyar Cheppedukkal-50*, Tanjavur, 1983.

Tiruvārūr copper-plate inscription of Marāṭhā king Sāmbhojī (1686 AD)
(Grantha script)

Courtesy: Se, Rasu, *Tanjai Marattiyar Cheppedukkal-50*, Tanjavur, 1983.

Bibliography

Primary Sources

Annual Reports on Epigraphy

Epigraphia Carnatica

Epigraphia Indica

Indian Antiquary

South Indian Inscriptions

South Indian Temple Inscriptions

Travancore Archaelogical Society

Uttankita Sanskrit Vidya-Aranya Epigraphs (vol. I)

Literary Sources

Krishnaswamy Ayyangar, ed., *Kōiḷ-Oḷugu*, Tiruchi.

Tiruvenkatachariar, S., tr., *Madhurāvijayam of Gaṅgā Devī*, Annamalainagar, 1957.

Mishra, Satyadeva (ed.), *Amarakośa*, Varanasi, 1972.

Books

Bühler, G., tr., *The Laws of Manu*, Delhi, 1993.

Filliozat, Vasundhara, ed., *Vijayanagara*, New Delhi, 1997.

Gurumurthy, S., *Education in South India* (Ancient and Medieval Periods), Madras, 1979.

Gopinatha Rao, T.A., *Copper-Plate Inscriptions belonging to the Śrī Śaṅkarācārya of the Kāmakoṭi Pīṭha*, Madras, 1916.

Kangle, K.P., *The Kauṭilīyam Arthaśāstram*, Delhi, 1992.

Karashima, Noburu, *Towards a New Formation — South Indian Society Under Vijayanagara Rule*, Delhi, 1992.

Krishnaswami Ayyangar, S., *Sources of Vijayanagara History*, Annamalainagar, 1919.

Krishnaswami, A., *The Tamil Country Under Vijayanagara*, Annamalainagar, Madras, 1940.

Mahalingam, T.V., *Administration and Social Life Under Vijayanagara*, Madras, 1940.

———, *Economic Life in the Vijayanagara Empire*, Madras, 1951.

Majumdar, ed., *The History and Culture of The Indian People* (vol. VI — The Delhi Sultanate), Bombay, 1990.

Minakshi, C., *The Historical Sculptures of The Vaikuṇṭhaperumāḷ Temple*, Kāñcī, New Delhi, 1940.

Nagaraju, H.M., *Devarāya II and His Times*, Mysore, 1991.

Nagaswamy, R., *Tamil Coins — A Study*, Madras, 1981.

———, *Studies in Ancient Tamil Law and Society*, Madras, 1978.

———, ed., *South Indian Studies*, Madras, 1979.

Natarajan, B., *Tillai and Nataraja*, Madras, 1994.

Nilakanta Sastri, K.A., *A History of South India*, Madras, 1988.

———, *The Pāṇḍyan Kingdom* (From The Earliest Times to the Sixteenth Century), Madras, 1972.

———, *The Coḷas*, Madras, 1984.

Nilakanta Sastri, K.A. and N. Venkataramanayya, *Further Sources of Vijayanagara History*, Madras, 1946.

Pillai, K.K., *The Sucīndram Temple*, Madras, 2002.

Ramachandra Dikshitar, V.R., *War in Ancient India*, Delhi, 1987.

Raman, K.V., *Śrī Varadarājasvāmi Temple*, Kāñcī, Delhi, 1975.

———, *Sculpture Art of Tirumala Tirupati Temple*, Tirupati, 1993.

Ramesan, N., *The Tirumala Temple*, Tirupati, 1999.

Ramesh, M.S., *108 Vaiṣṇava Divya Desams* (vol. IV), Tirupati, 1996.

Rasu, Se., *Tanjai Maratiya Ceppedukal-50*, Thanajavur, 1983.

Saletore, B.A., *Social and Political Life in Vijayanagara Empire* (AD 1346-AD 1646), vols. I & II, Madras, 1934.

Sarma, Sree Rama, *Saluva Dynasty of Vijayanagara*, Hyderabad, 1979.

Sarojini Devi, Konduri, *Religion in Vijayanagara Empire*, New Delhi, 1990.

Sastry, Sadhu Subrahmanya, *Tirupati Sri Venkateswara*, Tirupati, 1998.

Sathyanatha Aiyar, R., *History of the Nāyakas of Madura*, New Delhi, 1991.

Seetha, S., *Tanjore as a Seat of Music*, Madras, 1981.

Sewell, Robert, *A Forgotten Empire* (*Vijayanagara*), Madras, 1988.

Sharma, Ram Sharan, *Aspects of Ideas and Institutions in Anceint India*, Delhi, 1968.

Singh, Sarva Daman, *Ancient Indian Warfare*, Delhi 1977.

Sreedhara Menon, A., *A Survey of Kerala History*, Madras, 1998.

Srinivasan, C.K., *Marāṭha Rule in the Carnatic*, Annamalainagar, 1944.

Srinivasan, T.M., *Irrigation and Water Supply* (*South India, 200* BC-*1600* AD), Madras, 1991.

Subrahmanian, K.R., *The Marāṭha Rājās of Tanjore*, Madras, 1928.

Vriddhagirisan, V., *The Nāyaks of Tanjore*, New Delhi, 1995.

Articles

Chhabra, B.Bh, N. Lakshminarayan Rao, M. Ashraf Hussain, "Ten Years of Indian Epigraphy (1937-46)" from *Ancient India*, Bulletin of the Archaeological Survey of India, No. 5, Jan. 1949, p. 57.

Dikshit, G.S., "Irrigation Tanks During Vijayanagara Times" from *Medieval Deccan History* (Commemoration Volume in honour of Purshottam Mahadeo Joshi), Bombay, 1996.

E. Hultzsch, "The Coins of the Kings of Vijayanagara," *IA*, vol. XX, p. 308.

Krishnan, K.G., "Sanskrit in Inscriptions of Tamil Nadu" from *Svasti Śrī*, B. Ch. Chhabra Felicitation Volume, New Delhi, 1984, pp. 21-23.

———, "Characteristic Features of Tamil Inscriptions" from *South Indian Studies*, Dr. T.V. Mahalingam Commemoration Volume, Mysore, 1990, pp. 206-15.

Mahalingam, T.V., "Epigraphical Wealth of Tamil Nadu" from *Forth Annual Congress of the Epigraphical Society of India*, Madras, 1978, pp. 16-22.

Nagaswamy, R., "Āḍavallān and Dakshiṇameruviṭaṅkar of the Tanjore Temple," *Lalit Kalā*, no. 12., October 1962, Lalit Kala Akademi, New Delhi, p. 36.

———, "Tanjore Nāyaka Bronzes," *South Indian Studies* II, ed., R. Nagaswamy, Madras, 1979, pp. 164-67.

Sethuraman, N., The Later Pandyas (1371-1759 AD), Paper presented at the Nineteenth Annual Congress of the Epigraphical Society of India, Tiruchirapalli, 1993.

Srikantha Sastri, S., "Development of Sanskrit Literature Under Vijayanagara" from *Vijayanagara Sexcentenary Commemoration Volume*, Dharwar, 1996 pp. 295-328.

Subrahmanian, V.S., "Characteristic Features of Sanskrit Inscriptions" from *South Indian Studies* (Dr. T.V. Mahalingam Commemoration Volume), Mysore, 1990, pp. 191-205.

Felicitation/Commemoration Volumes

Ācārya Vandana (D.R. Bhandarkar Birth Centenary Volume), Calcutta, 1982

Indian History and Epigraphy (Dr. G.S. Gai Felicitation Volume), Delhi, 1990.

Raṅgavalli, Recent Researches in Indology (S.R. Rao Felicitation Volume), Delhi, 1983.

Śāṁkaram (Professor Srinivasa Sankaranarayanan Festschrift), New Delhi, 2000.

Shri Malampalli Somasekhara Sarma Commemoration Volume, Hyderabad, 1976.

South Indian Studies (Dr. T. V. Mahalingam Commemoration Volume), Mysore, 1990.

Śrī Nidhiḥ: Perspectives in Indian Archaeology (Sri K.R. Srinivasan Felicitation Volume), Madras, 1983.

Studies in South Indian History and Culture (Prof. V.R. Ramachandra Dikshitar Centenary Volume), 1997.

Svasti Śrī (B. Ch. Chhabra Felicitation Volume), New Delhi, 1984.

Index